THE LIFE AND LIES OF
CHARLES DICKENS

THE LIFE AND LIES OF
CHARLES DICKENS

HELENA KELLY

PEGASUS BOOKS

NEW YORK LONDON

To my mother and father

THE LIFE AND LIES OF CHARLES DICKENS

Pegasus Books, Ltd.
148 West 37th Street, 13th Floor
New York, NY 10018

First Pegasus Books cloth edition November 2023

ISBN: 978-1-63936-533-3

10 9 8 7 6 5 4 3 2 1

Printed in the United States of America
Distributed by Simon & Schuster
www.pegasusbooks.com

'I have never seen anything about myself in Print, which has much correctness in it – any biographical account of myself, I mean.'

Letter from Charles Dickens to Wilkie Collins, 6 June 1856

CONTENTS

ACKNOWLEDGEMENTS

Second albums are notoriously difficult to make and producing this, my second book, has been a difficult process too. It's taken a long time and a lot of hard work, partly because Charles Dickens led a full, busy and *very* productive life, but partly also, inevitably, because of the pandemic. I'm grateful to both my agents, George Lucas and Sally Holloway, and to Sally in particular. She has read so many drafts and suggested so many improvements that were this in fact an album rather than a book she would certainly have earned herself a writing credit. Thank you, I couldn't have done it without you.

Thank you, too, to my publishers. To everyone at Icon – Duncan Heath, Sophie Lazar, Emily Cary-Elwes, Rhiannon Morris and especially Connor Stait, who has gone above and beyond – and to the team at Pegasus Books – Claiborne Hancock, Jessica Case and Nicole Maher: thank you. Thank you also to my eagle-eyed proof-reader, Alison Foskett, and to Anna Morrison and Faceout Studio for, respectively, the UK and US cover designs.

In writing a biography you inevitably incur debts – to scholars, to the biographers who have preceded you, to librarians, archivists, editors, curators, and everyone else who has helped to make the body of knowledge and material that you draw on. I hope that I have paid due credit where possible but there are many unsung heroes, including the staff at the National Archives, the London Metropolitan Archives, and the National Maritime Museum at Greenwich, who are without equal. More particularly, I'm grateful to Dominic Rainsford, editor of *Dickens Quarterly*, and Emily Bell, editor of the *Dickensian*, and to their reviewers, all of whom have shared their expertise when critiquing work I've published with them. Any mistakes that remain are mine.

Writing can be a lonely and sometimes rather joyless task, so thanks for cheering me up and cheering me on are due to Matthew and Catherine Bottomley, Cat Given, Karen Wigley, my nieces Anna, Sophie, Emilie, and Lily, my god-daughter Pippa, my next-door neighbour Pauline, all my lovely in-laws, and my sister, Vanessa. Thank you too to my parents, who have listened patiently to many lengthy lectures on Dickens.

And thank you, finally, but most importantly, to Dave and Rory, my best boys.

PROLOGUE: THE CONJURER AND THE CONJURER'S ASSISTANT (1843)

The weather has been exceptionally mild of late but in this Christmas season every party demands a good blaze and good cheer. What with the fire and the punch bowl and mounting excitement, they are all already too warm; the children pink-cheeked, the ladies, both young and older, hectically flushed. Mrs Dickens, so near her time that none of the married women think it altogether wise for her to have come, sits breathless and smiling, dabbing at her brow. As for the gentlemen, one or two of them are growing so very boisterous, so shiningly rubicund, that it seems not impossible they might drop dead of an apoplexy and ruin poor Nina's thirteenth birthday party – and almost certain that not all the glassware will survive the evening intact.

The hostess, Mrs Macready, whose actor husband is away on tour in America, grows fretful. The gentlemen are her husband's friends, for the most part, and kindly meaning to fill her husband's place, but how is she to control them? All these sticky-fingered children, her pretty rosewood tables, everyone growing impatient. How long are they to be kept waiting?

But there are promising signs at last – a head peers around the door, conversations fade, noisy masculine voices demand quiet, a wine glass is rung, a bawled cry of *Order!* and their evening's entertainment bounds into the room.

Dickens is brilliant, of course. He pulls coins from behind the ears of the birthday girl and magics up sweets. He burns a handkerchief and then draws it out from a wine bottle, unsinged. Will anyone lend him a pocket-watch? In a flash it vanishes, only to be discovered inside a locked tea caddy. He conjures a guinea pig, which gets loose and scurries about the floor, squeaking furiously, fur on end. He kindles a fire in a hat, sets a saucepan over it and – in no more than a minute – has turned raw eggs and flour into a hot plum pudding and shows off the inside of the hat, good as new. Everyone is amazed, astonished. The room rocks with laughter. There is a storm of applause.

Dickens bows, delighted.

His friend John Forster fetches and carries and holds the props.[1]

❧

You may think that you know all there is to know about Charles Dickens – and there have been so many biographies and biopics devoted to him, so many newspaper stories, that you can be forgiven for thinking so. John Forster may not be a name you're very familiar with, though, but if you're interested in Dickens you really should be.

The two men seem to have met towards the end of 1836, introduced by a mutual acquaintance, the novelist William Harrison Ainsworth.[2] They hit it off. Invitations and gifts of magazines quickly followed their first meeting.[3] By June 1837, Forster was helping Dickens in a contractual dispute.[4] From then on, for almost the entirety of Dickens's career, John Forster was there in the background, dealing with the practicalities, prompting and advising. Nowadays we might call him Dickens's literary agent. It was to Forster that Dickens usually confided new ideas and complained when his writing wasn't going well; Forster who read his first drafts and negotiated on his behalf with publishers. They socialised and holidayed together. Few other relationships in Dickens's life proved so enduring. While friends and business associates and even close family members were left rejected by the wayside, Forster remained within the circle of trust. Dickens may have taken up with other intimates, such as fellow novelist Wilkie Collins, but when he separated from his wife Catherine in the late 1850s, it was Forster he chose to negotiate terms for him. And Forster was the person Dickens selected to safeguard his manuscripts after his death.

The two men were close in age. Both, after toying with legal careers, turned their energies to literature, though with markedly different success. Forster was chiefly a bread-and-butter writer – a journalist, a critic, occasionally a biographer. In later life he also worked for the Lunacy Commission and acquired – most unexpectedly – a rich wife. He had a remarkable talent for getting close to other, more celebrated literary figures. While still a young man he befriended Charles Lamb (of *Tales from Shakespeare* fame), the poet Robert Browning, and Edward Bulwer-Lytton, who was a best-selling author in the late 1820s and 1830s.[5] He also became engaged to a then wildly famous poetess called Letitia Elizabeth Landon, known by her initials L.E.L. A decade his senior, with a spotty reputation, she eventually broke off the relationship and married another man.[6] Nor was Dickens the only author he represented.

Unlike modern literary agents, Forster didn't get a contractually agreed cut of any profits made by his writer friends. What motivated him, then, if it wasn't money? What hunger made him pursue, for decades, the role of unpaid helper and occasional conjurer's assistant?

Perhaps what those who befriend celebrities so often want: proximity, access, inside knowledge.

That, anyhow, is what everyone assumed Forster had managed to get. The first volume of his *The Life of Charles Dickens* appeared in 1871, eighteen months after the novelist's death, and the third and last volume in 1874. People might have joked at the time that the book ought more properly to have been called 'The Life of John Forster, with reminiscences of Charles Dickens', but they read it and believed it.[7] He was, after all, effectively Dickens's authorised biographer; he was in a position to know things. His biography remains one of the most influential ever to be written. You'll almost certainly be familiar with parts of what he wrote, even if you don't know where they originated from. A substantial proportion of what everyone knows about Dickens comes from Forster.

For instance, it was Forster who announced to the world that sections of Dickens's 1849–50 novel *David Copperfield* were pretty much straight memoir, revealing that the celebrated author had, like David, been forced into menial work as a child, taken out of school and made to labour in a boot-polish factory when his father was sent to debtors' prison. Forster is our only source for this story, as he is for a lot of other supposed facts about Dickens's life.

These days, though, locating and accessing archival material has become a great deal easier than it used to be. And the archives show that quite a number of Forster's facts are incorrect, or inaccurate. He gets dates wrong, and sometimes names, too. He makes no reference to events that we now know took place. Details seem to be ignored or invented; there are people missing from the story who really ought to be there.

Is it simply that Forster wasn't a very good biographer, or was he, instead, continuing to facilitate Dickens in the same way he'd been doing for years? While claiming to reveal the truth about his famous friend, was he actually helping to maintain Dickens's lies, keeping Dickens's secrets?

⁂

At the end of 1843, when Dickens performed his conjuring tricks at Nina Macready's birthday party, he was still in his very early thirties. But since he had been hurtled to fame with *The Pickwick Papers* in 1836, he'd already completed four other novels, among them such runaway successes as *Oliver Twist*, *Nicholas Nickleby* and that great early Victorian favourite, *The Old Curiosity Shop*. *A Christmas Carol* had just come out. He'd spent six months of the previous year touring the United States and Canada, fêted wherever he went. His name had appeared in the newspapers thousands of times. Even those who hadn't read any of his writing knew who he was.

But no one knew very much about him.

Take, for example, *A New Spirit of the Age*. This was a book of biographical essays about eminent early Victorians which was published in 1844. An essay on Dickens opened the book and the picture of him which accompanied it served almost as a frontispiece. The flattering suggestion is that he was the poster boy for the new Victorian age. The essay itself discusses his successes, to date, and his failures. It contains some sophisticated analysis of his writing. There's one thing missing, though. The other essays in *A New Spirit of the Age* mention where their subjects were born, who their family were, where they went to school: this one doesn't do any of that. We're told that, 'if ever it were well said of an author that his "life" was in his books, (and a very full life, too,) this might be said of Mr. Dickens'.[8] Actually it's clear that – after seven years of being a household name – Dickens's origins and background remained, as far as the public was concerned, almost a total blank.

And despite intense, continued press interest, this state of affairs more or less persisted. Dickens's stories were clearly often inspired by his early life – in fact, several quite unexpected aspects of his work turn out to be partly autobiographical – but he almost never wrote of his childhood without a protective veneer of fictionality, even when he wasn't writing fiction.

In the last decade of his life, Dickens produced a number of magazine essays which look like memoirs, and have sometimes been treated so. They aren't. There's the ostensibly confiding piece, 'Dullborough Town', in which he recalls his 'boyhood's home', offering details of his days there, games and small friends, and strange, dreamlike memories. It's wholly unreliable. He describes a made-up place, an amalgam of two neighbouring towns, Chatham and Rochester, and gives it the made-up name 'Dullborough'. Readers are led to understand that he had not revisited the haunts of his boyhood until just 'the other day', when in fact he visited frequently through his twenties and thirties, and in his forties had bought a large house only a couple of miles up the road, at Gads Hill. Dickens even brings a dead childhood friend back to life, and describes having dinner with her and her family.[9]

Parts of these essays probably are rooted in genuine recollections, but how, in the circumstances, can we trust anything that he says in them? They're about as truthful as an interview with *Hello!* magazine or an influencer's social media feeds, and Dickens was in some ways much more like a celebrity or a big-name influencer than an ordinary author. He was astonishingly, globally famous. He was a product, a brand: available for so many shillings and pence in whatever format the public preferred. Illustrations of his characters were available to purchase. Unscrupulous individuals took advantage of lax copyright laws to publish abridgements and continuations of his work, and stage unauthorised adaptations. More loyal readers could choose to consume his work by monthly or weekly instalment or in book form. They could buy his magazines, *Household Words* and *All the Year Round*. There was special Christmas-edition Dickens, which proved very popular. Eventually people could pay to go and hear him perform his stories aloud in dramatic readings. He went on tour. Even his burial ended up turning into a public event.

When it comes to that kind of fame, having a public persona is both good business sense and a psychological shield. It isn't surprising that Dickens should have worked so hard during his lifetime to control what people knew and thought about him – sending out press releases, briefing against former business associates and family members, concealing information that his public might not react well to.

But the gaps and elisions in Forster's biography suggest that Dickens also put considerable effort into controlling what people would think of him after his death.

For years we've been under the impression that we'd carefully ferreted out most of Dickens's secrets – his infamous involvement with the young actress Ellen Ternan, his father's imprisonment for debt, his childhood employment in the boot-polish factory – but that's not what happened. We didn't have to find these things out. Dickens told us. He chose to make them public. In his will, Ellen Ternan is the first beneficiary listed. The story about the debt and the boot-polish factory appears in a book written by the man Dickens himself had selected to write it; it's the story Dickens gave him.

In spite of the revelations it offered, Forster's *The Life of Charles Dickens* is less a biography than an exercise in posthumous brand management. Indeed, Dickens's influence over the book was such that there's some argument for viewing it as a collaborative venture between him and Forster. Maybe this is why it's proved so enduring, so influential. The problem is, though, that it doesn't get us much closer to the truth than Dickens's other purported excursions into memoir. It's not just that Forster's biography isn't the whole story – it was designed to distract and deceive.

Dickens the conjurer and his faithful assistant have been playing tricks on us all this time. They've been feeding us lies, directing our gaze away from what they wanted to keep hidden.

The story of Charles Dickens's life isn't the one we think we know.

Notes

1. Details drawn for the most part from Charles Dickens's letter to Angela Burdett Coutts, 27 December 1843, and Jane Carlyle's description of the same party. I have also included one or two other tricks with which Dickens is known to have been familiar. The guinea pig sadly died not long afterwards (Letter to Mrs Carlyle, 27 January 1844).

2. Best known nowadays as the author of *Rookwood* (1834), an immensely popular gothic-style novel featuring the highwayman Dick Turpin.

3. Letter to John Forster, probably March 1837; letter to the same, probably May 1837.

4. Letter to John Forster, date conjectured to be 9 June 1837. Unusually, both this and the above survive in manuscript.

5. Now largely – and largely deservedly – forgotten.

6. For more information on the fascinating Letitia, see Lucasta Miller's *L.E.L.: The Lost Life and Scandalous Death of Letitia Elizabeth Landon, the Celebrated 'Female Byron'* (Jonathan Cape, 2019).

7. See, for example, *Sheffield Independent*, 13 January 1872, page 8. All newspaper articles accessed 12–15 June 2023, via The British Newspaper Archive or, in the case of *The Times* of London, *The Times* Digital Archive (https://www.britishnewspaperarchive. co.uk and https://www.gale.com/intl/c/the-times-digital-archive). Transcriptions author's own.

8. R.H. Horne (ed.), *A New Spirit of the Age* (1844). Essay on 'Charles Dickens'.

9. As remarked in William F. Long, 'What happened to Lucy Stroughill', *Dickens Quarterly*, Vol. 29, No. 4 (December 2012), page 313 ff.

MUD (1812–22) 1

Chatham, Kent, engraved by William Miller after J.M.W. Turner (1832). (Royal Academy of Arts)

'Mudbank, mist, swamp', says a convict in *Great Expectations*, describing the estuary landscape that Dickens was familiar with for almost the whole of his life, 'swamp, mist, and mudbank'. To find one's way safely through such treacherous territory is always going to be a challenge.

Charles Dickens was born in Portsmouth, on 7 February 1812, and passed much of his childhood in Chatham, one of a string of towns clustered close together along the muddy estuary of the River Medway in Kent. As an adult he returned to Kent, buying a house overlooking the Thames, where the river glides wide and unhurried past the marshes on either side out into the North Sea. Salt air, ebb and flood, these feature in story after story. Often the water looms threateningly. There are a surprising number of drowned bodies.

But it's clear that there must be something lying hidden in the murky waters of Charles Dickens's childhood – something more than or different from what we've been told. The information we can gather from Forster's biography and from Dickens's own letters and scraps of memoir is inconsistent, contradictory. Inconvenient facts keep looming out of the fog. There's little ground that will bear any weight. Things don't join up.

For example, Dickens often used to claim that he had spent his boyhood in the cathedral city of Rochester, rather than where he had actually lived, in the neighbouring and notably rougher dock-yard town of Chatham.[10] The claim seems, on the surface, rather pointless, but he must have had a motive.

He exhibits, on multiple occasions in his writing, a peculiar evasiveness about Chatham. *The Pickwick Papers* traces its way carefully around the outskirts of the town, coming right up to the edge of it in one episode dealing with an abortive duel, and in another moving to the military exercise ground on its further side but never entering its streets. In writing *A Child's History of England*, published between 1851 and 1853, Dickens manages to mention Rochester a dozen times, and Chatham not at all, not even when dealing with the famous Dutch raid of the late 1660s, in which the English fleet was attacked while anchoring there. Chatham must be the 'garrison-and-dockyard town' on the London–Dover road central to an allegation put during an important court case in *A Tale of Two Cities* (1859) – there is no other – but the name is omitted. *The Mystery of Edwin Drood* (1870) describes the area around Rochester Cathedral, and the journey from Rochester to the capital, with near forensic accuracy, but Chatham is snipped neatly out of the picture.

This is far from the only subject on which Dickens's accounts of his childhood turn out to be less than wholly reliable. He told Forster that he retained detailed memories of his time in Portsmouth: the 'exact shape' of a military parade ground, the garden of the house he had lived in and the fact it was snowing on the day they left the town.[11]

Yet according to the letter Dickens wrote as an adult to his German translator, he lived in London between the ages of two and six. Can these memories of Portsmouth possibly be those of a child of two, or even younger, one who soon after moved away? It seems very unlikely. At any rate, according to the letter, Charles returned to live in the capital again when he was twelve, or perhaps even thirteen. But according to Forster he was already working in a factory in central London by his twelfth birthday, and before that he had been living for some time in Camden, then just outside London. The letter itself doesn't survive and the transcript may not be entirely correct, but there appear to be quite considerable discrepancies.[12] Dickens definitely did go to a day school in London, Wellington House Academy, but how long for – whether it was for as much as two years, beginning quite early in 1824, or whether he was still there as late as the first months of 1827 – is a moot point, his school contemporaries recalling different dates which don't necessarily agree with his own versions.[13] Even the most famous part of the story, the debtor's prison and the boot-polish factory, doesn't really hold together – or at least not the way he and Forster tell it. So what did happen in Charles's childhood?

❧

We tend not to think of Charles Dickens as a forces child, but he was one. He grew up in dockyard towns, and moved from one to another at the will of his father's superiors. Without the navy, he might not even have existed.

John Dickens, Charles's father, was the second son of an elderly butler and a by-no-means youthful housekeeper, upper servants in the household of John Crewe, one of the MPs for Cheshire. The butler was so elderly, indeed, that it doesn't seem to have surprised anyone that he died just a couple of months after John was born.

Though the pair had worked and married in London, and their children were christened there, Mrs Dickens's job was based, at least part of the time, at the Cheshire estate, Crewe Hall.[14] It must have made for a strange upbringing for John and his elder brother William.

Charles's mother, Elizabeth Barrow, came from a family which had its roots in the West Country. Her relations were both musical and mechanically minded, with one holding a patent on a piano design.[15]

What brought together the son of a Cheshire housekeeper and the daughter of a London piano-manufacturer was the navy. And the navy influenced their lives in other respects, too.

Full-scale conflict between Britain and France had begun in 1793 and didn't finally end until more than two decades later, in 1815. The urgent need to maintain and increase British naval power meant that the government poured money into the Royal Navy, into ships, dockyards and men. They also recruited an army of additional clerks to try to make sure the money ended up where it was meant to. Among these clerks were Elizabeth's father, Charles Barrow, her brother Thomas and her husband-to-be John Dickens.[16] Thomas Barrow and John Dickens appear to have been office mates from at least as early as 1806.[17] We don't know precisely when John met his new colleague's family, but Elizabeth, born at the end of 1789, might have been no more than sixteen when she was first introduced to him. She was still only eighteen when they married. One wonders how many other young men she got the chance to meet, how much mature consideration she can have been able to give to her choice of husband. And one wonders, too, whether John would have married her if he'd known the perilous basis on which her family's apparent ease and security really rested.

The two Barrows, father and son, and John Dickens worked in the Navy Pay Office at Somerset House on the Strand. The clerks employed there managed the sailors' wages, pensions and dealings with creditors. They also inspected, and in many cases executed, sailors' wills. Enormous sums of cash and forests' worth of paperwork passed through their hands.[18] It was a highly responsible job and was viewed by the Barrow family as giving them status, becoming part and parcel of their identities.

When Charles Dickens's parents got married in June 1809, the ceremony took place in the church of St Mary le Strand, which sits marooned on a sliver of land in the middle of the road just opposite the main entrance of Somerset House. And when Grandfather Barrow died in 1826, his obituary noted that he was 'late of the Navy Pay Office', despite the fact that he left under something of a cloud. The pride his family so evidently felt was not passed on to Dickens, however. And there are a couple of possible reasons why.

We know that John Dickens worked in the 'Wages' branch for the majority of the time that he was employed by the Pay Office; we also know that sometimes he was based in London and sometimes at 'outports' – the dockyard towns of Portsmouth, where Charles was born, and Chatham, and possibly others as well. Finding out exactly *when* he moved from place to place is difficult to ascertain, however.[19] The recordkeeping was haphazard.

Fortunately for us, though, John and Elizabeth Dickens quickly developed some spendthrift habits. They rented a house which had 'a good kitchen and cellar', 'two excellent parlours', 'two good bedchambers' and 'two garrets in the attic' – pretty luxurious for a young family just starting out.[20] Another luxury Charles's parents chose to spend their money on was taking out birth announcements in the newspapers. This means we know not only that their first two children, Fanny and Charles, were born in Portsmouth, but that their next son, Alfred, died there late in 1814, aged five months, of 'water on the brain' – hydrocephalus.[21] By April 1816, at least some of the family were in the capital – the birth announcement for the fourth of the Dickens children, another daughter, Letitia, locates the family in 'Norfolk Street' in London.[22] There is a plaque on the wall of what was once 10 Norfolk Street (now 22 Cleveland Street) which states that 'Young Charles Dickens twice lived in this house 1815–16 and 1828–31' (that is, when he was aged three to four, and again when he would have been in his late teens). Actually, the proof isn't totally solid for his having lived there during either of these two time periods.[23] All we can say with any certainty is that Charles spent his earliest years in Portsmouth, and may have lived in London for a period as a small child, around the year 1816. By this point he would have been four, or thereabouts.

How long he remained in London we don't know.

Hostilities had finally ended in 1815, leading, in the navy, to several rounds of lay-offs and reductions in personnel. John Dickens was lucky to keep his job at all and may well have had to accept several short postings, one of which could have been in Sheerness, a dockyard on the Isle of Sheppey, off the Kent coast.[24] At any rate, he was in Chatham at some point before autumn 1817, employed in the Pay Office in the dockyard there.[25]

Chatham dockyard was in its glory days when John Dickens arrived, money still flooding in even though the war was over. The town was essentially an armed camp. It was intensely militarised, circled by forts: Elizabethan Upnor Castle across the river from the dockyard and Fort Amherst, Fort Clarence and Fort Pitt studded along the ridges of high ground behind it. A plan of Chatham, dated June 1816, shows one long high street and a few cross roads pinched in between a 'gun wharf' and the foot of the hill on which Fort Pitt is perched.[26] Another plan, of April 1821, marks parcels of land claimed by the navy, the army and the 'ordnance' (artillery), and a great swathe designated 'exercising ground', reserved for drills, training and displays.[27] There were soldiers everywhere – marching, on manoeuvres, lounging around in the streets. Convicted prisoners were brought from all over the country to the prison hulks moored in the Medway estuary – decommissioned ships, stripped of sails and masts, notorious for their harsh conditions, used either as temporary holding places for those sentenced to transportation or to house men used as forced labour. Travellers on the road between London and Dover were constantly passing through. Ships were arriving and leaving.

The Dickens family set up home in a road called Ordnance Terrace, also known as 'Ordnance-row', which sits below Fort Pitt. An advertisement of 1814 describes one house in the terrace as 'A commodious newly erected Dwelling-house, eligibly situate in Ordnance-row, Prices Dale, Chatham, and containing two chambers, two parlors, two kitchens, an inclosed garden 80 feet long [...] amply supplied with water'.[28] This sounds pleasant enough, though it's noticeable that Ordnance Terrace can't have been any bigger than their first family home in Portsmouth. With a growing brood of children and a couple of servants living there, as well as

Mrs Dickens's widowed sister Mary Allen (who apparently moved in with them), it can't have been too roomy. Later the family moved to St Mary's Place, in a slightly more central location but still well within sight of the surrounding fortifications. A noisy, crowded house, and outside, beyond the garden, barracks, drawbridges, sea-walls, 'sally ports' and sentry points – a place which, as the closest major naval dockyard to the French coast, had lived for years in expectation of attack and siege – this is where the young Dickens grew up.

In common with most dock towns, Chatham had an established Jewish population, while newspaper reports of 1820 mention the presence of a group of 'Turks' involved in an affray at Chatham's Fountain Inn.[29] Of the foreign prisoners of war who had passed through the town before the coming of the peace, some elected to remain. The Royal Navy was a famously colour-blind employer, at least of ordinary seamen, and a handful of people of colour appear in local newspaper reports in the 1810s and 1820s, their ethnicity being deemed worthy of note, but seldom of particular comment.[30] Whatever the source of the shocking attitudes to race that can be found in some of Dickens's later writing, they were not the result of a monocultural upbringing. The town teemed with people from all walks of life, religions and ethnicities from all over the globe.

It's possible that the Dickens family flirted with Baptist ideas during their time in Chatham. Young Charles attended a school run by a young Baptist schoolteacher, William Giles, whose father presided at the chapel neighbouring their house in St Mary's Place. Though the establishment was given the sonorous name of 'the Classical, Mathematical, and Mercantile School', there were other, far better-established schools in the neighbourhood – the cathedral school in Rochester, for instance, which took young choristers, and the Sir Joseph Williamson Mathematical School, at which the sons of many dockyard employees were educated for future jobs related to the yard, the sea or the river.[31] Giles was exceedingly youthful for a headmaster, only just out of his teens, and he hadn't attended university – indeed, he wouldn't have been able to attend either Oxford or Cambridge, which both required students to be members of the Church of England.[32] It's hard to see why – if religion wasn't a factor – the Dickens parents would have considered his school the best available option for their young son. Perhaps it was simply a matter of convenience or of cost.

John and Elizabeth Dickens continued to have their children baptised at the dockyard church and if they were drawn to Non-conformist worship, the effect on Charles seems not to have been a positive one. In an essay published in 1860, Dickens – or his journalistic alter ego – describes how, as a child, he was 'violently scrubbed from the neck to the roots of the hair as a purification for the Temple' before being 'carried off [...] to be steamed like a potato in the unventilated breath of the powerful Boanerges Boiler and his congregation'.[33] As an adult, Dickens disliked religious show, whether in the Roman Catholic or the Protestant church. His fiction holds up to mockery a number of characters who are charismatic, low-church preachers, expressing disapproval of the influence they could come to exert, particularly over women.

There are other stories about this period in Chatham which indicate the Dickens parents in fact held rather relaxed attitudes towards their children's moral education – for example, the suggestion that the two eldest, Charles and Fanny, were encouraged to sing publicly in the Mitre Tavern in Chatham.[34] It's true that a patriotic anthem or two at a semi-official dinner is a very different proposition to children prancing around singing saucy comic songs like real-life versions of *Jane Eyre*'s little Adele Varens, but neither is likely to have been universally approved by members of the Baptist communion.

Even if the young Charles wasn't taken to sing at the Mitre, there were plenty of events in the local community which might have struck the imagination of a future novelist. The year before the Dickens family arrived, fourteen people, most of them young women, drowned in the River Medway when a jaunt turned into disaster.[35] The majority of the victims were Baptists; the Dickenses would certainly have been made familiar with the story. A soldier was 'found frozen to death on the Marshes near Upnor', just across the river from Chatham – not far from the marshes where, in *Great Expectations*, we first meet Pip, on Christmas Eve, 'a small bundle of shivers'.[36] Convicts really did escape from the prison hulks.[37]

A servant accidentally set light to herself and, running panicked upstairs, spread the flames to her mistress and to a child.[38] An elderly woman named Elisabeth Moore 'threw herself into a well in Jenkins's Dale, Chatham, and was killed'.[39] A couple of days before Charles's tenth birthday, an 'unfortunate girl of the town' (that is, a young woman involved in prostitution) was found dead just around the corner from their old house.[40] The body of a heavily pregnant woman who had vanished from the Duke of York public house was discovered at the bottom of its well, her soldier husband later being brought back from overseas to be convicted for her murder and hanged.[41]

In March 1820, when a fire devastated the centre of Chatham, Dickens would have been eight. He might have slept through the alarm being given in the night, but the fire carried on well into the morning so he must have seen it: the ruined buildings, the soldiers, the inefficient fire engines, the faces of the adults grimy with soot, marked by the night's work and terror.[42] A contemporaneous report records that 38 houses were destroyed, including those of the baker, 'Mr. Watson, a linen-draper' and 'Mr. Cohen, a pawnbroker', and the town's 'principal inn', the 'Sun-tavern', the roof of which 'fell in with a tremendous crash', leaving 'only a very small part of the walls [...] standing'. A burning cinder blew '150 yards' from the High Street to land on a 'large stack of hay'. For two hours, between four and six o'clock, 'the confusion which reigned in the town was beyond description'; people were emptying their houses of furniture and valuables and the flames were only brought under control by pulling down buildings to create firebreaks.[43] The inhabitants of Chatham were lucky that the damage wasn't worse and that no lives were lost.

In the preface to *Nicholas Nickleby*, Dicken happily relates how he'd heard about one of the book's subjects, the cruelties of the infamous boarding schools in Yorkshire, when he was a little boy near Rochester Castle. But he never mentions any of these other events, not even in his 'autobiographical' essays. They offer obvious potential inspiration for the opening chapters of *Great Expectations*, and the smudgier outlines, perhaps, of the off-stage demise of the mother of Rosa Bud, the heroine of *The Mystery of Edwin Drood*, who we're told drowned during a boating party; for the death of the prostituted Nancy in *Oliver Twist*; for the minor character who spontaneously combusts in *Bleak House*; for the virtuous factory worker Stephen Blackpool's fatal plunge down a hole in *Hard Times*. Fire and collapsing buildings feature in a number of Dickens's fictions, most notably in *Little Dorrit* (1855–7), where the hero's childhood home creaks ominously throughout the novel, until it eventually falls in on itself.

In his biography, Forster makes all kinds of assertions about which people or experiences inspired Dickens's writing. Mr Micawber, he tells us, is based on Charles's father; Mrs Nickleby his mother. None of these stories from Chatham, despite being possible inspiration for a number of memorable incidents in Dickens's novels, make it into Forster's book.

Why?

෧෨

I've already mentioned that the record keeping at the Navy Pay Office was haphazard. The accounts were an absolute mess. This wasn't unusual. At the time, bookkeeping was an emerging art and checks were *ad hoc*. None of the branches of the British armed forces seem to have kept a very close eye on their finances. The various Pay Offices were filled with bags of coins, wads of banknotes and chests packed with cash, opening up hundreds of small cheats and ways to game the system. Unofficial 'borrowing' seems even to have been tolerated to some extent. In short, the temptations were vast and quite a few people succumbed.

One of them, as has been known for years, was Charles Dickens's grandfather Charles Barrow, who in 1810, two years before the author's birth, was discovered to have misappropriated between £5,000 and £6,000 (over £400,000 in today's money).[44] But he was small fry compared with some of the other offenders, in more powerful positions. When the accounts of the Paymaster of Marines could finally be made sense of, they showed a deficit of £280,000 (the equivalent of a good £18 million) – and that was just up to the year 1804. So though a Writ of Extent was issued against Barrow, permitting the state to seize what little of his property there was to seize, and a 'criminal information' was filed against him, proceedings of 'outlawry' were still being pursued two years later, in 1812.[45] By then he seems to have put himself out of harm's way; the report states he had 'absconded' and he wound up living in Douglas, on the Isle of Man, where he may have had relations, and where he was safe from the reach of the English criminal or civil courts.[46] He died there in 1826.[47] It's uncertain whether he ever met his grandson and equally uncertain whether Charles knew what it was his grandfather had done or had any idea why he was in exile. The subject can hardly have been an easy one, however, nor one to which the family cared to allude very often.

In spite of Charles Barrow's disgrace, both his son, Thomas Barrow, and his son-in-law, John Dickens, continued to be employed by the Navy Pay Office. Mud sticks, though. Neither man's career exactly took off. And on New Year's Day 1822, a few weeks before Charles turned ten, scandal reared its head again – and, for a second time, the Dickens family were touched by it.

Britain was six years into the peace but – as was despairingly discussed in parliament – the various dockyards were proving even more expensive to run than they had been at the height of the war in 1813.[48] A wide-ranging audit was instituted to work out where the money was going.

One of the places the auditors visited was the Navy Pay Office at Chatham, where accounting shortfalls had been building up. John Dickens's boss, an employee of many decades' standing called John Slade, welcomed them in, ostensibly calm. He indicated that he had the money that was wanting, and that they should begin to count some of it out from the bags on his desk. While they were doing so he left the building and was soon discovered dead, having shot himself. It turned out that about £8,000 was missing.

On the surface it's a juicy story – and, we might think, strikingly similar to the scene in *Martin Chuzzlewit*, written twenty years later, in which the vicious, thuggish Jonas Chuzzlewit, about to be arrested for murder, offers the arresting officer a bag of money for 'only five minutes in the next room', eventually committing suicide. Though the information about Slade was widely reported at the time, it has only recently attracted scholarly attention and discussion has so far been limited.[49]

We have a full account of both the death and the fraud, as not only was a Sheriff's Court of Inquiry held locally in order to work out what property the dead man had left, but Slade's sureties attempted to wriggle out of paying their bond, meaning that we have the records of the subsequent court case and, in the National Archives, the papers collected by a lawyer tasked with looking into the affair.[50] Taken together, the picture they paint is one of temptation, thoroughgoing incompetence and perhaps also widespread corruption. Slade had previously lost money in a bank collapse, a financial vulnerability which seemed to have attracted neither attention nor concern. Reports suggest that a sum of £10,000 or more 'cash in hand' was regularly delivered to the building he was in charge of.[51] Witnesses from other departments related how, on more than one occasion, they had discovered that packets of banknotes made up in the Chatham pay office were 'light' – a bundle of what was meant to be £10 notes, say, bulked out with lower denominations. The only person these irregularities were reported to was Slade himself; no record was made at the time, no concerns raised with superiors up in London.[52]

John Dickens was by all accounts, and in spite of his manifold failures as a father, a very affable man; popular, clubbable. If there were rumours circulating in the dockyard he was likely to have heard them. Given how small the Pay Office at Chatham was – Slade's deputy described it as 'a suite of 3 rooms' opening into each other – it's difficult to believe that neither John nor his colleagues noticed anything was amiss.[53]

Three more children had joined the Dickens family during their time in Chatham. Harriet, born in 1818, was followed by two more sons, Frederick in 1820 and another Alfred in 1822.[54] Most biographers suggest Harriet died as a baby, not unreasonably since the silence surrounding her is almost total; however, she survived babyhood – indeed, survived the dangerous years of early childhood. Though her famous brother seems not to have mentioned the fact to his biographer, Harriet turns out to have lived on until August 1827, to the age of nearly nine, after the family had moved to London, after the debtors' prison.[55] I'll talk more about her death later on. Here I want to try – perforce tentatively – to flesh out her life a little.

Forster knew Dickens for over three decades, and knew his parents and siblings too. If the subject of Harriet ever came up in a conversation that he was privy to, it looks like it was rapidly shut down again – or surely he would have signposted readers of his biography to the parallels between this loss and several which appear in Dickens's fiction. At this point in time, by far the likeliest reason for people to avoid referring to a legitimate relation was that the individual in question had some form of additional need, a physical or mental impairment. It wouldn't matter very much whether it was a serious developmental disorder or, say, deafness caused by childhood measles; the silence descended like a shutter either way.

The first Alfred Dickens had died of 'water on the brain' in Portsmouth in 1814, a condition which can be associated with neural tube defects (such as spina bifida, for example). With one child affected, there is a high chance of recurrence in subsequent offspring. We know that Charles's nephew Henry Burnett, his sister Fanny's son, had a disability. Born in 1839, Henry is sometimes considered to be the inspiration for the frail, lame Tiny Tim in *A Christmas Carol* (1843) and for Dickens's other, subsequent portrayals of disabled characters. But memories of Harriet could be in the mix as well, and might have been influencing Dickens's writing from even earlier in his career. Both *Nicholas Nickleby* (1838–9) and *Barnaby Rudge* (1841) give prominent roles to characters with additional needs, talking at some length about the challenges they face and their particular vulnerabilities – and the former was finished before Henry Burnett was even born.

There is a real possibility, then, that Harriet's health may have been poor for years, and that she may have required extensive medical care. And it's definite that, whether from extravagance or unavoidable expense, or both, the family's finances started to become increasingly convoluted around this time. John Dickens was awarded a long-service pay increase while he was in Chatham. But he also started on the downward spiral which would lead, in 1824, to his being imprisoned for debt. He borrowed money left and right, including from a James Milbourne in London and from former neighbours in Chatham. He also seems, as Michael Allen has revealed, to have borrowed from his boss John Slade, the debt noted in a report connected to Slade's death, dated 10 January 1822.[56]

This is the only place John Dickens's name appears in the whole, well-documented set of events surrounding the fraud in the small office he'd been working in for years. He's not mentioned as a witness at the court of inquiry, nor as an onlooker; nor were his evidence or his opinion, or his recollections, sought for the civil case against Slade's sureties. The subject of his debt to Slade doesn't seem to have been followed up either, though the money might have rightly been the government's and recoverable.

Michael Allen is confident that John Dickens was recalled to the capital in June 1822.[57] Certainly a reference book published at the end of 1822 puts him back in London, and in a different department of the Navy Pay Office, one which dealt with seamen's wills rather than wages, and still as one of the 'junior clerks'.[58] The move looks like an effective demotion, though in the context of the restructuring that was going on, and John's retirement a few years later on the grounds of ill health, it needn't necessarily have been one. But some whitewashing of events in Chatham definitely did go on. For one thing, Slade was christened, or re-christened, after his death, enabling him to be given a Christian burial and, though attitudes to suicide had begun to soften, this was by no means standard practice.[59]

Given the apparent conspiracy of silence over Slade's careless-ness with the money entrusted to him over several years, and the coincidence of timing, one possible explanation for John Dickens's move to London, and to a different department, is that he informed on Slade in the hope of avoiding repaying the money he'd bor-rowed. Another possibility we can't discount is that he had been tempted himself. With a – probably – sick child, with such inade-quate oversight, knowing how much his father-in-law had managed to get away with before he was found out, it is conceivable. In that case Slade might have discovered that someone else had their fin-gers in the till, and the so-called debt John Dickens owed might not have been a debt at all, but a repayment, or even a form of black-mail. Given the connection to the Crewe family, John Dickens's superiors might just about have been willing to cut him some slack in any of these circumstances – while removing him from the easy temptations of the wages office, and barring him from any more senior roles.

This is, of course, speculation, but the sequence of events, when combined with Charles Dickens's curious reluctance to mention his links to Chatham, is inescapably suspicious. And even if John Dickens hadn't done anything wrong, there's surely a chance that his son – an impressionable, fanciful little writer-in-waiting – may well have worried that he had, and carried that worry on into adulthood.

Dickens is, in his novels and stories, fascinated by fraud, yet he is also sympathetic to small-scale fraudsters in a way that he is not to more ambitious ones. In *David Copperfield*, the creeping, "umble' Uriah Heep ends up in prison for attempting to defraud the Bank of England; in *Dombey and Son* (1846–8), the corrupt manager Carker has an unfortunate encounter with a train after taking down the titular firm. But Carker's brother, who previously defrauded the same firm, is treated with tenderness by the author, permitted, by means of an extended metaphor, to make his smaller but repeated embezzling sound not only almost accidental but something that happened to a poor unfortunate victim who 'missed his footing [...] slipped a little and a little lower [...] and went on stumbling still, until he fell headlong and found himself below a shattered man'. The name of this small-scale fraudster is, incidentally – but perhaps not coincidentally – John.

I mentioned earlier that Chatham appears, unnamed but identifiable, in a court scene in *A Tale of Two Cities*. The evidence which relates to Chatham is given by a character going by the name of John Barsad, who, it's suggested, is 'in regular government pay and employment, to lay traps'.[60] It emerges in cross-examination that Barsad has not only been 'in a debtors' prison', but has 'borrow[ed] money of the prisoner' he accuses and not paid him back. We might think the surname, so close to 'bastard', indicates a strength of emotion that even the most passionate, imaginatively engaged writer doesn't always feel about their characters. And then there's the identical place, the same first name, the similarity of having been imprisoned for debt and of the fact of owing money to the accused; if this is nothing to do with John Dickens, then it is quite the coincidence.

Coincidences do happen. Dickens made full use of them in his fiction and in real life they happen all the time. Dickens's suspicions of his father, if he nourished them, are, of course, not proof of anything.

But he may well have nourished them. At ten, going to a local school in a compact, highly interconnected town, he must have heard some garbled version of the Pay Office scandal from his schoolmates and it's possible that he was left alone in Chatham to brood on it. Only possible, however. As usual with Dickens's childhood, if we're looking for certainty we have to fall back on archival records.

John Dickens was definitely in Chatham on 11 December 1821 – the day that he and his wife witnessed the marriage of her widowed sister, Mary Allen.[61] Mary's new husband was called Matthew Lamert, a forces surgeon who had children from a previous marriage and who was soon afterwards posted to Ireland.[62] Mary went with him and was dead before they had celebrated their first wedding anniversary, 'in child bed, of twins'.[63] But that was far from the end of the connection between the Dickens and Lamert families.

We know from the announcement of the birth of baby Alfred, in March 1822, and the record of his baptism at the dockyard church in the April that Mrs Dickens, at least, must have been in Chatham until then, but when she and the children moved to London we don't know. In one essay Dickens relates leaving his boyhood home alone, 'packed' into the stagecoach in 'damp straw', and 'forwarded, carriage paid, to the Cross Keys, Wood-street, Cheapside, London'. There was, he writes, 'no other inside passenger' and he was left to eat his 'sandwiches in solitariness and dreariness, and it rained hard all the way'.[64]

This story supports another, which is that Charles boarded for a time with his Chatham schoolmaster, William Giles, the rest of the family having moved away without him. The source is Giles's sister, who also lived in Chatham in the early 1820s and knew the Dickens family; there's no reason to doubt her.[65] Forster, though, relates an affecting vignette about Dickens's head teacher the 'night before we came away' 'flitting in among the packing-cases to give me [...] a keepsake', a book by the eighteenth-century writer Oliver Goldsmith. This sounds more as if Charles went at the same time as the rest of his family.[66] We have letters in which Dickens refers to Giles with, seemingly, great fondness – though also one in which he appears rather offended with his old teacher.[67] If he did board, it was probably during the second half of 1822, and perhaps on into 1823. This doesn't exactly tally with the story that has him living in Chatham for six or seven years, which would take us into 1824, but then, as I've said before, none of the stories about Dickens's early life tally exactly.

Let's keep the mental picture of Charles as a lonely little boy in the coach. Even if it isn't true, this has proved perennially popular with biographers. It's attractive. It not only looks familiar, it fits into what we know is coming. It's just like in the novels. David Copperfield travels alone by 'stage-cutch' from Suffolk to London, the journey taking a day and a night. In *Bleak House*, Esther Summerson is left to make her way to school all on her own, on the Reading stagecoach. Before leaving, she buries her doll in the garden of the house she grew up in, recognising that her childish days are over. Stagecoaches come to represent, in Dickens's fiction, not just a separation from family and friends, but a breaking with the past which cannot be undone or reversed, the end of childhood innocence and the beginning of adulthood. From the point that they clamber up into the vehicle, Dickens's characters are swept into the bewildering currents of the grown-up world.

So: a boy, certainly not a large one and no more than half-educated, one whose home had vanished, whose grandparents and aunt had disappeared overseas, who might have been aware of the existence of rumours and secrets and money trouble but was not yet able to comprehend any of them fully. A boy who, with an older sister and four younger siblings, one possibly with additional needs, was unlikely to have been the chief focus of his parents' attention. A boy whose family had left scandal behind them and had financial disaster waiting not so far ahead.

Many people are lucky enough to have firm and fond memories of childhood. They don't need to invent. Dickens did.

Notes

10. See, for example, the 'Author's Preface' to *Nicholas Nickleby*, where Dickens talks of having been 'a not very robust child, sitting in bye-places near Rochester Castle'; letter to Angela Burdett Coutts,

23 October 1850 ('I have an idea of wandering somewhere for a day or two – to Rochester, I think, where I was a small boy –').

11. John Forster, *The Life of Charles Dickens*, volume 1, page 3.

12. 'My father holding in those days a situation under Government in the Navy Pay Office, which called him in the discharge of his duty to different places, I came to London, a child of two years old, left it again at six, and then left it again for another Sea Port town – Chatham – where I remained some six or seven years, and then came back to London with my parents and half a dozen brothers and sisters, whereof I was second in seniority.' Letter to J.H. Kuenzel, transcript, date conjectured to be 1838.

13. See, for example, Chapter 10 of Robert Langton, *The Childhood and Youth of Charles Dickens* (1883).

14. See marriage record for 'William Dickens' and 'Elizabeth Ball', St George's Hanover Square, 1781 and burial record for William Dickens, also at St George's, dated 18 October 1785. 'Jno. Dickens', son of 'Wm.' and 'Elizth.', was baptised on 20 November 1785 at St Marylebone alongside his older brother William. John's birthdate is given as 21 August of the same year. This indicates John was not a posthumous child, which has sometimes been suggested. We can't necessarily assign significance to the fact that the boys were baptised only after their father's death. Accessed via Ancestry (https://www.ancestry.co.uk). All documents located through Ancestry accessed 12–15 June 2023, transcriptions author's own.

15. Charles Barrow belonged to the firm of Culliford, Rolfe & Barrow, piano manufacturers. His wife, Charles Dickens's maternal grandmother, was a Culliford by birth. Occasionally antique instruments made by the firm come up for sale.

16. It's sometimes suggested that John got the job through the patronage of his mother's employer, the MP John Crewe. For more information on the relationship between the families, see Michael Allen, 'The Dickens/Crewe connection', *Dickens Quarterly*, Vol. 5, No. 4 (December 1988), page 175 ff.

17. John Dickens and T.C. Barrow are both listed as 'extra clerks' in the Navy Pay Office on page 159 of *The Royal Kalendar or Complete and Correct Annual Register for England, Scotland, Ireland, and America, for the Year 1807*. The information in this would have been correct for the year 1806.

18. 'The Pay Branch, to pay seamen's wages and the yards. The chief person emoyed [sic] in this branch, has a salary of 660l., and is called deputy-paymaster. The residue of the business is committed to the officers next mentioned, and with their places their salaries are specified ... the one at Sheerness paid "330l", the one at Chatham, "440l." ... In the office in London, the first clerk, who superintends the making up of accounts, has 495l; and there are several other clerks, with salaries from 275l. to 101l. ... The Inspector's Branch, to inspect and examine all wills and powers of attorney, and to see that they are duly executed, according to act of parliament, and to grant certificates as an authority for the payment of wages due to the parties', John Adolphus, *The Political State of the British empire*, Vol. 2 (Cadell and Davies, 1818), page 249.

19. In the *Royal Kalendar*, for example, a directory of public employees published annually, the names of a large proportion of Navy Pay Office employees are listed, down to the housekeeper and messengers. Readers are told the sub-departments to which each person belongs, and, in the early years, what they are all paid, but not – for the more junior of the employees at least – *where* they are based.

20. See the sales particulars for 'Mile-End Terrace', given in the *Hampshire Telegraph*, 29 June 1812, page 3. It is stated that the house was 'late in the occupation of Mr. John Dickins'.

21. *Statesman*, 1 November 1810, page 4 and *Hampshire Telegraph*, 5 November 1810, page 3; *Morning Post*, 10 February 1812, page 4 and *Sun*, 10 February 1812, page 4; *London Courier and Evening Gazette*, 9 September 1814, page 4.

22. *Morning Chronicle*, 25 April 1816, page 3.

23. There were two Norfolk Streets in London. The other one, which was off the Strand, included among its inhabitants a 'surgeon and accoucheur', that is, a specialist in delivering babies: John Paternoster, who lived at No. 30. See *Johnstone's London Commercial Guide and Street Directory corrected to August 1817* (1818), pages 355–6. Paternoster's name also appears in an 1811 directory, at the same address. See *Holden's Annual London and County Directory 1811*, three volumes, no page numbers, arranged by city and alphabetically. Hydrocephalus – the condition which Charles's deceased younger brother had suffered from – can result from an extremely difficult labour or from inept interventions. That John

Dickens might have employed a London specialist to care for his wife during her next confinement is not far-fetched.

24. A claim which appears in various newspapers as early as May 1852. If he believed it to be wrong, Dickens never corrected it; he may not have been sure.

25. 'John Dickens, Chatham' appears in the list of subscribers for the second edition of *The History and Antiquities of Rochester and its Environs*, by Samuel Denne and William Shrubsole, the preface to which is dated November 1817.

26. National Archives, MFQ 1280/1, 'Plan of the Rights of Chatham Lanes and Gibraltar Guard House, June 1st 1816'.

27. National Archives, MFQ 1280/2. Plan dated 13 April 1821.

28. *Kentish Weekly Post*, 4 October 1814, page 4.

29. A man died as a result, stabbed by one Hassan Hussein. The verdict at the inquest was 'justifiable homicide'. There appears to have been both friction and cultural misunderstanding. The commander of the garrison issued an order 'that all Turks coming on shore for the future, shall be searched [...] and deprived of arms', *General Evening Post*, 29 July 1820, page 1.

30. See, for example, *Evening Mail*, 7 November 1810, page 2 (an account of a stabbing in Sheerness); *Kentish Weekly Post*, 18 April 1815, page 4 (the death of Mr Chatham Cuffy at Brompton); *Kentish Weekly Post*, 28 May 1824, page 4 (reference to a labourer employed at Sheerness); *Globe*, 15 July 1825, page 3 (mention of William Pascoe, a companion of the explorer Belzoni).

31. *Manchester Courier and Lancashire General Advertiser*, 4 December 1830, page 1.

32. Giles had been born in 1799.

33. 'City of London Churches', *All the Year Round*, 5 May 1860. 'Boanerges' is the name which Jesus gives to two of the apostles, denoting 'sons of thunder' (*Mark* 3.17).

34. Robert Langton, *The Childhood and Youth of Charles Dickens* (London, Hutchinson & Co., 1891), pages 34–5. See also John Forster, *The Life of Charles Dickens*, volume 1, page 10: 'He told a story offhand so well, and sang small comic songs so especially well, that he used to be elevated on chairs and tables, both at home and abroad, for more effective display of these talents.'

35. *Kentish Weekly Post*, 20 September 1816, page 4.

36. *Kentish Weekly Post*, 9 January 1818, page 4.
37. John Fuller escaped twice from the Sheerness Hulk (see *John Bull*, 14 January 1822). In August of the same year, when Charles may still have been in the area, three convicts escaped at once (*Kentish Weekly Post*, 30 August 1822, page 4).
38. *Kentish Weekly Post*, 23 February 1821, page 1.
39. *Kentish Weekly Post*, 29 September 1820, page 4.
40. At Chapel Steps, which was situated close to the New Road and Ordnance Terrace. *Kentish Weekly Post*, 15 February 1822, page 4.
41. *Morning Advertiser*, 22 October 1818, page 3.
42. This event also puts a rather different complexion on the passage in the early *Our Parish* where Dickens sardonically describes how the 'parish engine' [i.e. fire engine], called to 'a regular [real] fire', 'came up in gallant style – three miles and a half an hour, at least; there was a capital supply of water, and it was first on the spot [...] but it was unfortunately discovered, just as they were going to put the fire out, that nobody understood the process by which the engine was filled with water'.
43. *The Times*, 4 March 1820, page 2.
44. Modern equivalent figures are from the Bank of England's inflation calculator.
45. This as reported in the *London Courier and Evening Gazette*, 1 September 1812, page 2. Barrow's household furniture was apparently seized and sold.
46. Charles Barrow's mother was, before her marriage, Ann Cassteels, a surname which occurs fairly frequently on the Isle of Man, though it isn't unknown elsewhere. Other origins have been suggested.
47. There is a notice of his death in one newspaper that in the circumstances I think you'll agree exhibits breathtaking cheek: 'Sunday-week, in Athol-street, Douglas, Isle of Man, much respected, Mr. Charles Barrow, late of Somerset-house, London, aged 66 years.' *Cumberland Pacquet*, 7 March 1826, page 3.
48. *Morning Post*, 19 March 1822, page 2.
49. The first scholarly piece appears to be Michael Allen, 'Suicide, fraud and debt: John Dickens's last days at Chatham', *Dickens Quarterly*, Vol. 33, No. 4 (December 2016), pages 269–290.
50. National Archives, PMG 73/1, formerly P.M.G. 61/1.
51. *Public Ledger and Daily Advertiser*, 20 February 1822, page 3.

52. 'About three years since, an order came from Sheerness for a sum of money amounting to two or three thousand pounds, which was delivered to him by Mr. Slade, and he was sent with it to the Clerk of the Cheque at Sheerness. The next morning the principal clerk in the Cheque-office at Sheerness arrived at Chatham, and stated that a considerable deficiency had been discovered in the […] notes sent the preceding day.' *Morning Advertiser*, 19 February 1822, page 1.

53. Letter from John Otley, PMG 73/1.

54. For the birth of the child who is almost certainly the mysterious Harriet, see *Morning Post*, 18 September 1818, page 4 and *Morning Chronicle*, 18 September 1818, page 4. Harriet Ellen Dickens was baptised on 3 September 1819 at St Mary's Church in Chatham, nearly twelve months after her birth. All her siblings were baptised within a month or two of their arrival. Possibly the delay suggests the family were temporarily influenced by the Baptist tradition of adult or believer's baptism.

55. 'Harriet Ellen Dickins', of St Pancras, buried on 24 August 1827, age nine. Burial Register, accessed through Find My Past (https://www.findmypast.co.uk). All documents located through Find My Past accessed 12–15 June 2023, transcriptions author's own. Harriet's dates were first ascertained only relatively recently. I believe the first article to be William F. Long, 'Defining a life: Charles's youngest sister, Harriet Ellen Dickens (15 September 1818–19 August 1827)', *The Dickensian*, Vol. 1110, No. 492 (Spring 2014), page 24. For some reason the information has failed to filter out over the past decade and you'll struggle to find any significant discussion about Harriet or the effect her death might have had on the rest of the family.

56. '£227.10. – from a Mr. John Dickens I believe formerly of the Navy Pay Office […] M^r. Slade appears to have received lately two instalments of this debt amounting together either to £31.6.6 or £32.18.6 from M^r. Thomas Barrow of the Navy Pay Office who can probably give more information upon the subject.' This is Allen's transcription, from his article on the Slade case, mentioned above. I didn't come across this particular document when I looked through the bundle but it's possible that I overlooked it.

57. Michael Allen, *Charles Dickens' Childhood* (St Martin's Press, 1988), Chapter 4, page 71.

58. According to the 1823 *Royal Kalendar*, page 169.

59. Baptism record for John Slade, age 60, 8 January 1822. The burial record is dated the same day. Medway Archives, P153/1/50, page 184. Accessed through Find My Past.

60. The name John Barsad is, we later learn, assumed.

61. Medway Archives, P85/1/53, 1821–1824, page 101, accessed via Find My Past.

62. The spelling of the family name was erratic. It also appears as 'Lamerte', 'la Mert' and 'La'Mert'.

63. *Morning Chronicle*, 4 September 1822, page 4.

64. 'The Uncommercial Traveller', *All the Year Round*, 30 June 1860 (sometimes called 'Dullborough Town').

65. Robert Langton, *The Childhood and Youth of Charles Dickens* (Manchester, 1883), page 62 ff.

66. John Forster, *The Life of Charles Dickens*, volume 1, page 16.

67. See, for example, letter to the Rev. William Giles, 31 October 1848; letter to same, 16 September 1855.

BOOT-POLISH (1824)

2

Playbill advertising *Heart of Mid Lothian, or, the Lily of St.Leonard's* [and] *Doctor Faustus and the Black Demon, or, Harlequin and the Seven Fairies of the Grotto* at the Adelphi Theatre, London, 1824. (Victoria & Albert Museum)

We're approaching one of the best-known chapters in Charles Dickens's life story, the one which tells how, early in 1824, when his father was imprisoned for debt, Charles himself was not just put to work but was left, to all intents and purposes, alone in London to fend for himself. He had just turned twelve. He pasted labels onto jars of boot-polish in a factory on the banks of the Thames – by Hungerford Stairs, which, in the middle of the nineteenth century, vanished under Charing Cross Station. In other words, when Dickens wrote about the hopeless, spendthrift Micawbers being imprisoned for debt in *David Copperfield* (1849–50), he was sharing with his readers a moment of profound personal trauma. Meanwhile, the section of the novel where the young hero is taken from school and put to work washing out wine bottles and pasting labels on them in a 'warehouse […] at the waterside', close to 'some stairs […] where people took boat' is barely varnished memoir.

This was the major revelation in John Forster's biography of Dickens. When it first burst upon the public, in December 1871, eighteen months after Dickens's death, the press had a field day. Though it had been generally assumed that parts of the novel were loosely based on Dickens's own experiences – David is, after all, a novelist – no one seems to have had any idea that this section was one of them, still less that it came so close to the truth. If Dickens's family knew, or suspected, they never said, though one or two of them were wise after the event. And, so far as we're aware, Dickens himself never spoke or wrote openly of this period in the boot-polish factory during his lifetime – save to Forster.

By his own account, given in *The Life of Charles Dickens*, Forster first stumbled on the truth around 'March or April 1847', and he only did so because he happened to mention to Dickens an anecdote he'd been told by an acquaintance named Dilke, who knew John Dickens from the Navy Pay Office. The anecdote implied that Dickens 'had some juvenile employment in a warehouse near the Strand; at which place Mr. Dilke, being with the elder Dickens one day, had noticed him, and received, in return for the gift of a half-crown, a very low bow'.[68]

Dickens was apparently 'silent for some minutes' and it was only 'some weeks later' that he returned to the subject. The story didn't all come out then; Forster admits to having gleaned it over time, from various sources. Forster mentions conversations with Dickens, a fragment of memoir written by him – which has vanished – and the 'proof-sheets' of *David Copperfield* which had been 'interlined' (that is, annotated) 'at the time', presumably just before or during the publication of the story, which took place in 1849 and 1850. Forster was confident both that he had remembered accurately, and that, as he boasts, he had succeeded in 'separat[ing] the fact from the fiction'. I'm not sure he ought to have been.[69] By the time Dickens started talking to him about this period of his life, it already lay nearly 25 years in the past. Another twenty years would go by before Forster published his biography.

According to Forster, sometime in 1822 the Dickens family took a house in Bayham Street in Camden Town. The family consisted at this point of the two parents, John and Elizabeth, Charles, Charles's sisters Fanny and Letitia, and the two younger brothers, Frederick and Alfred. Forster does not mention Harriet – he hardly ever does mention her – but she must presumably have been there, too. Forster does, however, mention two other members of the household: a servant girl from the Chatham workhouse whose name we don't learn, and a lodger named James Lamert – a step-nephew acquired when Mrs Dickens's sister had married Matthew Lamert at the end of 1821.[70]

The families do seem to have quickly become close; John and Elizabeth Dickens's seventh child had been christened with the names 'Alfred Lamert', suggesting that Matthew may have stood godfather, possibly by proxy if he had already left for his new job in Ireland.[71] Uncle Matthew may also have inspired some of the military characters Dickens wrote about later, but the way Forster tells it, Cousin James was by far the more significant presence in his life in the early 1820s. Supposedly James used to take Charles to see plays and there's a lovely little anecdote included in the biography about him giving the younger boy a toy theatre.

Forster describes the new house as 'a mean small tenement, with a wretched little back-garden abutting on a squalid court' and the area 'about the poorest part of the London suburbs'.[72] Actually, from the little we can gather, the houses in Bayham Street seem to have been pleasant enough, and fairly inexpensive given how close they were to London, even if the area was a little rough and ready.[73] Camden was where heavy waggons stopped on their way into London, at one end of the Great North Road – the pulsing artery leading from Scotland through York to the heart of the capital. There were (probably in consequence) a number of inns in the vicinity, including one called Mother Redcap, which hosted a tea garden popular with proper city-dwellers.[74] But the inns, the drunks, would hardly have come as a shock to the Dickens family after all the years they'd spent in Chatham.

And much of Camden Town was, in the 1820s, still new. The local alms-houses had been built only in 1817; some of the churches weren't yet finished. Go around a couple of corners and you'd find sheep grazing in a field.[75] The extensive green spaces nearby weren't open to the public – what is now Regent's Park was still being developed, having not quite completed the shift from royal hunting ground to public amenity, while London Zoo was not even in the planning stages – but still they would have ensured that the local air quality was fairly good; better than in the smog-choked city centre. In fact, in a report of a local coroner's inquest in the autumn of 1822, Camden Town is described as one of 'the villages in the vicinity of London' – not much in keeping with what Forster writes of it.[76] Perhaps his description is coloured by what the place became later, rather than what it was then.

Forster quotes Dickens as saying that his father 'appeared to have utterly lost at this time the idea of educating me at all, and to have utterly put from him the notion that I had any claim upon him, in that regard, whatever. So I degenerated into [...] making myself useful in the work of the little house; and looking after my younger brothers and sisters.'[77] But nearly all the detailed remembrances of this period centre on visits to an uncle in Soho and a godfather in Limehouse and walks in the city; the picture of Camden remains vague. It would appear that Charles made no friends of his own age there, recalled no adventures. It's hard to shift the suspicion that either he didn't spend very long in the area – only a few months perhaps, or maybe just the school holidays – or that something may have been blanked out.

We've seen that Dickens's parents were already in financial trouble, and that they had a tendency to keep making impractical decisions like paying to take out birth announcements in the newspapers. It's all of a piece that, at the end of 1823, they should have decided to send their eldest child, Fanny, to study at the newly founded Royal Academy of Music. They also moved from Camden Town nearer to the city centre, to a house at Gower Street North; 'number four', Forster says.[78] He states that Mrs Dickens planned to set up a school of some sort there. This is a less ridiculous idea than he makes it sound, though in the end nothing came of it. Her family were, after all, musical and had run their own business making pianofortes, while one of her sisters-in-law was an artist. There were worse-qualified teachers about in the 1820s. Gower Street was also home to an 'Academy for Dancing' at Number 3, which suggests a potential source of pupils.[79] Whether the street was necessarily a step up, socially, is difficult to judge. A would-be comic piece in the *New Monthly Magazine* insinuated that it was believed to be 'genteel and out of the common way' only by those who had previously lived in such places as 'Hatton-garden' and 'the Minories' – that is, two impoverished areas of the city in which immigrant and minority communities had often made their homes.[80] It does seem to have attracted residents from bohemian backgrounds. We don't know exactly when the Dickenses moved out, but by the middle of 1825 Number 4 was occupied by a singer at Drury Lane Theatre, a Miss Graddon.[81]

In the light of the family's ongoing financial issues, however, and what came soon after, the move looks simply ill-judged. So does sending Fanny to the Royal Academy when it must have been unclear, even to the most phlegmatic of parents, how long they would be able to pay the fees. Perhaps both decisions were desperate last gambles with what credit or familial generosity they could still call on.

But it was too late.

Now, as related by Forster, comes the nadir of Charles Dickens's life, a humiliation from which he never fully recovered. While his sister Fanny was busy preparing for her future career, studying – and boarding – at the Academy, Charles was sent to work in a boot-polish factory, at the suggestion of his step-cousin James Lamert, whose own cousin (and brother-in-law), George, had bought into the business. Soon afterwards John Dickens was imprisoned for debt in the Marshalsea. Elizabeth Dickens accompanied her husband, going to live in the prison, together with the younger children. Both she and the children would have been free to come and go more or less as they pleased during the day, like Amy Dorrit in *Little Dorrit* (1855–7). It was only John Dickens who was incarcerated. However, Forster tells us that instead of remaining with his mother and siblings, twelve-year-old Charles was inexplicably abandoned in the city, left to share a room with two other unwanted small boys in the house of a family acquaintance. Forster suggests John Dickens must have paid for his son's lodgings, but why did he do so? If John and Elizabeth Dickens were concerned about their eldest son getting into bad company in prison, did they imagine that was the only place bad company might be met with? Could nobody in the extended family find a corner for one pre-pubescent boy? Not the Lamerts? Not any of his aunts or uncles, of whom several lived in London? Not his own grandmother? Surely the money that went towards his lodging would have been better spent on his schooling?

According to Forster, young Charles's days consisted of long hours spent in a 'crazy, tumbledown old house' with 'rotten floors and staircase' and, shudderingly, 'old grey rats swarming down in the cellars'. He would breakfast on a penny loaf and penny bottle of milk, lunch on stale pastries sold cheap or 'a slice of pudding', and eat bread and cheese for his supper. He wandered alone into coffee-houses or, on rare occasions, restaurants and shops, buying a plate of beef, or bootlaces, or sometimes a glass of beer. For friends, he had the other boys in the factory – 'Bob Fagin' (whose name he would later borrow) and someone called 'Poll Green'. He saw his family only on Sundays and had, for the rest of the week, 'No advice, no counsel, no encouragement, no consolation, no support, from any one', only the 'pots of paste-blacking', which he wrapped, 'first with a piece of oil-paper, and then with a piece of blue paper', then tied 'with a string', 'clip[ping] the paper close and neat, all round, until it looked as smart as a pot of ointment from an apothecary's shop', before gluing on the printed labels. On and on, day after day. It's a tale of outrageous parental favouritism – the money had been found to educate the eldest daughter, while the eldest son was not merely put to work but kept there, even after the parental debt had been dealt with, the Marshalsea escaped. When we read

of Charles finally confessing his unhappiness and his mother trying
to insist he be sent back to the factory again, it's almost painful.[82]

But how much of it is true?

A number of scholars of Dickens have tried and failed to locate
James Lamert in the public record. It's been conjectured both that
he may have been illegitimate and that he was actually George
Lamert, for whom we have a partial – though not complete –
bureaucratic paper trail.

It seems likely that neither conjecture is correct. We'll probably
never know for sure whether 'James Lamert' was the invention
of Dickens or of Forster; an attempted concealment, a genuine
mistake or a detail altered to strengthen the similarities between
Dickens's experiences and those of his fictional alter ego David
Copperfield, whose schoolfriend is called James Steerforth. We
can stop looking for him, though; the evidence suggests he never
existed.

The recently digitised service record of Matthew Lamert,
Dickens's uncle-by-marriage, gives the identities of all six of his
children, none of whom are called James.[83] They are, in birth order,
Sophia, George, John, Joseph, Hannah and Rebecca. John looks to
be the best fit with the information Forster offers us in the biography.[84] How much of that information can we believe, though?

Who and what can we trust in this narrative?

Well, we are reasonably sure, from the records of the Marshalsea
prison, that John Dickens entered the gaol on 20 February 1824.
This is likely to have followed a short period in a 'sponging house',
where debtors were kept while they made any last-ditch attempts
to raise funds. Though the death of John's mother, in April, soon
offered the prospect of his inheriting some money, and therefore
gaining a route out of prison, it was by no means the end of the
matter. A petition for relief (a hearing to arrange payment or insol-
vency) wasn't scheduled until the end of May; in December 1824
someone seems to have been attempting to arrange a meeting of
John Dickens's creditors in Rochester.[85]

And putting 'James' to one side, we can also be confident that
there was a link between the Lamerts and a boot-polish factory on
the banks of the Thames. Both George Lamert (one of Charles's
step-cousins) and a man called William Woodd or Woody (who

was married to another of his step-cousins, Sophia Lamert) had interests in one. Their partner in the business, though largely silent, was Jonathan Warren, a member of a family who had won considerable market share with their boot-polish. Just as Forster's biography relates, the Lamert/Woodd-owned factory was based – for a period, anyway – at Hungerford Stairs, Strand, in a house with a '30' painted on it. Since they sold polish branded as 'Warren's', the address enabled a crafty, if morally questionable, marketing plan – that of stealing custom from a close relation of Jonathan Warren's, Robert Warren, whose business was based at 30 The Strand and with whom he was, not surprisingly, in disagreement over ownership of the brand. With a careful choice of font size for 'Hungerford Stairs', the addresses on the packaging from the two different factories could be made to look almost identical.

There any certainty ends.

For a start, one London schoolfellow of Dickens's at Wellington House Academy suggested that Dickens had joined the school in the spring of 1824, soon after he himself had done so, and 'not later than June'. This agrees with the recollection of a second pupil, that Dickens had attended for two years, in 1824 and 1825.[86] Forster reports one fellow pupil who remembered that Dickens lived in 'one of the now old and grimy-looking stone-fronted houses in George Street, Euston Road', near the 'Orange Tree Tavern' – which sounds a lot like the house at 4 Gower Street North.[87]

But Forster suggests that Dickens was working at the boot-polish factory for months, after John Dickens came out of the Marshalsea, well into the summer of 1824. And he is also definite that Dickens's time at Wellington House Academy came *after* the family had left Gower Street North.[88] Possibly the family somehow managed to return to the house later in 1824, or had sublet it. Or, of course, there is the episode in Forster's biography where the young Dickens, desperate to avoid a new work acquaintance finding out where he really lives, winds up knocking on the door of a stranger's house, as if it's his own.[89] Perhaps that episode is essentially true but in fact involved a schoolfellow and Charles pretending he still lived in his old house. Yet another schoolfellow states that he lived 'in a very small house in a street leading out of Seymour Street, north of Mr Judkin's chapel', that is, Johnson Street, so if he did pretend it wasn't to everyone.[90]

Or perhaps there's a simpler answer, that Charles started his time at Wellington House earlier in 1824, before he moved from one house to the other, and that Forster is in error.

Forster does make some errors. It really doesn't seem likely that Charles can have stopped off on his way back to 'the borough' (that is, the neighbourhood of the Marshalsea prison) to buy a glass of the 'best – the *very* best – ale' to celebrate his birthday, as Forster's narrative encourages us to believe.[91] His birthday, 7 February, fell a fortnight before his father was imprisoned there. The episode might have occurred while his father was still in a sponging house, although that would make young Charles a cold-blooded little blighter, quaffing a celebratory ale when his family was trembling on the verge of disaster.

Similarly, Dickens recalls for Forster the family of an 'insolvent court agent', with whom he lodged in Lant Street, near the Marshalsea, at some point during this period: 'a fat, good-natured, kind old gentleman [...] lame' with 'a quiet old wife' and a 'very innocent grown-up son' (that is, intellectually disabled). And he gave Forster the impression that they 'still live very pleasantly as the Garland family' – a reference to the cheerful elderly couple in *The Old Curiosity Shop* who employ Little Nell's friend, the humble yet honest Kit.[92] There was an insolvent court agent living in Lant Street, one Archibald Russell, but he was a widower, having lost his wife in 1820 and a son the following year.[93] I've found no record of his remarrying.[94]

Might Forster have misunderstood? Might Dickens have misremembered?

If Dickens filled in gaps, made assumptions, conflated events or backdated memories when talking to Forster 25 years or so after the event, perhaps we shouldn't be surprised. It would, after all, have been a stressful time in his life. Perhaps we shouldn't be taken aback that he doesn't seem to remember what was actually written on the labels he spent so many hours pasting onto jars, or how much he was paid.[95] Perhaps we should simply view it as normal that he recalls in detail the backstories of some of the men and boys who worked at the factory – that one 'lived with his brother-in-law', that another's father was 'a fireman, and was employed at Drury Lane theatre' where 'another relation [...] I think his little sister, did imps in the pantomimes' – but not how he himself was related to the factory owners.[96] The fact that in the summer of 1824 the business moved from the waterside to the more salubrious surroundings of Covent Garden stayed with him, but not the move itself.[97] The distance isn't a significant one, so maybe this is natural. Perhaps it's also natural that the demise of Jonathan Warren, who dropped down dead in a nearby shop in August 1824, necessitating an inquest, should have made no impression on the young Dickens at all.[98]

Taken altogether, though, all these gaps and inconsistencies, all these small errors, do rather work to undermine the idea that Forster's biography offers a full and accurate picture of what happened to Dickens in 1824. And there's one other gap in the story.

Forster tells us that, during his time working in the factory, the young Dickens haunted the area known as the Adelphi.[99] It's here we find the Adelphi Theatre, which, in its modern 1930s incarnation, still occupies the same site on the Strand, just a few minutes' walking distance from both Hungerford Stairs and Covent Garden.

What he doesn't tell us, and may very well not have been aware of, is that during the 1823–4 season the Adelphi was showing a new pantomime called *Doctor Faustus and the Black Demon, or Harlequin and the Seven Fairies of the Grotto*. A physical copy of one of the playbills featuring it survives and is reproduced at the start of the chapter. The play was a unique retelling of the Faustus legend, with fairies, a harlequinade, a charmless, racist characterisation of a Chinese servant and 'a panoramic representation of the bombardment of Algiers'. As was usual, the play featured quite a number of scenes set in different places, some real, some imaginary, all listed in the advertisements.[100] Among the imaginary were the 'Silver Palace of the Golden Isles' and a 'Coral Grotto'; among the real, the pier at Brighton and 'Jonathan Warren's Blacking Warehouse, Hungerford Stairs'.

Sadly, we have no idea how the blacking warehouse was presented in the play, or which characters were shown, though the scenes are likely to have been got up expensively and elaborately.[101] But we do know that it was being staged all the way through the early part of 1824, until at least April.[102] This means it was on, at the Adelphi, when Dickens is supposed to have been working at the factory at Hungerford Stairs and, during his leisure hours, haunting the area around the theatre. As is well documented, Dickens loved the theatre, even as a child.[103] The idea that he somehow missed seeing advertisements for the play, or forgot about it, that it wasn't talked about among the youthful employees whose place of work it featured, that it didn't stick in his mind at all, is quite hard to believe.

The picture of the young Charles as an inexplicably neglected child labouring forlornly in a warehouse by the river while his father languishes in the Marshalsea prison is terribly affecting, but can we be sure that it's accurate?

⇛⇝

Awareness of Harriet and her probable health issues might already incline us to view Charles's parents with less disapproval than formerly. And actually it is possible to piece together a different timeline of events, one in which John and Elizabeth Dickens appear a lot less wantonly neglectful of their eldest son than they do in Forster's narrative.

We could, for example, have Charles coming up to London later than the rest of the family after a period boarding at his school in Chatham – which is what his headmaster's sister recalled. This might take us quite a way into 1823. There might then have been a break from schooling before the move to the house in Gower Street North late in 1823. Then, in 1824, rather than starting work, perhaps Charles went to school at Wellington House Academy. That would explain both why one of his schoolfellows seems to have remembered him living in Gower Street North and others as being present for most of 1824, and why he himself recalled so little about events at the factory during the period Forster tells us he worked there, not when or how it moved to better premises, not the pantomime in the nearby theatre which featured it as a setting, not the dramatic death of one of the main business partners. Even if Charles did spend some time living in paid lodgings, his weekdays would have been regimented and disciplined and his education kept up. There would have been no abandonment, no melodramatic neglect or forcing of Charles into lowly employment at a tender age.

Plenty of parents are guilty of favouritism, but we wouldn't, then, need to believe that Dickens's mother and father had been quite so blatant as to send their eldest son to work aged twelve while keeping his elder sister at music school, or quite so negligent as to leave him almost alone in the city while keeping his younger siblings safe.

And there is another, less melodramatic version of Dickens's employment in the boot-polish industry. It's said that when, some years later, he was trying to break into journalism, one of his uncles claimed, in a letter of recommendation, that he had 'assisted Warren the blacking man in the conduct of his extensive business, among other things had written puff [i.e. promotional] verse for him'.[104] Not all biographers accept this as true – mostly because it comes via a man called John Payne Collier, who, though he moved in the right circles at the right time, is a known literary forger. Even those few biographers who do accept his version of events have generally treated it as family soft-soaping.

At a time when the majority of people were obliged to walk considerable distances going about their daily lives, on roads that were often unpaved, and where street drainage was still supplied in many places by filthy open 'kennels' (drains and sewers all in one), there was a lot of money in boot-polish. The competing companies – including both of the businesses which used the Warren name – found it well worth their while to invest in large and costly newspaper advertisements, complete with illustrations, stories, poems and acrostics. So working at Warren's, a company with family connections, would have offered the young Dickens both some money and a possible route into writing for a career, penning advertising copy and the like.

And you could fit it in. Perhaps we should envisage Charles undertaking his first job not as a small, piteous figure labouring in a rat-filled warehouse by the river but in more respectable premises and as a teenager. He could have been associated with the boot-polish business after he'd finished his schooling and before he started his training as a lawyer's clerk; we're not certain when his schooling stopped. This could have been when Forster's informant

Dilke encountered him. Charles might even have done piecework in his late teens alongside other employment.

Forster tells us of Dickens watching as his sister Fanny 'received one of the prizes given to the pupils of the Royal Academy of Music' and of how he was reduced to tears by the idea that he was 'beyond the reach of all such honourable emulation and success'.[105] He associates this event with the period in which Dickens worked at the boot-polish factory. But Fanny was awarded prizes not just in 1824 but in 1826 as well.[106] And she was praised in lavish terms at the 1827 prize-giving.[107] How can we possibly say that what Dickens was recalling for his friend was the first of these occasions, rather than the second or the third?

Dickens clearly talked to Forster about his childhood, but there's little proof that the narrative Forster gives us is correct. Most of the independent evidence we have suggests it isn't – not in every particular, certainly. It makes for a great story, though.

Long before he began on *David Copperfield*, Dickens had shown himself willing to approach the subject of boot-polish a number of times in his work, on several occasions mentioning Warren's by name, in connection with the employment they offered to authors. In 'Seven Dials' (1835), one of his first published pieces, there's a 'shabby-genteel man' who occupies the 'back attic' of an over-crowded lodging house, and who, since he 'never was known to buy anything beyond an occasional pen, except half-pints of coffee, penny loaves, and ha'porths of ink', is supposed to be 'an author' who 'writes poems for Mr. Warren'. In *The Pickwick Papers* (1836–7), the exuberant Cockney coachman Tony Weller, father to Mr Pickwick's sharp young servant Sam, is made to remark that 'Poetry's unnat'ral; no man ever talked in poetry 'cept a beadle on boxin' day, or Warren's blackin' or Rowland's oil'. In *The Old Curiosity Shop* (1840–41) another jobbing writer enlarges on what 'my poetry has done', for 'perfumers', 'blacking-makers', 'hatters' and 'old lottery-office-keepers' and offers to rewrite 'an acrostic' for a customer – 'the name at this moment is Warren, and the idea's a convertible one'.

It's difficult to see in these references the smarting sensitivity that you would expect, given what Forster tells us. If Warren's was such a painful spot in Dickens's life – so raw that years afterwards he had to cross the road to avoid the smell of corks being sealed onto polish bottles, as he supposedly told Forster in the late 1840s – why did he keep coming back to it on and off in print for a dozen years before-hand, often quite cheerfully?[108] Compulsion, perhaps, but plenty of what happens elsewhere in *David Copperfield* is fictional. Why assume that novel is necessarily a more accurate reflection of what Dickens felt or experienced than his earlier depictions of Warren's?

Whatever the truth about Dickens's employment in the boot-polish factory – whether it happened as Forster reports, or later on, in the advertising line, as the other version of the story goes, or whether it happened at all – we should exercise a greater degree of caution in talking and writing about this part of his life.

Forster's version of the story has dominated nearly every bio-graphical discussion of Dickens for 150 years. It's served to send hundreds of researchers haring off in search of 'James Lamert', someone who appears never to have existed.[109] And it's succeeded in hiding a fact which I think has to affect – and maybe alter – our understanding of more than one of Dickens's novels.

Matthew Lamert's service record reveals, as we saw, the iden-tities of his children, Dickens's step-cousins. The same document enables us to work out why the local parish records for the fam-ily are far scantier than one might expect: Matthew was born in Germany, and several of his children were born overseas. They were also Jewish.[110]

Matthew Lamert's first marriage, to Sarah Lamert, took place, it turns out, in the Great Synagogue in London in 1798, with Matthew then going by his original name, which was Moses.[111] Matthew seems to have been keen to assimilate, changing his name, marry-ing into Dickens's family, perhaps being a godfather for Charles's second-youngest brother Alfred Lamert Dickens. Most of his six children followed his example and married in church, though one at least chose to marry a spouse who was also of Jewish ancestry.[112]

Was Dickens aware of his uncle's background? If he wasn't when he was a child, I suspect he could hardly failed to have known in later years.

It would have been easy to keep track of the Lamerts, with their unusual surname and given that most of them shared the Dickens family's *penchant* for placing announcements in the births, marriages and deaths columns.[113] And there was another member of the Lamert family whose name appeared in the newspapers all the time. This was Abraham Lamert, familiar to the public in the first half of the nineteenth century from newspaper advertisements. Abraham had a well-publicised line in proprietary medicines, inherited from his father Isaac – the 'Cordial Balm of Zura', the 'wonderful ointment, the Poor Irishman's Friend' – which he claimed cured anything from blindness to venereal disease. From time to time he mentioned his relationship to Matthew in advertisements.[114] His address, also given in the advertisements, was in Spitalfields, one of London's unofficial Jewish quarters, close to where both the Sephardi synagogue, Bevis Marks, and the Great Synagogue were located. After Abraham's death in 1836, and some serious financial wobbles, a new generation of Lamerts took over, and by the 1860s they seem to have operated chiefly as specialists in sexual health.[115] They kept going with the advertisements.

While we're on the subject of the Lamerts, it's also worth touching on Dickens's pen name, Boz, and how we ought to say it. According to Forster's *The Life of Charles Dickens*, it was originally the family nickname of Charles's 'youngest brother Augustus', short for 'Boses', that is, 'Moses [...] facetiously pronounced through the nose'. Forster claims the inspiration came from a character in the popular eighteenth-century work *The Vicar of Wakefield*.[116] But we know now that Moses was the original name of Matthew Lamert, who I suggested might have been Alfred Lamert Dickens's godfather – it appears evident, at least, that Alfred was named for him. Is it not possible – even likely – that either Dickens or Forster has garbled the story here, that it was *Alfred* who was nicknamed Moses, as a nod to his uncle's origins? Not a very tactful one, since the 'facetious' mispronunciation is strongly reminiscent of nineteenth-century 'jokes' about Jewish accents, but nevertheless an acknowledgement of sorts. And if we're correct in thinking this, what should we make of Dickens's decision to use the name 'Boz' himself? Have we been labouring under a misapprehension, not only about its pronunciation, but its meaning?

&∞§

For a century and a half, readers have been encouraged to follow Forster in viewing the riverside factory section of *David Copperfield* as autobiographical. But now that we know more about the Lamerts, do we extend autobiographical readings to other Dickens novels, to episodes where children find themselves in the company or care of characters who are Jewish? Should we interpret Oliver Twist's misadventures with the Jewish fence, Fagin, as, potentially, a form of concealed memoir? Surely not. Dickens clearly gave Forster the impression that he liked the Lamerts, whereas *Oliver Twist* draws on ancient, noxious veins of anti-Semitism.[117]

The character of Fagin is introduced as 'a very old shrivelled Jew, whose villainous-looking and repulsive face was obscured by a quantity of matted red hair'. Dickens manages to refer to him as 'the Jew' another six times over the course of the next three-and-a-half paragraphs and a further 100 times over the rest of the novel. Fagin is only one of a group of criminal conspirators against Oliver – not the worst or the most violent – but he alone is left to carry the can, so far as the novel is concerned. Everyone else, including Oliver's half-brother, gets to cheat justice one way or another. Fagin, meanwhile, encounters not 'the faintest sympathy' in the courtroom and finds himself sentenced to hang, dreading the dawn, eventually driven mad by the waiting. He has no friends to mourn him, no consolation of religion offered him. Why is he the only character treated this way? It's difficult to believe that his race is irrelevant.

If *Oliver Twist*'s anti-Semitism is bad, *The Old Curiosity Shop* is worse. Its main villain is a 'malicious dwarf' named Quilp who has nefarious designs on the body and imagined inheritance of the young and innocent Little Nell. Fleeing him, she is driven across England, dependent on the dubious kindness of strangers, finding rest only on her deathbed. Quilp's helpers, the corrupt lawyer Sampson Brass and Sampson's sister Sally, are Jewish; their ethnicity not – this time – ever explicitly stated but clearly indicated. Almost the first thing we're told about Sampson is that he is 'from Bevis Marks', the location of the main Sephardi synagogue in London.[118] The Brass siblings are written in anti-Semitic shorthand; readers are told of one's 'reddish' hair, of the other's 'cringing manner' and noticeably large nose, while their surname, given Dickens's often eccentric, memorable efforts, is crassly straightforward – 'Brass', money. The pair are horrible. They keep a nameless child locked in their house as an unpaid and underfed skivvy; Sally's own daughter, we gather, and, we're given to understand, Quilp's, too, possibly the product of rape.[119] However, unlike Little Nell, this girl gets to end the novel not just alive but happy, gaining a name (Sophronia, 'Sophy' for short, like the oldest of the Lamert siblings), an education, a 'little cottage at Hampstead' and a fond husband who, though he suspects the truth about her origins, experiences, we're told firmly, 'no uneasiness' on the subject.

Sophy's happy ending offers an oddly sunny, almost post-racial postscript to the ugly attitudes that appear elsewhere in the novel and, indeed, elsewhere in Dickens's writing. So too does the fact that Dickens gave his fourth son, another Alfred, born several years after the novel appeared, the nickname 'Sampson Brass'.[120]

In his 2019 study of the imitations and piracies which were the bane, not just of Dickens's career, but of several popular Victorian writers, Adam Abraham suggests that one way in which the pirated versions of *Oliver Twist* differed from the original was in being even more egregiously anti-Semitic.[121] This introduces the depressing possibility that, regardless of his personal views, regardless of his relationship with the Lamerts and the fond memories he seems to have had of at least some of them, Dickens chose to include racist tropes in his work because there was a market for it. For many people that might make the situation even worse.

Other, cheerier expressions of Dickens's attitude to his Lamert cousins may be found in two later novels. One is of course *Our Mutual Friend* (1864–5), where the disabled 'Jenny Wren' is befriended by the Jewish Mr Riah, and the orphaned Lizzie Hexam finds refuge and honest employment with a Jewish family. The other, perhaps less obvious one, is *A Tale of Two Cities* (1859), in which it seems that we may be intended to read Lucie Manette's ridiculous but kindly companion Miss Pross as Jewish.[122] Again, though, I'm unsure how much difference, if any, either of these more positive portrayals makes.

It may be that *Our Mutual Friend* best expresses Dickens's feelings about what happened to him in the last months and years of his childhood. It may be that *David Copperfield* does, or *A Tale of*

Two Cities, or *Oliver Twist*, or Forster's biography, or that all of these stories did so, at different times and in different ways. There is no way, though, that Dickens's anti-Semitism should be minimised. Given the facts, we absolutely cannot brush it off while murmuring some bromide about ignorance, or widespread Victorian attitudes. Even if it was partly a smokescreen, intended to distract from his Jewish relations, it doesn't stop it being anti-Semitism – though it makes it more complicated, closer to home than we've previously believed.

In fact, almost everything to do with Dickens's early years turns out to be more complicated than we've been led to think.

We're accustomed to thinking that – just as Forster insisted – *David Copperfield* offers a lightly concealed, but fundamentally truthful account of Dickens's own experiences in the boot-polish factory and that those experiences were searingly, scarringly terrible; a humiliating psychic wound. The idea that they may not have taken place at all, or not the way we've thought; that Dickens's life, aged eleven to thirteen, may have been quite different; that he may have deliberately edited events to make his resentment of his parents appear more justified than it really was or to conceal his relations: it's disruptive, challenging. But it's liberating, too.

Forster's biography may not offer us much in the way of reliable facts; what it does do is show us that Dickens moved on from just not sharing information about his childhood. He started manipulating his life story for posterity, and always in a way which was likely to appeal to the public and to make him the object of sympathy.

Forster's insistence on seeing this period as the central, shaping trauma of Dickens's life leads him to present what came before, and after it, as comparatively straightforward and unproblematic. This, presumably, is what Dickens wanted us to believe, too. We've already seen, however, that Chatham was not without its share of problems. Nor were the years in which Dickens grew to adulthood.

Notes

68. John Forster, *The Life of Charles Dickens*, volume 1, pages 27–8.
69. As above, page 29.

70. As above, pages 16–18.

71. Medway Archives, Baptisms register, 3 April 1822. P85/1/25 1820–22, page 124 https://cityark.medway.gov.uk/wwwopacx/ wwwopac.ashx?command=getcontent&server=files&val-ue=P085-01-25(1).pdf). Accessed via Find My Past.

72. John Forster, *The Life of Charles Dickens*, volume 1, page 16.

73. An advertisement of 1818 describes 'No. 14 Bayham-street', Camden Town as having a 'parlour, kitchen, and stable' and as being 'in a most desirable and healthy situation', while one of 1826 lists three properties on the road as 'eight room Dwelling-houses, situated upon Lord Camden's estate' 'in the occupation of respectable tenants at very low rents' (*Morning Advertiser*, 16 May 1818, page 3; 9 October 1826, page 4).

74. It's possible that they served as inspiration for the description of the 'well-known rural "Tea-Gardens"' in Dickens's early story 'London recreations'.

75. The theft of five sheep from 'a Field situate at the rear of Mornington-crescent, Camden-town' was reported in the *Police Gazette*, 20 June 1829, page 3.

76. See *Morning Chronicle*, 21 November 1822, page 4. The inquest was to determine on the death of an elderly crossing sweeper who tended the road, and had been killed by a private carriage which, 'in trying to pass a one-horse chaise' had sped up to a pace of 'between nine and ten miles'. We might wonder whether there is, here, any suggestion of the child crushed to death by a carriage in *A Tale of Two Cities*.

77. John Forster, *The Life of Charles Dickens*, volume 1, page 18.

78. As above, volume 1, page 23. The house is now essentially in the middle of University College London.

79. See *Morning Post*, 10 October 1823, page 3; 18 March 1825, page 1.

80. Reprinted in the *Perthshire Courier*, 17 December 1824, page 4.

81. In an advertisement announcing a benefit performance for her, her address is given as '4, Gower-street North', *The Examiner*, 19 June 1825, page 13.

82. John Forster, *The Life of Charles Dickens*, volume 1, page 31 ff.

83. National Archives, WO 25/803/34, Folio 66.

84. Forster claims that the man 'relinquished' a 'commission in the army […] in favour of a younger brother' – which the youngest

brother, Joseph, would obviously have struggled to do (*The Life of Charles Dickens*, volume 1, page 29).

85. 'John Dickens, Gower-street North, clerk in the Navy Pay Office', See *Public Ledger and Daily Advertiser*, 19 May 1824, page 2. See also Andy Wood, 'In debt and incarcerated: the tyranny of debtors' prisons', https://www.thegazette.co.uk/all-notices/content/100938, which notes the planned creditors' meeting in Rochester, advertised in the *London Gazette*, 21 December 1824.

86. Robert Langton, *The Childhood and Youth of Charles Dickens* (1883, 1891), the chapter 'School Again'.

87. John Forster, *The Life of Charles Dickens*, volume 1, page 60. 'George Street' was north of the New Road, now the A501. Directly opposite it, immediately to the south of the New Road, came the short stretch of Gower Street North, running straight down into Upper Gower Street. George Street is now called 'North Gower Street', while 'Gower Street North' and 'Upper Gower Street' were both incorporated into 'Gower Street'. What's being described is the crossroads, which is where the Orange Tree Tavern was located. This is not so very far distant from Johnson Street/The Polygon, where Forster suggest the family was living when Dickens was at the school, but it seems unlikely that anyone could confuse the two houses. See Greenwood's Map of London, *Map of London, From an actual Survey made in the years 1824, 1825 & 1826. By C. and J. Greenwood*, 1827. There's a zoomable version available online, hosted by Bath Spa University.

88. The quotation comes from Forster's biography, *The Life of Charles Dickens*; perhaps the name changes the road underwent blinded him to what seems to contradict his narrative.

89. John Forster, *The Life of Charles Dickens*, volume 1, page 41.

90. As above, page 62.

91. As above, page 43.

92. As above, pages 39–40.

93. Death notice for 'Louisa, wife of A.C. Russell of Lant street Southwark', *Public Ledger and Daily Advertiser* 6 January 1820, page 4. Death and baptism records for Archibald Campbell Russell, 23 July 1821 (National Archives TNA/RG/8/75), 30 November 1799 (TNA/RG/5/31, D1-250). The couple had daughters, Elizabeth and Sarah, and another son, Joshua, who had married in 1822 and worked as a

solicitor (*Public Ledger and Daily Advertiser*, 19 October 1822, page 4, for the marriage; *Patriot*, 29 January 1834, page 1, for the employment, earlier references to the firm of solicitors in Lant Street named Russell presumably also being the same person). I haven't found any other child. Possibly I've missed him, or he was a nephew or the son of a housekeeper, but as ever, the evidence doesn't support either Dickens's recollections or Forster's assertions.

94. A number of websites relate that Dickens lodged with the 'vestry clerk of St. George's Church', though I have struggled to trace the original source for this piece of information. The Metropolitan Archives identify the vestry clerk's surname as Russell; it seems clear this is the right family. London Metropolitan Archives, Saint George the Martyr: Borough High Street, Southwark (https://search.lma.gov.uk/LMA_DOC/P92_GEO.PDF).

95. See John Forster, *The Life of Charles Dickens*, volume 1, page 32, where he refers only to 'a printed label'; also page 30.

96. As above, pages 32–3.

97. As above, page 47.

98. *Morning Advertiser*, 18 August 1824, page 2; *Bell's Weekly Messenger*, 22 August 1824, page 5.

99. John Forster, *The Life of Charles Dickens*, volume 1, page 42.

100. Writers of pantomimes tended to select 'topics that were close at hand and that were readily understandable and interesting to London audiences [...] Arrangers and comics were quick to point out products that were as dangerous as they were useful and to deride commercial practices and economic policies which produced undesirable consequences' (David Mayer III, *Harlequin in His Element: The English Pantomime, 1806–1836* (Harvard University Press, 2013; reprint), page 191).

101. The manuscript of the play which survives offers no details for the later scenes other than that they contained 'comic business'. Huntington Library, John Larpent Plays, LA2392.

102. 'Adelphi Theatre Strand. This evening will be presented the favourite Burletta of The Deuce is in Her. – A Grand Divertissement. – After which the admired Burletta of Married Bachelor. – To conclude with the Grand Pantomime of The Black Demon; or Harlequin and the Seven fairies of the Grotto', *Morning Advertiser*, 3 April 1824, page 2.

103. He claimed that he had been 'brought up [i.e. to London] from remote country parts in the dark ages of 1819 and 1820 to behold the splendour of Christmas Pantomimes', letter to the Sub-editor of *Bentley's Miscellany*, (?)March 1838.

104. John Payne Collier, *An Old Man's Diary, Forty Years Ago, Part IV, for the last six months of 1833* (Thomas Richards, 1872), pages 12–13. We can discount Collier's claim that Dickens was the author of one Warren's poems about a dove (as reported in *Dundee Evening Telegraph*, 18 July 1884, page 2). The poem he identifies as Dickens's work appeared in newspapers at least as early as 1817.

105. John Forster, *The Life of Charles Dickens*, volume 1, pages 46–7.

106. 'Pianoforte [...] 2d prizes, Misses Foster and Dickons [...] W.H. Phipps and Miss Dickons had the honour of receiving prizes for general good conduct', *Morning Post*, 2 July 1824, page 3; 'At the conclusion of the concert Sir J. Murray announced the rewards to the successful candidates' among whom were 'Misses Dickens, Foster [...] The medals and other rewards were paid for and bestowed in person by her Royal Highness the Princess Augusta', *Belfast Commercial Chronicle*, 12 July 1826, page 4.

107. *London Evening Standard*, 5 July 1827, page 1.

108. John Forster, *The Life of Charles Dickens*, volume 1, pages 49–50.

109. There's no indication that James was even a middle name. John Lamert's middle name was Thomas; Joseph's, according to his will, was Richard. See PROB 11: Will Registers, 1848–1849, Piece 2095: Vol. 10, Quire Numbers 451–500 (1849), accessed via Ancestry.

110. The first suggestion that the Lamerts were Jewish is Michael Allen, 'Locating Tom-all-alone's', *Dickens Quarterly*, Vol. 29, No. 1 (March 2012), page 32 ff. See also my article, 'Matthew Lamert's military record: clarifying the Lamert family origins', *Dickens Quarterly*, Vol. 38, No. 3 (September 2021), page 319 ff.

111. They were presumably cousins of some kind.

112. The youngest Lamert child, Rebecca, went to live in Ireland with her father and afterwards moved to Toronto, in Canada, where she died (see *Limerick Chronicle*, 7 April 1832, page 3; *Southern Reporter and Cork Commercial Courier*, 3 September 1839, page 3). Hannah married a vicar's son in 1850, on the Isle of Man (*Cork Examiner*, 9 August 1850, page 2). George married a woman called Harriet

Oppenheim; the evidence indicates she was from a Jewish family as well (see *Weekly Dispatch*, 4 February 1827, page 7). The Joseph Lamert who married Eliza Barnett at the Great Synagogue in 1834 seems to be a cousin of the same name. John went to live in Cork, in Ireland, where in fact he'd been baptised (on 9 April 1806). There are several references to a 'John Lamert' or 'Lamerte' in the Irish newspapers, and also a record of his marriage, to a 'Miss Wiseman' in St Peter's Church, in 1835 (*Southern Reporter and Cork Commercial Courier*, 21 February 1835, page 3). Joseph joined the 97th Regiment of Foot in 1825 (National Archives, WO 25/804/67, Folio 133). His will reveals that he later became a captain in the 78th Regiment of Foot.

113. Hence, for example, his ability to tell Forster about John resigning his army commission in favour of Joseph.

114. According to a newspaper puff letter: 'Having heard Dr Lamert of the 7th R.V.B., when lying in Gibraltar, during the sickness which raged there in 1813, mention he had a brother in London famed for his skill in complicated cases, induced me to believe you might be the person, which turned out to be correct' (*Aberdeen Press and Journal*, 16 July 1834, page 1, and elsewhere). There is a degree of uncertainty as to whether Abraham was in fact Matthew's own brother or his brother-in-law. Though Isaac Lamert's will (National Archives PROB 11/1721/91) describes John Lamert as his grandson it does not mention Matthew, or Matthew's other children. Perhaps there was a falling-out over religious issues.

115. See, for example, the London *Sun*, 20 January 1862, page 1, which advertises 'Dr La'Mert on Self-Preservation', but their advertisements appear frequently in different newspapers around the country. For a reference to Abraham Lamert's bankruptcy, see the transcript of the trial of Thomas Gore for theft and embezzlement, 9 May 1836, Old Bailey Online (reference number t18360509-1335, oldbaileyonline.org).

116. John Forster, *The Life of Charles Dickens*, volume 1, page 83.

117. Dickens did tone down the anti-Semitism in the novel slightly in the 1860s, after being taken to task by a Jewish reader, Eliza Davis. The Davises had taken over the rent of Tavistock House when Dickens moved out.

118. See the Sephardi Community webpage on Bevis Marks synagogue (https://www.sephardi.org.uk/bevis-marks/visit-bevis-marks/).

119. A passage making explicit the identity of the girl's mother was removed before publication, though there are heavy hints in the published text. See Gerald Grubb, 'Dickens's Marchioness identified', *Modern Language Notes*, LXVIII (1953), page 162 ff.

120. See, for example, letter to Frederick Dickens, 9 September 1846.

121. Adam Abraham, *Plagiarizing the Victorian Novel: Imitation, Parody, Aftertext* (Cambridge University Press, 2019).

122. Miss Pross has red hair, believed at this point to be a typically Jewish physical characteristic, and her brother's real name is, we are told, Solomon, though he has invented a new identity, that of John Barsad. 'Barsad' is described early in the novel as 'one of the greatest scoundrels upon earth since accursed Judas – which he certainly did look rather like' and elsewhere as having an 'aquiline, but not straight' nose with 'a peculiar inclination towards the left cheek', a feature which is mentioned several times.

WATCH WHERE HE SETTLES (1827–35)

3

Extract from the 'Deaths' column in the _London Evening Standard_, 21 August 1827. (The British Library Board. All rights reserved. With thanks to The British Newspaper Archive)

Many nineteenth-century novelists avoid grappling with the adolescence of their protagonists altogether, beginning the story when they are already young adults, or fast-forwarding them from, say, aged twelve or fourteen, to about eighteen or twenty in the space of, at most, a few paragraphs. Dickens sometimes does this – in _David Copperfield_, for example, and in Esther Summerson's narration in _Bleak House_. Sometimes he doesn't. Nell, the heroine of _The Old_

Curiosity Shop (1840–41), is fourteen when her story commences; several of the other characters in the novel are in their mid-teens, too. Florence Dombey's lonely adolescence occupies plenty of narrative time in *Dombey and Son* (1846–8). Both girls are vulnerable, unhappy, moved about from place to place, either through compulsion or the whims of adults, menaced by unwelcome sexual attention, unable to rely on their nearest relations. Following Forster, readers have been very keen to see David Copperfield's experiences as reflecting those of his creator. We might, now, also need to consider tracing some autobiographical echoes in the figure of Oliver Twist and, despite the difference in sex, in Sophy in *The Old Curiosity Shop*; possibly even, less distinctly, in Lucie Manette and Lizzie Hexam as well. Having done this, why not add Little Nell and Florence Dombey? There are echoes between their experiences and those of their creator. Like John Dickens, Nell's grandfather is hopeless with money. Florence Dombey has to watch a younger sibling die, as Charles did. Writers have to draw their inspiration from somewhere, whether that process is conscious or not; it's sometimes said that all characters are, on some level, versions of their authors.

We tend not to find it as easy to summon up sympathy for a hulking male adolescent as for a teenaged girl or pre-pubescent boy, and in many respects it is obviously correct to view girls and young children in general as being particularly vulnerable. Teenage boys aren't exactly safe, though, not in circumstances like the ones Charles Dickens seems to have found himself in.

The precise timeline of events is, as I explained in the previous chapter, difficult to pronounce on with certainty. We can say that Charles attended school in London for a time, at Wellington House Academy, but not when or how long for. He seems to have lost touch with all of his classmates, who retained only patchy memories of him at school – memories which, in some cases, as we saw, seem to suggest the possibility that he may have started there around the end of 1823 or beginning of 1824, when he was living in Gower Street North. On the other hand, he may, as Forster asserts, have been busy in the boot-polish factory then, and only have started back at school in 1825. And then there's the period during which Dickens *might* have worked with his Lamert step-cousins writing advertising copy for their business – although again, we can't be sure when or even whether this happened.

In 1827, not long after his fifteenth birthday, Charles seems to have started working as a clerk for the law firm of Ellis and Blackmore, staying there about eighteen months.[123] After this he was employed by another lawyer called Molloy (sometimes spelt Molley), but not for any significant length of time. By 1829, he had become a shorthand reporter. He was still only seventeen. From here he segued into journalism. He worked most often for a journal of parliamentary record called *The Mirror of Parliament* – a rival to Hansard run by one of his mother's brothers, John Barrow – and sometimes for the *True Sun* and *Morning Chronicle*.

John Barrow was among the more useful of young Charles's relatives, but the *Mirror* was to prove an expensive and ultimately unsuccessful endeavour. Uncle John also had complex familial arrangements – though still in possession of a wife, he had set up home with a mistress, with whom he proceeded to have a number of children.[124] We'll come on to Charles's own marital failings later, of which he had plenty, but it's worth bearing in mind how few solid, reliable male role models he had while growing up. One of Dickens's brothers ended up in the divorce courts; another abandoned his wife and moved to America, where he started a second family: the inescapable conclusion is that they grew up with some very strange ideas about marriage.

In his fifties, the overriding memory Dickens had of his early journalistic career was of movement: 'writing on the palm of my hand by the light of a dark lantern in a post-chaise and four, galloping through a wild country all through the dead of night', having 'been upset in almost every description of vehicle known in England'.[125] He recalled dashing around the country, covering elections, racing other newspapermen to be on the spot for an exciting story. This isn't entirely representative of those years. Shorthand reporting from the courts, or from the Houses of Parliament, involved long hours of waiting around and boredom. There were the court and parliamentary recesses to be filled, too. Dickens appears to have been employed in some part-time capacity by a Frenchman named André Fillonneau who later on would become one of his sister Letitia's in-laws.[126] Possibly this was connected to publishing, or even to advertising, since in 1834 we find an 'A. Fillonneau' connected to the *Town and Country Advertiser*.[127] Dickens may also have toyed with pursuing acting ambitions; certainly he penned dramatic pieces for private performance as well as comic poems to entertain acquaintances. He started publishing stories, too. It's possible that he even began drafting a novel, though we don't know whether any of it ever saw the light of day.[128]

It's small wonder, one way or another, that he struggled to settle.

Received wisdom has it that, after John left the Marshalsea prison in the summer of 1824, the Dickens family went first to Little College Street and then to 29 Johnson Street, in Somers Town, the district between Euston station and Kings Cross St Pancras. Again, this is usually identified as a 'low' neighbourhood. But an advertisement of the time describes '29 Johnson street, Somers-town' as one of 'Four genteel Residences […] let to highly respectable tenants at 120 l. per annum'.[129] It's possible that the advertisement exaggerates, of course, that the house had become less genteel, or was more densely occupied. It may be just that the house number is wrong – in 1829 John Dickens seems to be insured at a different house in the same street.[130] But it's also possible this is yet another example of John Dickens living beyond his means. In 1825 he retired from the Navy Pay Office on the grounds of ill health and, one suspects, because he had finally worn out the patience of his superiors. Navy pensions were by no means bad, and he began to pursue a second career in journalism, but the family's regular income was reduced.

There's some suggestion that in spring of 1827 the Dickens family were evicted for non-payment of rates and that they moved to a house around the corner in the Polygon, a terrace of houses constructed in a circle in the middle of Clarendon Square.[131] But the addresses in this small corner of the city seem to have been slightly fluid. In November 1827, the announcement of the birth of yet another child, their last, Augustus, stated that Mrs Dickens had been delivered of a son 'in Johnson-street, Clarendon-square'.[132] This might be a white lie, designed to conceal the fact that they'd been forced out of their home, though you can find this same formulation elsewhere. Perhaps there was no move. Perhaps the death of Harriet Dickens led to a reprieve. Not every landlord or government official in the nineteenth century was a heartless monster, after all, and a sick child, perhaps with a disability, dying young, leaving behind grieving parents, the mother visibly pregnant, might very well have stirred generosity.

Harriet died in August 1827, three months before the birth of Augustus.[133] In spite of their financial situation, her parents observed all the decencies. Notices of Harriet's death appeared in the *Evening Standard*, the London *Sun*, the *Morning Herald*, the *Morning Chronicle*, the *New Times* and the *Whitehall Evening Post*: 'On the 19th instant, Harriet Ellen, third daughter of Mr. John Dickens, aged 9 years.'[134]

Harriet was not the first sibling that Charles had lost. In 1814 his baby brother had died, an event he almost certainly did not consciously recall, since he was only two and a half when it took place. But when Harriet died he was fifteen; he cannot have been anything other than fully aware of her passing, and with a combination of adult understanding and adolescent sensitivity that would lead it to have a significant and lasting effect on him.

At that age, in anyone's life, the death of a sibling has to be a watershed and yet Dickens chose to conceal it – from Forster, presumably; certainly from us. If I'm right in my suggestion that Harriet had additional needs, then those needs are likely to have absorbed a good deal of the time and energy that her parents had to offer, and perhaps a fair amount of money, too. We know that Frances, Charles's older sister, also absorbed a lot of the family's financial resources in pursuit of her music career. Charles must sometimes have felt ignored, neglected. Add in bereavement, and you have the recipe for a truly toxic mixture of emotions. And he didn't have much opportunity to process them at the time.

Whether or not the story of the eviction has a basis in fact, the financial clouds do seem to have been gathering over the Dickens family yet again.

Between 1825 and 1827, most sources agree in fixing the family in Johnson Street. From 1828 onwards, they're all over the place. We can find traces of them in Norfolk Street, in George Street, Adelphi, at two addresses in Hampstead (North End and No. 3 Belle Vue).[135] We have an insurance record placing John Dickens back in Johnson Street again. Charles addresses letters from some of these locations, and also from '70 Margaret Street Cavendish Square', from 15 Fitzroy Street, from 18 Bentinck Street. He spends a week in Norwood with his uncle, and a fortnight at 'the Red Lion' in Highgate. One letter seems to refer to yet other lodgings in Cecil Street, near the Strand.[136] Trying to pursue Dickens from place to place during these in-between years is a hopeless exercise – we even have a couple of letters where he is seemingly negotiating a house purchase for an unnamed woman, an episode in his life not yet satisfactorily explained.[137]

Bentinck Street does appear to have been where some of the family resided, at least for a time, but several of the places I've mentioned may just have been accommodation addresses – the equivalent of an Amazon locker.[138] There are strong indications that this may have been the case with Margaret Street. The same goes for 10 Norfolk Street, in spite of the blue plaque currently affixed to the wall of the building declaring that Dickens lived there.[139] Where Charles slept, where he kept his belongings, that's anyone's guess.

If we're looking for sources of resentment and insecurity, though, there's no need to look to a little boy in a boot-polish factory: here they are. Only we have Harriet's death irrupting into the plot too, confusing our sympathies. In context, even John Dickens looks less feckless and more consumed by grief. This bit of the story isn't about Charles; it's about Harriet, and taking her out results in gaping holes.

This means that all we can really recover of Dickens's teenage years is glimpses.

Glimpses of a 'handsome', 'curly-headed', 'mischievous' lad; 'a healthy looking boy, small but well-built, with a more than usual flow of spirits' and 'a general smartness about him' playing silly games with his schoolfellows, 'pretending to be poor boys, and asking passers-by for charity' then laughing and running away, speaking gibberish in the street with the 'ambition […] to be considered foreigners'. Remarkable? Not noticeably so. Though one fellow pupil at Wellington Academy recalls him making up stories and putting on plays with his friends, another doesn't 'remember that Dickens distinguished himself in any way or carried off any prizes'. 'I cannot recall anything that then indicated he would here-after become a literary celebrity,' says a third.[140]

We can see glimpses of a taller boy, nearly but not quite a man, crossing the New Road, which ran between Islington and the Edgware Road, strap-hanging on the coaches, dodging between the carts and drays and, as time went on, admiring, perhaps, one of the new omnibuses which started to ply their trade at the end of the 1820s. Glimpses of him bored and daydreaming in a lawyer's office, struggling over shorthand, ploughing through improving books in the reading room at the British Museum. Glimpses of him sitting on the press benches in the House of Commons or, in the House of Lords, standing in 'a preposterous pen' where reporters 'used to be huddled together like so many sheep'.[141] Glimpses of him tumbling into love – or at least what he thought was love.

The object of Charles's youthful affections was a young woman named Maria Beadnell, the daughter of a banker. We'll meet her again in a later chapter, married to another man, carrying a bit of baby weight.

At this point, though, like Dickens, she was still waiting for her life to begin.

According to the local parish register, Maria was born late in December 1810, making her just over a year older than Charles.[142] Not much of an age difference, but probably enough to count. It seems probable that Charles met her via his sister Fanny. In letters Dickens presents himself as an unfavoured suitor to Maria's hand, subject to disapproval from her parents. Maria's father would not leave them alone together, he complains. Maria's mother got his name wrong. They can hardly have viewed him as a desirable mar-riage prospect, though, given his youth, his family obligations, his background and his less than ideal financial situation. What, then, did he have to offer Maria, aside from the lovelorn acrostics on her name and light comic verse about their shared social circle that he wrote for her at the time?

Infatuation is all-consuming in the moment; in retrospect it can appear almost incomprehensible, even absurd. By the time Dickens came to write *David Copperfield*, in his late thirties, he seems to have recognised the utter impracticality of his long-past passion. He told Forster that he had based his hero's feelings for dim, pretty Dora on his own early experiences.[143] And Dora and David have nothing in common. He's besotted with her but there's no real reason for him to be.

It happens as soon as he claps eyes on her, a *coup de foudre*. The 'lovely garden' she walks in, the 'house at Norwood' in which she lives, these offer perhaps more substantial, material attractions than she does herself. The garden is 'beautifully kept' with 'a charming lawn', 'clusters of trees' and 'perspective walks [...] arched over with trellis-work, on which shrubs and flowers grew in the growing season'. The 'wire-arched walks', the 'greenhouse' filled with 'beautiful geraniums', the 'garden-gate', the 'garden-seat', a 'lilac tree': these are solid, tangible. Dora, by contrast, is nebulous, 'a Fairy, a Sylph'; a creature of David's imagination, insubstantial as gossamer. She's ludicrously insulated from real life. A suggestion that she might consider learning to cook makes her faint. The realities of getting money, of marriage and the loss of a child crush her.

Maria Beadnell was perhaps no more real to Charles than Dora is to David. Marrying her was a dream; she was a dream, the prize he longed to attain, not a flesh-and-blood person. She was what motivated him to work and to write, at least according to what he told Forster:

> it excluded every other idea from my mind for four years, at a time of life when four years are equal to four times four; [...] I went at it with a determination to overcome all the difficulties, which fairly lifted me up [...] and floated me away over a hundred men's heads [...] – And so I suffered, and so worked, and so beat and hammered away at the maddest romances that ever got into any boy's head and stayed there [...][144]

As with some of the other information that Dickens gave Forster, we might wonder whether this is all the truth.

The first adult letter of Dickens's that we possess, written when he was nineteen, is addressed not to Maria but to a friend of hers, a Miss Mary Anne (or Marianne) Leigh. The tone might possibly be read as flirtatious: 'I have to apologise for not keeping my promise last night [...] I called at Beadnells *on purpose to fetch you* this Morning,' he writes, 'but you had just gone which vexed me very much as I had anticipated not only the pleasure of walking with you but also of picking that bone that we have to discuss which I will embrace the first opportunity of doing.' He signs off with 'I remain (what shall I say) Yours truly?'[145]

We find Dickens writing to Mary Anne Leigh again, and referring to her, too, after some kind of falling-out with Maria. This time the tone is easier to ascertain. He writes to Miss Leigh with all the self-importance of a young man who believes himself injured, returning her 'Album (which I regret to say want of a moment's time has quite prevented me writing in)', and taking her to task for telling people he had confided in her – even though it seems that he had done so.[146] And he writes to others of Miss Leigh's 'malice', of her 'duplicity and disgusting falsehood', says that 'she has for some reason and to suit her own purposes, of late thrown herself in my way [...] – For instance on the night of the play after we went up stairs I could not get rid of her'.[147] He insists that he never thought of Mary Anne romantically.

Indeed, according to Dickens's letters from this period, more than one of the women he encounters are given to telling the most dreadful lies about him. 'I long to give you my opinion of that Miss Evans,' he writes to a friend, Henry Kolle, 'and to communicate some monstrously strong circumstantial Evidence to prove that she must tell the most confounded -- [...] I shall leave your imagination and observation to supply the blank.'[148] The missing word is, of course, 'lies'. We know almost nothing about Miss Evans, other than that Dickens doesn't seem to have liked her very much, but in 1835 he published a short story called *Miss Evans and the Eagle*. In it, the fictional protagonist's manners and morals leave much to be desired and her flirtatious behaviour leads to her fiancé getting into a fight at a pleasure-garden. Whether or not there's any connection remains unclear. Similarly it may be meaningless coincidence that, in *David Copperfield*, the drunken, light-fingered maid David and Dora employ shares Mary Anne Leigh's first name.

Dickens's behaviour through this whole episode with Maria Beadnell is not exactly edifying. But then, why would it have been? If he's quick to accuse people of lying, that's probably, as we've seen, because he was already inured to lies, surrounded by them – lies about his criminal grandfather and terminally unreliable father, lies about where he lived. If Dickens's actions, and reactions, seem immature, that's because he was. He was so inexperienced – still a teenager when he met Maria and just 23 when he got engaged to another woman.

Dickens can't have been the only young man who, frequently seeing the same two or three sisters, cousins or friends together in the same surroundings, not getting to know any of them well, lacking any opportunity for real privacy, found his romantic interest misinterpreted – or, indeed, divided. It must have been easy for misunderstandings to develop, whether intentionally or not. Dickens explores several such situations in his fiction – sometimes for comedy, as in the breach of promise case which features in *The Pickwick Papers*, and sometimes with greater seriousness, as in *Martin Chuzzlewit* (1843), where a character suddenly proposes to one sister after appearing to court the other – a foretaste of his cruel, sadistic personality.

Quite why the relationship with Maria foundered we don't really know, nor whether anyone aside from Dickens himself considered it a relationship. There's the falling-out glanced at in Dickens's letters, but given how young they both were that may have been a storm in a teacup. Maria's parents could have disapproved and torn the two young lovers apart. She didn't marry until 1845 – by which point she was 34 and Dickens had been married to someone else for nearly a decade. Even so, she seems to have lingered in Dickens's imagination for a long time. His memories of her contributed to Dora, in *David Copperfield* (1849). He entered into an impassioned – and potentially compromising – correspondence with her in middle age. After meeting her, though, he had, he told Forster, metamorphosed her into Flora in *Little Dorrit* (1855) – silly, embarrassing and, what's worse, fat. Dickens's first pieces of published fiction appear so soon after the relationship with Maria had drawn to a close that we might well choose to see her as an inspiration for them, too. But he had other inspirations.

Dickens's first piece of published fiction, 'A Dinner at Poplar Walk', appeared in the *Monthly Magazine* when he was still only 21, at the end of 1833. It is a slight, mildly comic confection in which a 'clerk', proud of his position at 'Somerset House', is persuaded, much against his better judgement, to go to dinner with relatives who nourish expectations.

Other sketches and short stories followed: descriptions of fairs or city streets; comedies set among socially mobile city dwellers, equally out of their depth at a dinner party they are hosting or travelling via steamer to a seaside resort; farcical misunderstandings and contrasting tales of woe. Many of the stories were set in the urban and suburban landscapes where Dickens had spent his teens: Somers Town, Camden Town, 'Fitzroy-square', Cecil Street, Norwood. Some appeared in the *Monthly Magazine*; most found a home in the publications of the author's new employer, the *Morning Chronicle* – an established liberal newspaper. At first the stories appeared without any name attached, then Dickens started making use of his pen name, 'Boz'. Within little more than two years he had three dozen sketches under his belt.

Several of them touch on financial insecurity. In 'Shabby-genteel People', published in 1834, the narrator writes of being 'haunted by a shabby-genteel man' in the 'British Museum' and suggests a common occupation for such types is being 'a clerk of the lowest description, or a contributor to the press of the same grade'. In 'The Boarding House', a young lady marries in order to land her new husband with her debts. Darker still is 'A Passage in the Life of Mr Watkins Tottle', which appeared early in 1835. Mr Tottle is financially embarrassed; his attempts to improve his situation by marrying money are doomed to failure. The friend who has bailed him out washes his hands of him. Tottle ends by drowning himself.

We don't have to go far to find where Dickens got his ideas.

In 1834 John Dickens was again arrested for debt. The family couldn't pay their landlord. Charles was called on – as if he, at 22, could solve matters, as if it was either sensible or fair for him to start taking on debt himself in order to save his father. Tellingly, it took a while for him to start worrying about his father's absence, 'knowing', he wrote resignedly in a letter, 'how apt he is to get out of the way when anything goes wrong'.[149]

It was an aptitude he was starting to acquire himself. Soon after the family's finances hit crisis point again, Dickens outlined a plan for his fourteen-year-old brother Frederick to live with him in bachelor quarters in Furnival's Inn, Holborn, 'to instruct and provide for as best I can'.[150] It seems this isn't exactly what happened, though. Once Dickens was established in his own flat, we find him suggesting that Henry Austin (later his brother-in-law, the husband of his sister Letitia) should move in with him; Frederick isn't mentioned at all.[151]

Can we blame him?

No. Charles was in no position to take on the entire responsibility for Fred, still less for his mother and other siblings. He was just starting to progress in his career and had begun travelling for work – the *Morning Chronicle*'s reports on an election in Essex in January 1835 seem to have been his.[152] There were trips to the West Country. He wanted to get on, so he had to get away. It's understandable, forgivable.

It's understandable, too, that he should have proved willing to grab at any opportunity that presented itself, any handhold that seemed to offer some promise of security and advancement, no matter who he neglected or elbowed aside, no matter the finer feelings of those he might have trampled on. Whether we can forgive the damage he did along the way, the lies he told, is another question altogether.

☙❧

Charles Dickens's relationship with Catherine Hogarth is often seen as a rebound from his involvement with Maria Beadnell, but that's not all there was to it. Catherine had no fortune, so we can acquit Charles of having the purely mercenary motives of a Watkins Tottle. Portraits of her when young show a pretty woman with a delicate, pensive face. And looks aside, she held other attractions for a young man with writing ambitions. Three years Dickens's junior, one of ten siblings, she had been born in Edinburgh but lived in various English towns before, in 1834, her family finally settled in London. Her father, George Hogarth, was a lawyer and journalist with a particular interest in music criticism and had also been a business partner of the famous Scottish novelist Sir Walter Scott. One of her uncles had been Scott's publisher and had a claim to have discovered him. Her mother's father, George Thomson, had known the poet Robert Burns.

Dickens would have met George Hogarth as a more senior employee when he joined the *Morning Chronicle* and seen him promoted to editor of its sister paper the *Evening Chronicle*. He would have been introduced to the Hogarth family in their house at Chelsea, then a pretty village outside London. The reflected glory of Burns and Scott, so near, must have seemed bright. In 1835, when he proposed, he was a young journalist and writer with an eye to progressing in his career and acquiring useful connections and George Hogarth's daughter was excellent marriage material – a sensible, pragmatic choice of bride. Dickens clearly fell for the entire package. As to the extent to which he fell for Catherine herself, or how long he continued to feel that he had made a good match – who's to tell? Even in the letter where Dickens announces to one of his uncles that he is getting married, 'Miss Hogarth' appears squeezed into the middle of a sentence, with publishers and Dickens's own growing reputation on one side, and her father ('one of the most eminent among the Literati of Edinburgh') on the other.[153] There is nothing about her beauty or good nature; almost nothing about her as an individual at all. Might Dickens have picked out one of Catherine's sisters instead, if they'd been older? With the benefit of hindsight the answer is a resounding yes. Might we even suspect that he saw the girls as, on some level, interchangeable? There's some evidence for that, too.

Dickens's story *The Four Sisters* was published in 1835, the year he became engaged to the eldest of four sisters, and in that context it appears rather alarming to modern eyes. The sisters in question are, we're told, 'so completely identified, the one with the other' that the neighbours aren't sure which of them is actually getting married, one even going so far as to suggest that the prospective groom 'was of Eastern descent, and contemplated marrying the whole family at once'. In the church, we're told, '*all* the Miss Willises knelt down at the communion-table, and repeated the responses incidental to the marriage service in an audible voice'. It is only when the youngest sister gives birth that the neighbourhood can rest easy, while the twenty-first-century reader is left to decide whether they have been reading a sweet funny story about sisterly closeness or the disturbing tale of a semi-incestuous *ménage à cinq*.

The first readers of *The Four Sisters*, however, are likely to have reacted quite differently.

It's difficult for us nowadays to switch off our cultural disapproval of the idea of sexual relationships between men and their sisters-in-law. In Britain, as in many countries, the taboo is well-established. In the 1830s, though, respectable young persons tended to interact in situations which were tightly controlled and supervised; things might not be noticeably different after they had made a choice. Some degree of chaperonage was expected even once couples were engaged, and often siblings were drafted in to supply this, a halfway house between parental surveillance and leaving unmarried people alone together. If, after marriage, someone became even closer to a new in-law, perhaps spent weeks or months in the same household, they might have found themselves wondering whether their choice had been the right one. Add in the high maternal mortality rate and it's not really any wonder that marriages between brothers- and sisters-in-law were, if not exactly approved of, at least tolerated, and took place fairly frequently. However, in 1835 a new Marriage Act had specifically made such marriages illegal, unless carried out abroad.[154]

Until Dickens was 23, then, a man's sisters-in-law were not exactly fair game, but nor were they forbidden fruit. We've already seen that Dickens, while professing himself in love with Maria Beadnell, nevertheless managed to get entangled with at least one of her friends. But later the very year that he proposed to Catherine, the law declared that marrying her would place her three younger sisters completely off-limits, forever out of reach.[155] *The Four Sisters* suggests, at the very least, that the acquisition of these new relations played on his mind.

From this point on, Charles Dickens's story is intertwined with the stories of all four of the Hogarth sisters. The eldest, Catherine, he married. The second, Mary, is said to have died in his arms. Georgina, the third, was later to sacrifice not just years of her life but also her reputation for him. Dickens's relationship with the youngest sister, Helen, meanwhile, eventually deteriorated into mutual loathing.

Late in her life, long after she had separated from her husband, Catherine Dickens requested that his youthful letters to her be preserved for posterity, so that people could see that once upon a time he had loved her.

Are they proof of that? Sadly, no.

Even the letters Dickens wrote to Catherine during their engagement are full of excuses – he is sorry – he has to work – he is tired – and complaints about her 'sudden and uncalled-for coldness' and 'sullen and inflexible obstinacy', her 'hasty temper', how difficult her handwriting is to read, even. To these gripes are added baby talk and pet names that read more as attempts to create intimacy than evidence of it. He sends her millions of kisses, calls her 'dearest darling Pig', 'Mouse', 'Titmouse', 'Wig', asks her repeatedly not to be 'coss' (i.e. 'cross'). The two of them seem, indeed, to be patching up quarrels so very often that you have to wonder whether they would have stayed the course of a longer engagement.

In the event, the engagement was shorter than the couple had anticipated. Early in 1836 John Macrone, a new but already successful publisher, still only in his twenties, issued a collection of Dickens's short pieces as *Sketches by Boz*. A second volume followed at the end of the year. The publications included pictures by George Cruikshank, a well-known political caricaturist who had moved on to book illustration and would later work on *Oliver Twist*.

The adverts for *Sketches by Boz* carried a glowing recommendation from the editor of the *Morning Chronicle*, for which Dickens was working at the time ('Evidently the work of a person of various and extraordinary intellectual gifts'). Reviews, while positive, were more temperate. *The Examiner* complained that there was 'too much' 'caricature of Cockneyism' but admired the author's 'quick' 'perception of the ludicrous', 'rich vein' of humour and 'little touches of pathos'.[156] The *Sun* called the sketches 'full of promise'.[157] Sales were, similarly, good rather than stellar; no indication of what was to come, but the money he received for the copyright was enough for Dickens to marry on, especially since he had also been commissioned to work on what would end up becoming his first full-length work, *The Pickwick Papers*, the first instalment of which appeared in March 1836.

Catherine and Charles would face a number of challenges in the early years of their marriage – family bereavement, miscarriage, mental health problems and, sooner than these, perhaps more terrifying than any of them, fame. It was coming at them: pitiless, unstoppable. They weren't ready for it. No one is. Everything was about to change for them, forever.

Notes

123. Forster quotes Edmund Blackmore as recalling that Dickens 'came to me in May, 1827, and left in November, 1828' (*The Life of Charles Dickens*, volume 1, page 66).

124. William J. Carlton, 'Dickens's literary mentor', *Dickens Studies*, Vol. 1, No. 2 (May 1965), page 54 ff. John Barrow's mistress was Lucina Fidelia Arabella, wife to Alfred Nicholson, and one of five illegitimate daughters of Luke Pocock. The eldest sister had been born in India. See Will of Luke Pocock of Cudham and Keston, Kent, National Archives, PROB 11/1764/178.

125. Speech given at the anniversary dinner of the Newspaper Press Fund, as recorded in the *Evening Standard*, 22 May 1865, page 3.

126. See, for example, his letter to André Fillonneau, date uncertain, which refers to 'the amount due for the last two weeks'. Fillonneau married Amelia Austin on the same day as Henry Austin married Letitia Dickens, and in the same church (St George Bloomsbury, 15 July 1837, marriage records accessed via Ancestry).

127. *Newcastle Journal*, 12 April 1834, page 4. The reference is to a dissolution of a business partnership but the publication appears to have continued in some form until 1836.

128. In a letter to his friend Henry William Kolle, seemingly of December 1833, Dickens mentions a plan to 'cut my proposed Novel up into little Magazine Sketches'.

129. *Morning Advertiser*, 17 October 1822, page 4.

130. 'John Dickens' is insured for 1829 at '13 Johnson Street Somers Town'. London Metropolitan Archives, 74/SUN/ MS 11936/521/1086718.

131. A claim which proves difficult to verify.

132. *Morning Post*, 13 November 1827, page 4; *English Chronicle and Whitehall Evening Post*, 13 November 1827, page 3; *Morning Herald*, 13 November 1827, page 4; *Public Ledger and Daily Advertiser*, 14 November 1827, page 4.

133. 'Harriet Ellen Dickins', of St Pancras, buried on 24 August 1827, age nine. Burial Register, accessed through Find My Past. She wouldn't have turned nine until September. Perhaps she was looking forward to her birthday.

134. London *Sun*, 21 August 1827, page 4; *London Evening Standard*, 21 August 1827, page 1; *Morning Herald*, 21 August 1827, page 4; *Morning Post*, 21 August 1827, page 4; *New Times*, 21 August 1827, page 4; *Morning Chronicle*, 21 August 1827, page 4; *English Chronicle and Whitehall Evening Post*, 21 August 1827, page 3; *Englishman*, 26 August 1827, page 4.

135. The Belle Vue address comes from a number of newspaper reports (for example, *Public Ledger and Daily Advertiser*, 1 December 1831, page 3).

136. Dickens to H.W. Kolle, tentatively dated to April/May 1832.

137. Letters to Charles Molloy, perhaps February and March 1834. Perhaps the nameless woman is his mother, perhaps some other female relation. It's highly unlikely that, at just nineteen or twenty, he could even have considered setting up a mistress.

138. An advertisement from a gentleman and wife looking for 'board and lodging' directs their letters to be sent to 'B.G., 70 Margaret-street Cavendish-square, London' (*Kentish Gazette*, 14 January 1834, page 1). Five years later a young woman looking for a position as a lady's maid requests potential employers to 'Direct to H.B., 70, Margaret-street, Cavendish-square' (*Morning Post*, 29 September 1839, page 8).

139. 10 Norfolk Street, a grocer's shop, with rooms for rent, was used as an accommodation address by other people during the 1820s, including when the Dickenses were supposedly living there. Charles put it down as his residence in his applications for reader's tickets from the British Museum, and the last time he did so was in May 1831. The 1831 census, however, taken at the end of May, states that there were twelve people in the house, seven of them female and five male, and comprising five family groups. The men were, supposedly, all over the age of twenty. Charles

had only just turned nineteen, though it's possible he might have fibbed. However, this really doesn't look like the Dickens family and certainly not all of them.

140. John Forster, *The Life of Charles Dickens*, volume 1, pages 57–63.

141. Speech given at the anniversary dinner of the Newspaper Press Fund, as recorded in the *Evening Standard*, 22 May 1865, page 3.

142. The register is more informative than is often the case: 'Maria Sarah, the daughter of George & Maria Beadnell was born the 27th December 1810 & baptized the 20th January 1811.' Ancestry, register for City of London, All Hallows Lombard Street.

143. John Forster, *The Life of Charles Dickens*, volume 1, pages 72–3.

144. As above.

145. Letter to Miss Mary Anne Leigh, 7/8 March 1831.

146. Letter to Miss Mary Anne Leigh, probably 17 May 1833.

147. Letter to H.W. Kolle; letter to Maria Beadnell, both probably 14 May 1833; letter to Maria Beadnell, probably 16 May 1833.

148. Letter to H.W. Kolle, probably shortly before Christmas 1832.

149. Letter to Thomas Mitton, probably 20 November 1834; letter to the same, probably 21 November 1834.

150. Letter to Thomas Beard, from internal evidence November 1834, perhaps 29th.

151. Letter to Henry Austin, date uncertain but probably early in 1835.

152. Letter to Henry Austin, probably 7 January 1835; letter to Thomas Beard, 11 January 1835.

153. Letter to Thomas Barrow, 31 March 1836.

154. They remained illegal until 1907 for a man who wished to marry his deceased wife's sister, and until 1921 for a woman wishing to marry her deceased husband's brother.

155. The law was passed at the end of August 1835; though we have no definite date for the engagement, it had certainly happened before then.

156. *The Examiner*, 28 February 1836, pages 4–5.

157. *Sun*, 15 February 1836, page 3.

THE SUMMERHOUSE (1836–41) 4

'Mr Winkle Soothes the Refractory Steed' – one of
the last illustrations Robert Seymour completed
for *The Pickwick Papers.* (Classic Image/Alamy)

On his wedding day in April 1836, Charles Dickens was a minor journalist and short-story writer who had just embarked on a new collaborative project, *The Pickwick Papers*. Within weeks he found himself working alone. Soon after he was to become 'the inimitable Boz'.[158] By the time 1836 had turned into 1837, and Catherine had given birth to their first baby, Charles Culliford Boz (known as Charley), Dickens was famous, hailed as 'a comic novelist of the first order',[159] his work 'need[ing] no recommendation'.[160] Extracts from *The Pickwick Papers* appeared in all the newspapers. A well-known publisher, Richard Bentley, courted him, offering him a job as editor of his eponymous magazine, *Bentley's Miscellany*, and the chance to publish a new novel in it in serial form. Dickens accepted, which, since he already had one publisher for *Sketches by Boz* (Macrone) and another for *The Pickwick Papers* (Chapman & Hall), brought the number of publishers for this young writer to three.

By 1838, foreign journalists were writing articles about him. By 1839, he was a 'public character'; everything he did was news (the *Manchester Courier*, for instance, saw fit to report that he had visited a church in Brighton).[161] Everyone connected with him was news. The fact that 'A brother of the celebrated Mr. Charles Dickens has been appointed to a small place in the Excise' was suddenly worth reporting.[162] Fans could purchase a 'lithographic print' of their new favourite author.[163] Literary locusts descended on his work, producing piracies and parodies and unlicensed theatrical adaptations for which he received not a penny. Meanwhile, newspapers were solemn about suggestions that *The Pickwick Papers* was modelled a little too closely on a series of comic sketches in the *New Sporting Magazine*, collected and published in book form in 1838 as *Jorrock's Jaunts and Jollities*. While professing itself unconvinced by the claims, the *Morning Advertiser* declared that '[W]e know not how Mr. Dickens can avoid some explanation'.[164] He had arrived. Thousands of people were watching him. They wouldn't stop watching him for the rest of his life.

Fame comes at a cost. For Dickens, it seems, the cost was not only the ability to be honest about himself and any hope of a genuinely happy marriage, it was very nearly his sanity.

☙❧

Events could have played out entirely differently if it were not for what happened behind the summerhouse in the garden of No. 16 Barnsbury Place, Islington, within less than three weeks of Charles and Catherine's wedding day. On Wednesday 20 April 1836, a maidservant, Eliza Kingbury, discovered the body of her employer there, weltering in his own blood, with a gun beside him. The scene sounds gruesome in the extreme; later reports suggest that the man's heart had been almost entirely destroyed and that three pieces of broken rib were embedded in the small portion of it which remained.[165]

The dead man was Robert Seymour, 'a gentleman well known', according to the *Morning Post*, 'for his admirable productions as a caricaturist and artist'. Well-known, well-regarded, married with children and, at 39, still in the prime of life, Seymour's 'humorous sketches' filled 'the print shop windows'.[166] According to the evidence of a nephew at the inquest, he had also suffered from depression for years. Seymour comes into the story because, at the time of his death, he was illustrating *The Pickwick Papers*. Or, rather, a promising young sketch writer called Charles Dickens had been employed to write entertaining copy for Seymour's comic pictures.

The collaboration didn't last long, and in Seymour's suicide note he exhorted his wife Jane to 'Blame [...] not anyone, it is my own weakness and infirmity. I don't think any one has been a malicious enemy to me.' But the fact that Dickens had written to Seymour on the Thursday before the older man's death, suggesting a meeting – and criticising one of the pictures Seymour had offered for the second instalment of the project – has led to persistent insinuations that he might bear some responsibility for the illustrator's death, that something Dickens said, or did, or his mishandling of their work disagreement, helped to tip a vulnerable man over the edge.[167]

At the time of his death, Seymour was far the better known of the two. He was the senior partner in the project; his engravings were meant to be the main attraction. And his death was an opportunity for Dickens – as it turned out, a moment of golden good fortune. Dickens seized it. But accusations from the bereaved family were to dog him for the rest of his life – that the inspiration for *The Pickwick Papers* had been shared between illustrator and writer, and that the praise should have been shared likewise, along with some of the profits.

Pictures were an important element in the appeal of Dickens's fiction, and the Seymours were not the only people to claim that sometimes it was the illustrations which had inspired the writing rather than the other way about. After Dickens's death, his most famous illustrator, George Cruikshank, produced a short pamphlet titled *The Artist and the Author* (1872), in which he claimed to be 'the originator of Oliver Twist' and also asserted his substantial contribution to the work of another author he had illustrated, William Harrison Ainsworth – the man who had introduced Dickens to John Forster. Clearly Cruikshank may well have been exaggerating; equally clearly, though, given that *Oliver Twist* was published – and, it seems, written – in instalments over the course of a year and a half in 1837–8, it's impossible that his illustrations didn't have some influence on what Dickens wrote, if only a subconscious one. The same argument could be applied, though not anything like as strongly, to the half-dozen illustrations of Seymour's which appeared in *The Pickwick Papers*, and any other sketches which he prepared and showed to Dickens.

There is, besides, another possible source for the Seymour family's bitterness. Seymour's illustrations were used in the second instalment of the novel, published in May 1836, the month after he had taken his own life. One showed 'Mr. Pickwick in Chase of his Hat' at a military display: tubby, fussy, irresistibly comic. The second illustrated another amusing episode in which Pickwick's friend Mr Winkle 'Soothes the Refractory Steed'. In the text, though, these scenes are separated by a more sombre one in which Pickwick, admiring the river on a sunny morning, encounters a 'dismal man' who speaks of suicide:

'You have seen much trouble, sir,' said Mr. Pickwick compassionately.

'I have,' said the dismal man hurriedly; 'I have. More than those who see me now would believe possible.' He paused for an instant, and then said abruptly –

'Did it ever strike you, on such a morning as this, that drowning would be happiness and peace? [...] The calm, cool water seems to me to murmur an invitation to repose and rest. A bound, a splash, a brief struggle; there is an eddy for an instant, it gradually subsides into a gentle ripple; the waters have closed above your head, and the world has closed upon your miseries and misfortunes for ever.'

In the circumstances it seems tasteless to have printed this passage alongside pictures which had been completed by Seymour so close to his death and it must have been immensely hurtful to those the artist had left behind. And if Seymour had read the passage in the days immediately preceding his decision to take his own life, then for a family appalled, grieving, flailing about for reasons, Dickens's words might have seemed one. And perhaps Dickens himself might have wondered whether he could have had such power, a thought at once intoxicating and horrific.

One definite legacy of the terrible scene behind the Islington summerhouse was that Dickens became militant about shutting down any other potential route by which people could claim to have influenced *The Pickwick Papers*. Sometime in the summer of 1837, he wrote to an acquaintance – the father of Maria Beadnell, in fact – to reject some offered suggestions:

> – if I were in the slightest instance whatever, to adopt any information so communicated, however much I invented upon it, the World would be informed one of these days – after my death perhaps – that I was not the sole author of the Pickwick Papers – that there were a great many other parties concerned – that a gentleman in the Fleet Prison perfectly well remembered stating in nearly the same words – &c &c &c. In short I prefer drawing upon my own imagination in such cases.[168]

There is arrogance here in Dickens's expectation that the 'World' would care about him when his first full-length work hadn't even been finished. Or perhaps not – *The Pickwick Papers* was, as I said, a phenomenon. We also find fragmented sentence structure, a darting, ever-proliferating anxiety ('&c &c &c') and, more startling, a 25-year-old man, with a wife and small baby at home, contemplating his own death. It's true that, although copyright law was not at all well established at the time and piracies commonplace, Dickens's period in a lawyer's office – and the experiences of his Lamert cousins, who spent years in a quagmire of lawsuits over ownership of the Warren brand – might have left him with a healthy fear of litigation, of being involved in expense and reputational damage even if he won his case. It seems likelier, though, that he had been made anxious, not by abstract possibilities, but by the very real and already angry Seymours.

If Dickens's early life had offered the perfect training for a liar, it's here, as fame swept him away, that he began to put his training to serious practical use.

By the following year he had come up with a new and improved version of events. Now he was claiming that not just *The Pickwick Papers*, but everything he had achieved so far had been due solely to his own efforts.[169]

In the letter of 1838 which Dickens wrote to a German translator describing his childhood and life thus far, he doesn't just avoid referring to Seymour, he avoids mentioning any of the assistance he had received in the early years of his career. He claims to have been 'induced to join the Mirror of Parliament' while glossing over the small detail that one of his uncles owned it.[170] He explains that his father-in-law is 'Mr. Hogarth of Edinburgh, a gentleman who has published two well-known Works on Music, and was a great friend and companion of Sir Walter Scott's', but not that Mr Hogarth was also a senior employee of the newspaper company which had done so much to champion *Sketches by Boz*. As we saw in Chapter 1, this letter contains one of the vanishingly small number of references to spending his childhood in Chatham that Dickens seems ever to have committed to paper, but it could hardly be termed truthful. Towards the end it deteriorates into a list of all the ways in which he had been special even from his childhood: 'I was a great reader,' he boasts, 'being well versed in most of our English Novelists before I was ten years old'; 'I wrote tragedies and got other children to act them'; 'I won prizes at school'; 'I am positively assured I was a very clever boy'. None of this comes across as jokey, it seems entirely serious; the simple story of how a remarkable boy became a famous man.[171] It's Dickens beginning to take control of his brand.

But though brand management necessitated ignoring Seymour and his contributions to *The Pickwick Papers*, the older man's suicide behind the summerhouse in Islington haunted Dickens. It flits through his fiction for years afterwards, a pale, persistent ghost.

In one later scene in *The Pickwick Papers*, a 'trembling old lady' sitting in what is variously described as an 'arbour' or 'summer-house' spends an unpleasant few minutes expecting to be attacked by a servant boy. Pickwick's clever Cockney servant Sam Weller suggests that he might be 'a gen'l'm'n myself one of these days, perhaps, with a pipe in my mouth, and a summer-house in the back-garden'. In *Nicholas Nickleby* (1838–9), the hero's mother and sister encounter a madman while sitting in a summerhouse in the garden of their cottage in Bow. In *The Old Curiosity Shop* (1840–41), one favoured resort for the repulsive villain Quilp is a 'summer-house', 'a rugged wooden box, rotten and bare to see, which overhung the river's mud, and threatened to slide down into it', its 'table scored deep with many a gallows and initial letter'. Fleeing London, the novel's heroine Nell and her grandfather pass 'many a summer house innocent of paint and built of old timber'. Summerhouses continue to carry negative connotations through almost all Dickens's novels. A 'summer-house' is listed among a number of 'Plans, elevations, sections, every kind of thing' shown off by the hypocritical architectural tutor Pecksniff in *Martin Chuzzlewit* (1842–4). There are some 'rotten summer-houses' in *Dombey and Son* (1846–8). In *David Copperfield* (1849–50), we have a couple, one the setting for the sad recital of the fate of 'Em'ly', seduced and betrayed by David's friend Steerforth. *Little Dorrit* (1855–7) describes an urban 'wilderness patched with unfruitful gardens and pimpled with eruptive summerhouses'. 'Sundry summer-houses' are pulled down in a small spot of civil unrest in *A Tale of Two Cities* (1859). Wemmick, in *Great Expectations* (1860–61), also mentions a 'summer-house' – a rare positive reference.

In *Nicholas Nickleby*, begun in 1838, the theme of suicide is introduced in the opening paragraphs. We're informed of Nicholas's grandfather 'seriously revolving in his mind a little commercial speculation of insuring his life next quarter-day, and then falling from the top of the Monument by accident'. Then, still early on in the novel, while Nicholas is travelling up to the school in Yorkshire where he has been offered a job, an accident to the stagecoach requires the passengers to wait for some time at an inn. During this enforced pause we're given two tales-within-the-tale, one of which is about a German baron who, driven to distraction by the pressures of marriage and children, converses with 'the Genius of Despair and Suicide'. The threat of suicide lurks throughout the novel until close to the end, when the hero's vindictive uncle, Ralph Nickleby, hangs himself.

The Old Curiosity Shop opens with a narrator describing how he loves to walk about London at night. Almost the first places that he particularises are 'the bridges':

> where many stop on fine evenings looking listlessly down upon the water with some vague idea that by and by it runs between green banks which grow wider and wider until at last it joins the broad vast sea – where some halt to rest from heavy loads [...] and where some [...] pause with heavier loads than they, remembering to have heard or read in old time that drowning was not a hard death, but of all means of suicide the easiest and best.

The narrator soon vanishes but, as in *Nicholas Nickleby*, the idea lingers right to the end of the story, where a coroner's inquest brings in an incorrect verdict of suicide on Quilp, who has, the reader knows, accidentally drowned in the river. Quilp is (probably anachronistically) 'left to be buried with a stake through his heart in the centre of four lonely roads'.

Suicides (achieved or attempted) were technically treated as crimes in England until the early 1960s, a prohibition rooted in religious concepts of life as a gift from God. The Victorians often termed suicide 'self-murder' and, like most other murders, suicides were reported in lurid detail in the newspapers – exactly what modern best practice suggests should *not* happen, since it's believed to increase suicidal thoughts.[172] One popular method was cyanide, readily available in the form of prussic acid or 'hydroceanic acid' and used as a medication. In the 1830s it was recommended (at very low dosages) to treat respiratory problems, including asthma and tuberculosis, and as an alternative to opium; it was also taken 'to raise ... spirits' but was considered both dangerous and addictive.[173]

Dickens himself may well have been a lifelong prussic acid addict. He admitted to taking it during his early twenties and, come 1868, when he was in his fifties, he was apparently promising his dentist that he really would desist.[174] Laudanum, too, was easy to buy. Death by drowning, in an age when few people could swim strongly, was never far to seek. In London, the Thames always beckoned. The city was very close to being a perpetual suicide cluster.

It seems that Dickens was aware of what we might now call social contagion. Ralph Nickleby's fatal decision comes almost immediately after he's passed by a graveyard where a suicide whose inquest he once sat on was buried. Dickens tells us how, though the character 'could not fix upon the spot among such a heap of graves', 'he conjured up a strong and vivid idea of the man himself, and how he looked, and what had led him to do it; all of which he recalled with ease. By dint of dwelling upon this theme, he carried the impression with him when he went away.'

This might be an example of Dickens's acute psychological insight, decades ahead of his time. It might also be due to his obsession with Seymour. There is evidence to suggest, though, that it comes from personal experience, that he had undergone a mental health crisis during the late 1830s, perhaps even had thoughts of harming himself.

৯৽৽৻

In May 1837, Catherine Dickens's sister, Mary Hogarth, died, possibly of heart failure. Her death was sudden; totally unexpected. Since Charles and Catherine had married, just over a year before, she had spent much of her time living with them. She died in their house and apparently in Charles's arms. Only hours before, they'd been at the theatre together. It must have come as a terrible shock.[175]

Even so, his reaction was extreme. He threw himself into an orgy of grief, proving incapable for a time not only of carrying out his editing job, but even of meeting his deadlines for the next instalments of *The Pickwick Papers* and *Oliver Twist*. The contrast between his reaction to this death and his reaction to Seymour's is striking.

Dickens mourned Mary greedily. Her funeral, he wrote to one of his publishers, Edward Chapman, 'will be no harder time to anyone than myself' – as though he had as much right to mourn as the dead girl's parents and siblings, perhaps even more.[176] In another letter he thanked God that he had been with Mary when she died, and that 'the very last words she whispered were of me'.[177] She had been 'the dearest friend I ever had', with 'not a single fault', beautiful, young, 'far above the foibles and vanity of her sex and age'.[178] A few months later we find him writing to Mary's mother of the 'mournful pleasure' he would take in wearing a present, presumably a piece of mourning jewellery woven from the dead girl's hair. There is, he declares, a 'melancholy pleasure' in remembering the times 'we were all so happy'. Mrs Hogarth was, he says elsewhere, prostrated by grief, but still, this letter is extraordinary. When it speaks of grief and loss the vocabulary is conspicuously cheerful (pleasure, joy, happy, proud, pleasant, precious). When it moves on to what ought to be a positive event, even in the midst of such sadness, his wife's 'coming confinement' with a new baby, Dickens writes of anticipating what a 'truly heavy time' it would be – for him. He mentions he had been wearing a ring of Mary's 'since she died', only taking it off to wash his hands.[179]

Quite what Catherine, Mary's sister, Dickens's wife and the mother of his son, felt about all this noisy self-indulgence, we can only speculate. Not even the miscarriage she experienced in the immediate wake of her sister's death, or her third pregnancy, conceived scant weeks afterwards, seem to have elevated her any higher in her husband's mind than being 'a fine-hearted, noble-minded girl' – evidently in no way to be compared to her dear departed sister.[180]

Quite what we should feel about it is difficult to determine, too.

In her 2010 book, *The Other Dickens: A Life of Catherine Hogarth*, Lillian Nayder points out that, though Mary's feelings and thoughts tend to be elided from biographical discussion, her letters indicate what would now be considered a perfectly normal attitude to her brother-in-law rather than hero-worship or romantic feelings.[181] We can probably discount any idea of a torrid affair, or of any obviously inappropriate behaviour while Mary was alive. But having looked briefly at the group dynamics of 1830s courtship and the new restrictions which were brought in on marriage between in-laws, we can, I think, see that Dickens could have found himself falling in love with Mary, or imagining – or morbidly fearing – that he could do so. Taking into account how easy it must have been for people to mistake their affections at the time, we might even find it in ourselves to feel a little sorry for him – if it weren't for the fact that he quite frequently developed crushes on women in subsequent decades.

It's clear from Dickens's letters that during the period that he was engaged to Catherine, meetings with his then-fiancée were frequently meetings with her sister as well. His brother Fred, a year younger than Mary, sometimes made a fourth member of the party. They were together often, not just during the months of the engagement, but afterwards, when Mary spent long periods staying with her sister and her sister's new husband. Though the Hogarth parents were alive and well, such an arrangement would not have surprised anyone at the time. The married sister could enjoy the benefits of ready-made companionship, help and childcare, and the unmarried one gained access to a wider circle of acquaintances and thus potential suitors, while also acquiring useful household knowledge. As the Hogarths had only recently settled in London, they might have been especially keen for Mary to get to know more people.

Catherine Dickens conceived her first child rapidly after her wedding; the dates suggest a honeymoon baby. If she was any-thing like most other pregnant women, she would have been tired, falling asleep in the evenings, feeling sick. Mary, meanwhile, was frequently with them: slim, attentive and awake. When the baby was born, Catherine seems to have suffered from post-partum depression – and she was soon pregnant again.[182] And there, again, was Mary, active, helpful and not throwing up all the time.

Born in October 1819, Mary Hogarth was just over a year younger than Harriet Dickens would have been, had she lived. Again, if we are charitably inclined, we could explain away the odd behaviour Dickens displayed around Mary's death as motivated not by illicit love but by delayed grief for his real sister, unprocessed emotions rising to the surface. And Dickens's feelings about Harriet did, I suspect, get tangled up with his feelings about Mary.

But what seems just as significant is that Mary's death came at the end of what had been, for Dickens, thirteen incredibly demanding, disruptive months. He was still working on *The Pickwick Papers*, but he had begun editing a magazine, *Bentley's Miscellany*, and was publishing a new serial novel in it, *Oliver Twist*. He had produced two plays and penned the libretto for a (bad) light opera called *The Village Coquettes*. And then there were the stresses of his personal life. When a couple hasn't lived together before, marriage requires considerable adjustment. Both Charles and Catherine were the first among their siblings to marry; they may have had little idea of what to expect. The arrival of their first child Charley, in January 1837, necessitated the family's removal from the bachelor apartment in London to Chalk, near Gravesend in Kent, and a hefty commute up to town for his father, possibly on the steamer service which ran up and down the Thames. The location offered flexible transport options – in one letter Dickens bemoans the fact that between a lengthy meeting and an appointment with an estate agent, he had 'missed the steamer, and shall have to go back by a Dovor coach' – but however he made the journey, it was a tiring and time-consuming one.[183] After that came a search for a suitable house to rent in London, and yet another move. John Dickens remained a liability, so much of one that eventually Charles arranged for his parents, and Augustus, to go and live near Exeter, giving up several days of his time to go down there and sort out the cottage for them himself.[184]

Ally this to the whole Seymour situation and the stresses of new-found fame, as well as possible substance abuse, and it wouldn't be surprising if Dickens's mental health had started to buckle. There were multiple demands on him – professional, financial, psychological, physical. Mary's death may simply have been the final straw, his unbalanced reaction not a sign of sexual rapaciousness or pathological narcissism, but rather a symptom of mental illness.

Madness was much feared in the Victorian era. It was also something of a cultural obsession. Mental health issues were common, probably even more so than now. Pregnancy carries a risk to a woman's psychological well-being as well as to her physical health; frequent pregnancies exacerbate that risk. Debt was easy to get into and very difficult to escape. Job security was all but non-existent, and while there was social care of sorts, in the work-houses, it was deliberately made as unappealing as possible. Added to this were the environmental factors; there were frequently adul-terants and pollutants in food, furniture, wallpaper and paint. The advent of factories, added to domestic wood and coal fires, meant that air quality was terrible, particularly in cities – something which has long been noted to correlate with a greater incidence and severity of psychological disorders. Thyroid problems, diabetes, hypertension, urinary tract infection; all can manifest with cogni-tive impairment or apparent dementia. Doctors had only the haziest ideas of how to manage any of these conditions and certainly didn't understand the mechanisms underlying them.

Even properly prescribed drugs may have led to temporary derangement. You probably know that mercury was used to treat sexually transmitted diseases such as gonorrhoea and syphilis, both of which were at epidemic levels throughout Dickens's life-time. Mercury was also the main ingredient of something called calomel and of 'blue pills'. People didn't quite pop these like ibu-profen or paracetamol but they resorted to them a lot as purgatives. At one point during Charles and Catherine's engagement, Dickens relates being 'taken [...] extremely unwell', with a bad headache and 'dizziness' which 'affected my sight'. His response was to buy what he calls a '5 grained pill [...] decidedly the most power-ful piece of calomel I ever ventured upon'.[185] The usual dose was three grains. We also find him urging calomel on Catherine when she's unwell.[186] People might readily have found themselves taking enough to cause serious side-effects when all that was wrong with them was a fever or constipation. God only knows, meanwhile, what was in some of the medicines and ointments widely adver-tised in the press.

There were plenty of asylums. Some offered kind and thought-ful care to inmates; many more were grim, to be avoided if at all possible. 'Lunatic keepers' were kept well-employed in private houses. We meet a couple in Charlotte Brontë's *Jane Eyre* (1847). Some encounter the Nickleby family while recovering a wandering charge. David Copperfield's childhood home ends up being 'occupied only by a poor lunatic gentleman, and the people who took care of him'. These anonymous patients offer a melancholy contrast to Mr Dick, who lives with David's aunt Betsey Trotwood and is, despite his monomania about Charles I, both cheerful and manageable.

If Dickens experienced a bout of mental illness, then it might well have been managed privately. We needn't imagine him raving, either; few of his 'mad' characters are shown doing so. Dickens's obsession with his dead sister-in-law seems to have been handled as gently as Mr Dick's monomania is. Mourning jewellery, traditionally ornamented with the deceased's hair, was made to order and wasn't cheap. Mary Hogarth was one of a large family. Nevertheless, the Hogarths made sure that Dickens received a piece. She can't have had very many personal possessions – at least, not ones that were suitable for giving to a man. Dickens's in-laws managed to find at least one for him, though; a pen-wiper, which they gave to him as a 'New Years' token'.[187] He'd already appropriated a ring of hers, as we saw.

In a note prefixed to the delayed instalment of *The Pickwick Papers*, which appeared a month late, in July 1837, Dickens listed a number of rumours about him which (he said) were circulating: how, 'By one set of intimate acquaintances, especially well informed, he had been killed outright; by another, driven mad; by a third, imprisoned for debt; by a fourth, sent per steamer to the United States; by a fifth, rendered incapable of any mental exertion for evermore'.

I suspect this is the first instance of the strategy he was to employ again later in his life: that of deliberately confusing the public – concealing the important fact, the unwelcome story, conjurer-like, in a flurry of extraneous information. If there were whispers about debt or death, they were not widely reported. All I can trace are suggestions, in several newspapers, that Dickens was unwell; depressed. One refers to his 'indisposition'.[188] Another announces that 'poor Boz has fallen under affliction. The buoyant wit whose *bijouterie* [i.e. examples of the jeweller's art] have soothed many an aching heart, is warped awhile by sickness'.[189] A third mentions 'the susceptibility of his finely-toned mind', explaining that he 'has been unable, from mental suffering, to bring out the June number of the Pickwick papers' and 'has been compelled to seek a short interval of rest and quiet'.[190]

It was only a short interval. Though Macrone had cancelled a book contract in return for the rights to *Sketches by Boz*, Dickens still had two publishers to keep happy. One of them, Chapman & Hall, felt themselves obliged to buy up the copyright to *Sketches by Boz* in order to stop Macrone republishing it in monthly instalments, which would have diluted the market for Dickens's new work with them. It cost them £2,000, the equivalent of close on £200,000 today. Gallingly, Macrone died not long afterwards. Dickens had to keep delivering.

He had started writing *Oliver Twist* (for Bentley) when he was about halfway through *The Pickwick Papers* – which appeared with Chapman & Hall; part way through *Oliver Twist* he began *The Adventures of Nicholas Nickleby*, which ran from 1838 to 1839 (Chapman & Hall again) – though he was under contract to produce another two novels with Bentley. Eventually Bentley agreed to count *Oliver Twist* as one of the two novels he had contracted for, with the second to be a historical work called 'Gabriel Vardon', set against the backdrop of the anti-Catholic Gordon riots of 1780. Dickens edited the memoirs of a famous clown called Grimaldi – for Bentley – and a comic work, *Sketches of Young Gentlemen* – for Chapman. These both appeared in 1838. A companion volume to the latter, *Sketches of Young Couples*, appeared in 1840. If you find all this confusing, you aren't alone. Dickens himself seems to have struggled to keep track of who had rights to what and what exactly he had agreed to do.[191] It's clear that he took on far too much work, much more than he could hope to complete at all, let alone to a consistently high standard. Like a lot of newly famous people, he struggled to say no. Besides, the financial insecurity of his childhood cast a long shadow.

By the beginning of 1840, Bentley had grown tired of waiting for 'Gabriel Vardon' and tried to force Dickens's hand by advertising it. After much toing and froing, renegotiation of contracts, threatened legal action and possibly even rumblings of blackmail, the matter was more or less resolved.[192] The novel was not published by Bentley but eventually appeared, after

The Old Curiosity Shop, as *Barnaby Rudge*, published by Chapman & Hall in 1841.

At around the same time that Bentley was losing his patience with Dickens, rumours flared up once more. Dickens was Catholic.[193] And – again – Dickens was mad.

An association with Catholicism was not as damaging in 1839 or 1840 as it would have been a decade earlier, the passage of the 1829 Roman Catholic Relief Act having removed the prohibition against Catholics sitting in the House of Commons. But Catholicism was far from universally tolerated. The Relief Act had not passed unchallenged and, besides, the rumour invited speculation about Dickens's family background, which – as we've seen – he probably wouldn't have wished to encourage for a number of reasons. The Catholicism story was, so far as we can tell, simply a misapprehension and it soon dissipated. Questions over Dickens's sanity remained.

Dickens, or his friends, attempted to turn the rumour into a joke. Pieces appeared in the press suggesting that someone had misheard a reference to his love for his new pet raven and thought that he was 'raving', and also that the rumour had been 'disseminated more widely on purpose [...] by the emissaries of a certain London publisher, who owed Boz a grudge' – Bentley, that is, enraged that Dickens had reneged on their publishing deal.[194] Another report suggested that the initial poor reviews of Dickens's most recent offering, *The Old Curiosity Shop*, had been organised, 'that the opposition to the work was of a very systematic kind'.[195]

Dickens also addressed the issue in a preface when the novel was published in book form:

It may be some consolation to the well-disposed ladies or gentleman who, in the interval between the conclusion of his last work [i.e. *Nicholas Nickleby*] and the commencement of this, originated a report that he had gone raving mad, to know that it spread as rapidly as could be desired, and was made the subject of considerable dispute [...] with reference to the unfortunate lunatic's place of confinement: one party insisting positively on Bedlam, another [...] Saint Luke's, and a third [...] the asylum at Hanwell.

This, Dickens suggests, is all 'invention' and 'absurdity', with no more basis in fact than the rumour of the duel in the old play *The School for Scandal*.

I don't think we can be sure that it *was* baseless. Bentley might have helped to spread the story after his association with Dickens had come to an end, but, as we saw, it had started several years before, in 1837, when the two men were on much better terms.

And besides the strange behaviour over Mary's death and a fixation, in Dickens's early novels, with suicide and madness, there are a number of letters written during these years which might easily have given rise to dark mutterings about his state of mind.

'I want a walk,' he writes sometime in 1837, in a letter to Thomas Beard, a former *Morning Chronicle* colleague in whom he had earlier confided about one of his father's recurring financial crises: 'The top of the Monument is one of my longings; the ditto of Saint Pauls, another.'[196]

Fast-forward three years, to February 1840, and we discover him producing some more alarming letters. They concern Queen Victoria, who had just got married, and they are undeniably odd. There are four of them altogether – two surviving only via extracts in Forster's biography, but two in manuscript which support them. One is addressed to a close friend of Dickens, the artist Daniel Maclise, another to a Thomas James Thompson, also a friend, but a less intimate one.[197] At first, the letter to Thompson looks as if it must be intended to be funny, that Dickens's claim that he and Maclise were 'raving with love for the Queen' and had gone to see her bedroom at Windsor Castle must be mocking the strange, prurient, personal interest that the British have been taking in their royals for centuries, long before there was any other type of celebrity; that delusion of familiarity which, in the mentally vulnerable, can all too easily tip over into obsession.

But it becomes less funny when you find Dickens writing to Maclise about how he hates his house and 'love[s] nobody here', that he has 'several times' wondered what would happen if he murdered his publishers. 'What if I murder myself?' he asks, a few lines later. 'All,' he decides, 'is difficulty and darkness.' He ends the letter by declaring that 'I am utterly miserable and unfitted for my calling. What the upshot will be, I don't know, but something tremendous I am sure. – I feel that I am wandering.'[198] A pattern of crosses follows, arranged in lines and circles.

The letter would suggest to some readers at least that its writer is genuinely and quite seriously unwell. The passages which Forster quotes in his biography may appear even more concerning. And though Forster insists we are dealing with one of Dickens's 'whimsical fancies', he nevertheless acknowledges that it was a 'daring delusion', 'a wonderful hallucination [...] which had then taken entire possession' of his friend, reaching 'the wildest forms of humorous extravagance' and pursued even in public, to the concern of bystanders.[199] If Dickens was simply joking, then given the rumours which had been circulating about him the joke is surely – at best – imprudent. Imagine if the press had got hold of this story, what they would have done with it. There comes a point where anyone in their senses would stop; these letters go miles past it. If people are already saying that you're mad, then pretending to be mad kind of proves them right. It isn't a normal, rational response. It doesn't look altogether sane.

ॐ⁓ॐ

In some quarters, the rumours were taken seriously.

By September 1841, Dickens was rapidly forming plans for a trip to America. Washington Irving, the American author of *The Legend of Sleepy Hollow* and *Rip Van Winkle*, had – Dickens said – assured him that a visit there 'would be such a triumph from one end of the States to the other, as was never known in any Nation'.[200] The two writers appear to have struck up a mutually worshipful correspondence and Dickens had started to receive American fan letters. That didn't mean that the trip was a good idea. Relations between Britain and America were never very friendly during Dickens's lifetime and were particularly bad at this point. In 1837, Canadian rebels had been pursued into American territory.[201] Towards the end of 1841, an American ship, the *Creole*, was hijacked by some of the enslaved people who were being transported on it and redirected to Nassau, in the Bahamas, a British colony. Slavery had in theory been made illegal through-out nearly all British territory in 1833 and the people on the *Creole* were permitted to go free – though some of the active participants in the hijacking were taken into custody for a time. The southern American states expressed their outrage. The newspapers talked of a possible war.

Catherine seems to have been deeply unhappy about the planned visit; Charles was himself daunted by the prospect of going so far away from his children and for so long. Nor was there any suggestion that this would be a commercial tour, like the ones which would come to dominate the later years of Dickens's life. The most he could expect to gain from it was extra fame in America and – he hoped – material for a travel book.

In October 1841, Dickens underwent surgery without anaes-thesia – treatment for an anal fistula. From his description it would appear that his fistula was either opened out or wholly excised, a procedure now known as fistulectomy.[202] Recovery must have been uncomfortable and the surgery itself agonising. Complications frequently result from operations like this even nowadays.

What concerned insurers for Dickens's proposed trip to North America, however, seems to have been neither this risky operation nor the very real possibility of war, but the question of his mental health. They were, Dickens complains, 'very particular in requiring an emphatic contradiction of the mad story'.[203]

This was wise of them because at this point, in the autumn of 1841, Dickens's obsession with Mary had returned in full force.

Burial space was at a premium in London, which may have factored into the Hogarths' decision to have Mary interred in a plot that Dickens clearly viewed as his property. He seems to have been happy enough to allow Mary's grandmother to be bur-ied there, too, but when Mary's brother died in autumn 1841 his reaction was peculiar. He could only manage a grudging letter to his in-laws offering them the use of the plot. He had, he wrote, 'always intended to keep poor Mary's grave for us and our dear children, and for you' but he would 'cheerfully arrange to place the ground at your entire disposal'. And, resentfully, shockingly so, when addressing a bereaved parent, he adds, 'Do not consider me in any way.'[204] His resentment seems to have been even more explicitly expressed in letters to Forster:

> It is a great trial to me to give up Mary's grave; greater than I can possibly express. I thought of moving her to the catacombs, and saying nothing about it [...] The desire to be buried next her is as strong upon me now, as it was five years ago; and I know (for I don't think there ever was love like that I bear her) that it will never diminish [...] coming so suddenly, and after being ill, it disturbs me more than it ought. It seems like losing her a second time.[205]

By this point she'd been dead four-and-a-half years – five years, if you were prone to exaggerated feelings.

Dickens may still have been on strong painkilling medication after his operation. As previously mentioned, there are the other drugs we're fairly sure he took frequently – prussic acid and calomel, both of which can affect thought processes and emotional reactions. But whatever the underlying or additional causes might have been, question marks over Dickens's mental health recurred throughout the late 1830s and early 1840s.

At not quite 30, Dickens was on the cusp of becoming globally famous. He received fan mail from across the Atlantic. His work had already been translated into French, German, Dutch, Danish, Italian, Czech and Polish.[206] Gratifying, of course, but daunting as well. Too much to take in. He wasn't a curly-headed schoolboy any longer, nor an embittered teenager ashamed of his father's inadequacies, resentful of his siblings. He wasn't Maria Beadnell's rejected suitor. He had made himself a new character to step into: 'Boz', 'The Inimitable', a phenomenon. He had published five novels and, by doing so in magazine serials, had helped to pioneer a new and popular form of storytelling. He had many clever and successful friends and a pretty wife who had brought him four children, Charley having been joined by Mary ('Mamie'), Katie and Walter.

The road to success as a writer had not been easy, however. Praise he'd received in abundance, but there had been bad reviews too, recurring complaints that his work was innately vulgar.[207]

One man who led a course of lectures on him might have been of the opinion that Dickens was 'peculiarly *the* author of the age', but he also mentioned that there was a 'notion' abroad 'that Dickens has produced his best works and passed the meridian of his powers', an idea which from this point on we find often repeated.[208] To reiterate: he wasn't yet 30.

The novel which had begun life in 1837 with the proposed title 'Gabriel Vardon' and finally appeared four years later as *Barnaby Rudge* didn't necessarily do much to contradict such opinions, or accusations. *Barnaby Rudge* bears many similarities to the other novels Dickens had worked on during the intervening years. The title character, Barnaby, broadly resembles Smike from *Nicholas Nickleby* – both have learning disabilities, both have a parent who has abandoned them. Barnaby is inveigled into criminal company in London, like Oliver Twist. Where Nicholas Nickleby's sister Kate narrowly escapes abduction, the two heroines of *Barnaby Rudge* are kidnapped and carried off. And the story is lumpy, uneven, the apparent romantic leads stiff and colourless, little more than names on the page. This is not just how it was viewed in hindsight; 'Insufferably heavy and tedious,' opined one provincial reviewer.[209]

Dickens had also made enemies as well as friends. There were the Seymours and his erstwhile publisher Bentley. Even Chapman & Hall didn't have unbounded faith in him. There was a serious falling-out in the summer of 1841; Dickens was deeply offended by the revelation that a punitive contract had been drawn up for him to sign.[210] The situation was rescued, but only just. In September 1841, an agreement was signed for a 'new work' to start appearing in the following November, for which it was stipulated that Chapman & Hall would pay an advance of £1,800 in the form of a monthly stipend – repayable from future profits.[211] Today that would be about £150,000. Almost immediately afterwards, Dickens announced that he was disappearing off to the States, a trip which from the point of view of his publishers was not only a distraction from his new work but also a commercial dead loss, since, in the absence of international copyright, they would receive no income from increased American sales at all.

John Dickens remained a cause of 'great grief and distress' as well as expense, directing at least one creditor to his son's publishers.[212] Charles must have feared that his parents would end up back in prison for debt, which, in addition to being upsetting and bureaucratically complex, would have been terrible publicity.[213] His surviving sisters, Fanny and Letitia, were both married by this point, but his brothers, Fred, Alfred and Augustus, remained to a degree dependent on their family. The younger two were still teenagers, and in need of guidance from someone. Their behaviour would inevitably reflect on him.

Perhaps it would be stranger, given all the circumstances, if his mental health had been robust. Even if there was, in fact, no foundation to the rumours about insanity or depression, fame had left him exposed, vulnerable.

He found himself trapped. The public knew what they wanted from him: the same but different. They hadn't much cared for his excursion into historical fiction. What they liked, it turned out, was stories set in the recent past, particularly those inspired and energised by his personal experiences. Only the more he wrote about himself, the more he risked revealing. And there were aspects of his personal history which could easily be used to turn public opinion against him, or which critics would latch onto: his father's time in debtors' prison; the scandals at the Navy Pay Office; the Lamerts; even, perhaps, the existence of his sister Harriet.

Dickens started on the construction of his public persona almost as soon as he became famous. He was remarkable. He was self-made. He was the noble victim of untruthful rumours. He had been careful to slide a reference to his 'Rochester' boyhood into the preface to *Nicholas Nickleby*. The virulent anti-Semitism in *Oliver Twist* and *The Old Curiosity Shop* had ensured that no one was likely to suspect that he had Jewish relatives.

Going to America might offer fresh material but the risks were larger, too. As Dickens became more famous, so his public became more curious and he came under more pressure to lie. The more he lied, the greater the danger that he might slip up or that someone might choose to reveal the truth. Even if we can understand why he might not have wanted to share his private affairs with all and sundry, his lies were now reaching an audience of hundreds of thousands, perhaps potentially millions of people. There was no taking them back. The stakes kept rising. Deliberately concealing salient information from his insurers about his mental health came with a real risk of involving himself in criminal fraud. Dickens might well have struggled to convince a court of law that he had been telling the truth when giving that 'emphatic contradiction of the mad story'.

He had learned another coping strategy from his father and grandfather besides habitual lying, however: that of removing himself from the situation.

Notes

158. The first references to the phrase seem to appear in the newspapers in the middle of 1836.
159. *Norfolk Chronicle*, 14 January 1837, page 2.
160. *Kentish Gazette*, 17 January 1837, page 2.
161. See a slightly critical reproduction of the piece in the *Morning Post*, 23 January 1839, page 3.
162. *Naval and Military Gazette*, 21 July 1838, page 11.
163. *Naval and Military Gazette*, 2 June 1838, page 14.
164. *Morning Advertiser*, 5 October 1838, page 3.
165. *Bell's Weekly Messenger*, 24 April 1836, page 5; *South Eastern Gazette*, 26 April 1836, page 3.
166. *Nottingham Review and General Advertiser*, 29 April 1836, page 2.
167. Letter to John Seymour, postmarked 15 April 1836. It appears to have been misdirected, since it is addressed to 11 Park Place West, Barnsbury Park, Islington. We don't know when Seymour received it.
168. To George Beadnell, conjectured from internal evidence to be sometime in July 1837.
169. We are not certain when either letter was written; both are roughly and tentatively dated from internal evidence.
170. Letter to J.H. Kuenzel, transcript, date conjectured to be 1838.
171. As above.
172. See https://www.samaritans.org/media-centre/media-guidelines-reporting-suicide/best-practice-suicide-reporting-tips

173. *The Lancet*, 28 March 1824, pages 425–7; *Morning Chronicle* 7 January 1834, page 2.

174. In a letter addressed from Furnival's Inn, where Dickens lived as a bachelor and in the first year of his marriage. We cannot be certain of the date. The later reference comes from the transcribed text of a letter from Dickens to his dentist, Samuel Cartwright, saying that he has 'taken the pledge to abstain from hydrocyanic acid' (2 December 1868, no manuscript). This is a phrase borrowed from the temperance movement.

175. Letter to George Thomson, 8 May 1837; many other letters.

176. Letter to Edward Chapman, 12 May 1837.

177. Letter to Thomas Beard, 17 May 1837.

178. Letter to Richard Johns, 31 May 1837.

179. Letter to Mrs George Hogarth, date conjectured to be 26 October 1837.

180. Letter to Richard Johns, as above.

181. Lillian Nayder, *The Other Dickens: A Life of Catherine Hogarth* (Cornell University Press, 2010).

182. 'Mrs. Dickens has been for some days past, in a very low and alarming state; and although she is a little better this morning, I am obliged to be constantly with her, being the only person who can prevail upon her to take ordinary nourishment.' Letter to Richard Bentley, probably 24 January 1837, Catherine having given birth just after the new year. It's a problem which tends to recur, and worsen, with subsequent pregnancies.

183. Letter to George Cruikshank, presumably early February 1837.

184. See letter to Catherine Dickens, 5 March 1839, and following letters to various correspondents.

185. Letter to Catherine Hogarth, date conjectured to be 4 November 1835.

186. Letter to the same, date conjectured to be 21 January 1836.

187. From the diary which Dickens kept, sporadically, 1838–41. Entry for Tuesday 2 January 1838.

188. *Liverpool Mercury*, 9 June 1837, page 7.

189. *The Lincolnshire Chronicle*, 9 June 1837, page 2.

190. *Dublin Evening Packet*, 17 June 1837, page 3.

191. For a taste of the complexities involved, see Dickens's lengthy letter to Bradbury & Evans, 8 May 1844, detailing the status of his various copyrights.

192. In a letter dateable to 29 January 1840, Dickens relates that he bumped into his illustrator Cruikshank in the street, 'and he told me that Bentley had told Ainsworth that if I did the New Work instead of Barnaby, he *intended to publish all the letters I had ever written him!!!*' [his italics and exclamation marks]. Two other letters to Richard Bentley, neither securely dated, might perhaps refer to potentially sensitive issues. 'I received the accompanying note from Mr. Hogarth [presumably Dickens's father-in-law] on Sunday, which I inclose for the edification of your ingenious informant,' says one. In another Dickens explains, 'I forgot to speak to you the other day respecting a gentleman who bears a letter to me from a friend, and whom I wish to give a letter to you.'

193. 'Mr Charles Dickens [...] is, it is said, a member of the Roman Catholic Church,' announced the *Exeter and Plymouth Gazette* on 30 November 1839 (page 4), while the *Coventry Herald* and *Newcastle Journal* both stated that 'It is not generally known that Mr. Charles Dickens is a member of the Catholic Church' (22 and 23 November 1839, respectively). The rumour appears to have originated with the Irish press.

194. *Exeter and Plymouth Gazette*, 24 October 1840 (page 4); widely reprinted elsewhere. Decades later a notably similar suggestion pops up in a letter written by Dickens denying reports that he is unwell; that a reference to his love of 'cricket' has been misheard as his being in a 'critical' state of health (To the editor of *The Sunday Gazette*, 13 September 1867).

195. *Londonderry Standard*, 24 June 1840, page 3.

196. Letter to Thomas Beard, dateable from internal evidence to 28 January 1837.

197. Thompson was a dilettante and a widower, who would later marry a young woman called Christiana Weller, on whom Dickens had developed one of his crushes. Christiana's sister, meanwhile, was to marry Dickens's brother Frederick.

198. Letter to Daniel Maclise, presumably, again, 13 February 1840.

199. John Forster, *The Life of Charles Dickens*, volume 1, pages 194–6.

200. Letter to William Hall, 14 September 1841.

201. This is the '*Caroline* affair', named after the schooner *Caroline*, which was burned by British forces.

202. 'I have been very ill for a week, and last Friday Morning was obliged to submit to a cruel operation, and the cutting out root

and branch of a disease caused by working over much which has been gathering it seems for years. Thank God it's all over and I am on the Sofa again', letter to Thomas Beard, 12 October 1841.

203. Letter to Thomas Mitton, 18 November 1841.

204. Letter to Mrs Hogarth, 24 October 1841.

205. John Forster, *The Life of Charles Dickens*, volume 1, page 264.

206. See 'Timeline of the European reception of Charles Dickens, 1833–2013', in *The Reception of Charles Dickens in Europe*, ed. Michael Hollington (Bloomsbury, 2013).

207. The *Morning Post*, which was growing to be an inveterate enemy of Dickens, criticised another writer for having 'we fear [...] read over much of the Ainsworth and "Boz" class of productions, and from them acquired a vulgarity of tone' (7 January 1842, page 3).

208. A Mr F. Rowton at the Eastern Literary and Scientific Institution, Hackney-Road, *Morning Advertiser*, 16 December 1841, page 2.

209. *Cambridge Chronicle and Journal*, 13 November 1841, page 4.

210. Letter to Chapman & Hall, probably August 1841.

211. Agreement dated 7 September 1841.

212. Letter to Thomas Latimer, 18 February 1841.

213. Imprisonment for debt was not abolished in England until 1869.

RUNNING AWAY (1842–3) 5

The first Royal Mail steamer, the *Britannia* (Cunard Steamship Company). (W. Ridley & Co., Ward & Co Ltd. National Maritime Museum)

On 4 January 1842, the steamship RMS *Britannia* set out from Liverpool for Boston, via Halifax in Nova Scotia. Among its passengers were Charles and Catherine Dickens, who planned to spend several months travelling in the United States and Canada. In the event they didn't return home until the end of June. Their children – Charley, who turned five two days after his parents left, Mamie (nearly four), Katie (two years and three months), and eleven-month-old Walter – were left behind in the care of their uncle Frederick Dickens, aged 21, and their fifteen-year-old aunt Georgina Hogarth. Fortunately for the children, Katie's godfather – Dickens's actor friend, William Macready – was on call for any emergencies. One of the complaints Dickens would make publicly about his wife in later years was that she had never been a very attached mother; this period of separation is unlikely to have aided matters.

Launched less than two years before, the *Britannia* had completed only eight transatlantic voyages. It was considered state of the art, but still the Dickenses might have had private qualms.[214] Less than a year before, in March 1841, a larger transatlantic steamer, the SS *President,* had been lost at sea.[215] The story attracted huge public and press interest, a precursor to the *Mary Celeste* or Flight MH370, and remained fresh in people's minds.

In 1865, Dickens was to be involved in a train accident at Staplehurst in Kent. That resulted in significant fatalities, and the episode features large in biographies. But this 1842 journey, too, might very easily have been the end of him – if, that is, his accounts of it are to be believed.

Apparently, a storm blew up; a bad one. The passengers, remembering the recent disappearance of the *President*, were terrified; nor were the crew sanguine. In *American Notes*, the travel book Dickens published on his return to Britain, he plays the storm for an odd combination of grand effect and laughs, describing how the ship 'stops, and staggers, and shivers [...] beaten down, and battered, and crushed, and leaped on by the angry sea' and how he himself was unshaven and unkempt, and 'pale with seasickness'. There's also a comic 'little Scotch lady' who urges the captain to attach 'a steel conductor [...] to the top of every mast, and to the chimney, in order that the ship might not be struck by lightning'.

In the letters he wrote soon after, though, the sense of peril is unleavened by any attempts at humour. To his brother Frederick, he wrote:

The sea ran so high all the way, that when we came into Boston, the funnel which was properly red, was *white* to the top, with the ocean's Salt. Such a battered looking ship as it was, you can hardly imagine. When we put into Halifax, the fragments of our broken life boat still hung upon the deck. The rumour ran from mouth to mouth, that we had picked up the wreck of one of the poor *President's* boats at sea; and the crowd came down for splinters of it, as valuable curiosities![216]

The account of the voyage preserved in Forster's biography is even more doom-laden: 'The head engineer, who had been in one or other of the Cunard vessels since they began running, had never seen such stress of weather; and I heard Captain Hewitt himself say afterwards that nothing but a steamer, and one of that strength, could have kept her course and stood it out.'[217] Forster relates that, in addition to the terrible storm at sea, Dickens described to him how the ship struck a mudbank on the approach to Halifax harbour, and that the crew were on the point of abandoning her:

The men (I mean the crew! think of this) were kicking off their shoes and throwing off their jackets preparatory to swimming ashore; the pilot was beside himself; the passengers dismayed; and everything in the most intolerable confusion and hurry. Breakers were roaring ahead; the land within a couple of hundred yards; and the vessel driving upon the surf, although her paddles were worked backwards, and everything done to stay her course [...] for half an hour we were throwing up rockets, burning blue lights, and firing signals of distress, all of which remained unanswered, though we were so close to the shore that we could see the waving branches of the trees.[218]

None of this, though, was reported in the press at the time.

In later years one of the other passengers on the *Britannia* agreed that the ship had had some narrow escapes, while another asserted that the majority of the passengers were never alarmed. Dickens was no stranger to steamers. He travelled on them fairly frequently. He had previously been across the English Channel in one. An ocean-going voyage was a different proposition, though.

All accounts agree that he spent the majority of his time either ill in his cabin, or in the ladies' saloon with his wife, her maid and another woman passenger, none of whom had made the Atlantic crossing before either. Perhaps, unwell and isolated, he simply worked himself up into a funk.

But according to Forster, Dickens made a point of warning that the perils he had undergone would be concealed: 'Of course you will not see in the papers any true account of our voyage, for they keep the dangers of the passage, when there are any, very quiet.'[219] That efficient PR machinery seems to have failed, however, and within only a few weeks. We know – because it *was* widely reported – that the next Cunard steamer to set out for America from Liverpool, the *Britannia*'s sister-ship *Caledonia*, was obliged to turn back to Ireland after eleven days at sea. One newspaper describes the ship as having 'encountered tremendous weather, which lasted for three days. Her bulwarks had been carried away, her paddle boxes stove in, and her decks swept. The rudder was completely twisted.'[220] The *Caledonia*'s failure to arrive in Boston on schedule meant that Charles and Catherine were left waiting eagerly for letters from home. It also gave Charles more opportunities for introducing borrowed excitement and strong emotion into his writing. Just as he keeps mentioning the *President*, so he repeatedly drags in the *Caledonia*, catastrophising, surrounding every reference to it with the language of disaster – 'it is much feared', 'terrible apprehensions', 'the worst suspicions'. 'It is a strange feeling,' he writes:

> to think of some odd little blotted scrawl which one of our small toddlers believed to be a letter, lying at the bottom of the deep sea, among drowned men, and fragments of fine Ships, and such serious, uncongenial company; but when I think how easily we might have been ourselves in that dread plight [...] I thank God we are here [...][221]

In our era of rolling global news and social media, Dickens's self-absorbed responses to others' disasters have become commonplace. It hadn't been him, but the important thing from his point of view was that it could have been. On the same sea and the same route, in a ship owned and run by the same company, he felt he had come close. Possibly this explains the dubious tales about the dangers he himself had undergone, not just a storm but nearly a shipwreck, too. They might be imaginative leaps into the experiences of those who had made the same journey before or after him.

This isn't the only time Dickens claims to have been involved in dramatic events of which there is no other record. There are various examples. He describes how he nearly drowned crossing a river in Scotland.[222] He encountered a mute child on the beach and turned him over to the nineteenth-century equivalent of social services.[223] His wife was rescued from a carriage drawn by a runaway horse.[224] Yet he was news; his family were news. When the stagecoach his father and one of his brothers were travelling in crashed off the road, the papers were full of it.[225] Would all these juicy items really have escaped the attention of journalists, as they appear to have done?

Perhaps he overreacted on the voyage. Perhaps his fears were morbid, a remnant of depression. Or perhaps it just made for a better story. Because with his proposed book about his American travels, Dickens was entering a crowded field.

There were a number of recent publications in which British writers shared their experiences of travelling in the United States and Canada. There was Adam Hodgson's *Letters from North America* (1824) and Captain Basil Hall's 1829 *Travels in North America*. The writer Frances Trollope, mother of the more famous Anthony, had lived in the United States for several years and had even planned, at one point, to join an ideal community, which turned out to be an ill-run, swampish nightmare. Her best-regarded work of non-fiction was her 1832 travelogue *Domestic Manners of the Americans*, and she had also written a novel called *The Refugee in America* (1833).[226] The economist and novelist Harriet Martineau was inspired to produce two separate works: *Society in America*, which appeared in 1837, and *Retrospect of Western Travel*, which came out the following year. Also published then was Andrew Bell's *Men and Things in America*. In 1839, Captain Maryatt, author of *The Children of the New Forest*, who was half-American on his mother's side, had published his *Diary in America*. And there were others. We know that Dickens had read at least two of these books before he went – Bell's and

Trollope's – because he briefly mentions some of their contents in a letter.[227] But he had also looked at another book, not about America, but about Britain: *The Glory and Shame of England*, by the American author C.E. Lester, which included, among general criticism of English manners and manufacturing, pages and pages of lavish praise of one Charles Dickens.[228]

When, in the 1860s, Dickens was gearing up for his second trip to America, he viewed the first, in retrospect, as having been ill-timed. Politically, it had been, as we saw. And personally, too, the timing was not ideal. His children were very small. There had been the fistulectomy and, added to that, considerable psychological and emotional stress. Looking back a quarter of a century later, he remembered himself, at 30, as having been ill-tempered: 'When I went to America in '42, I was so much younger, but (I think) very much weaker too,' he wrote. 'I had had a painful surgical operation performed, shortly before going out [...] I was less patient and more irritable then.'[229]

Reading the letters that he wrote in anticipation of this first trip, though, the overwhelming impression is one not of weakness or irritability, but of glee. The idea of America thrilled him.

One letter, written early in 1841, shows Dickens enchanted by the notion that his books were being read in what he describes as 'the backwoods of America [...] the vast solitudes [...] the green forests on the banks of the Mississippi'.[230] As for the notion that he might go there himself, it was astonishing. 'I can hardly believe I am coming,' he declared, dazedly, to his penfriend Washington Irving.[231] He jokes about the souvenirs he means to bring back for friends and acquaintances, 'such as a phial of Niagara water, a neat tomahawk, or a few scales of the celebrated Sea Serpent' which was supposedly sighted in the waters off the eastern seaboard; but you sense how enthralled he was about seeing, touching, breathing the air, treading the ground himself.[232] He promises pebbles, rocks, chunks of the new world, guaranteed genuine.

And in spite of the discomforts of the voyage, however ordinary or extraordinary they really were, the excitement flickered into life again when Dickens arrived in America. 'I can give you no conception of my welcome here,' he writes from Boston:

There never was a King or Emperor upon the Earth, so cheered, and followed by crowds, and entertained in Public at splendid balls and dinners, and waited on by public bodies and deputations of all kinds. I have had one from the Far West: a journey of 2,000 miles! If I go out in a carriage, the crowd surround it and escort me home. If I go to the Theatre, the whole house (crowded to the roof) rises as one man, and the timbers ring again. You cannot imagine what it is. I have 5 Great Public Dinners on hand at this moment, and Invitations from every town, and village, and city, in the States.[233]

This letter is addressed to one of his oldest friends, Thomas Mitton, whom he had known since their teens; perhaps this is why the tone is so naively delighted, so unguardedly boastful. But the excitement began to pall. Dickens was shown the sights – prisons, schools, libraries, factories, all interesting enough in themselves, particularly the prison that enforced solitary confinement, and the school for the 'deaf and dumb', but all places that Trollope, Hall and the others had written about before, that he had already encountered on the page. He visited 'the Senate, and the House of Representatives' and found the buildings 'very tastefully fitted up', and briefly met the President (John Tyler), but thought him 'worn and tired'.[234]

By contrast with her husband, it would seem that Catherine had a consistently miserable trip. Dickens's letters to his brother Fred and to Forster indicate that she was unwell, on and off, for almost the whole of their time away, suffering from a facial swelling that came and went for weeks on end and 'so bad a sore throat that she was obliged to keep her bed'.[235] He also reminds Forster of her 'propensity' for falling and tripping when climbing into boats and carriages; how she 'scrapes the skin off her legs; brings great sores and swellings on her feet; chips large fragments out of her ankle-bones; and makes herself blue with bruises'.[236] If the injuries weren't all to do with Catherine's feet, this could come across as an abusive husband's explanation of how his wife keeps walking into walls. As it is, the impression is one of impatience and irritation rather than sympathy with Catherine's poor health. Given the voluminous, bell-shaped skirts which were fashionable in the 1840s, we might also wonder why her husband didn't lend a helping hand.

Dickens admired American education, was pleased with the gallantry shown publicly towards women and was grateful for his reception, but still, he soon began to express a longing to be back home. There were so many people. He was so continually on display. He had, he complained, no time to himself: 'I thought it could scarcely be that I – I, the devoted one; the sacrifice – could have a morning to myself.'[237] He went to 'Boston, Worcester, Hertford, New Haven, New York, Philadelphia, Baltimore, Washington, Fredericksburgh, Richmond, and back to Washington again'.[238] Uncomfortable with encountering slavery in action, and with the unseasonably hot weather, he ventured only a short way into the South, and for a shorter time than had been intended. He may have grown cautious about travelling through slave-owning states when feeling about the _Creole_ affair was still running high.[239] And we can see in his letters a growing longing to be elsewhere. He didn't want to be paraded around the cities of the eastern seaboard, to bow and shake hands with this politician and that 'literary lady' and face staring strangers and earnest fans bearing letters of introduction, but rather to travel thousands of miles away into the wild, unsettled landscapes of his imagination.[240]

'I want to see the West,' writes Dickens at one point.[241] It is a cry from the heart; it was what he really wished for, the wilderness, with no one to pretend or perform to. Having determined to decline invitations to public entertainments, he could not resist one in St Louis, 'a town in the Far West, on the confines of the Indian territory'.[242] He looks forward, he tells his friend Maclise in another letter written the same day, to:

> the heights of the Alleghany Mountains which we are about to ascend [...] the small cabin of the canal boat in which we embark [...] the surface of the Lakes we have yet to traverse [...] the silence of the broad Prairies we shall shortly cross [...] the gloom of the Great Mammoth Cave in Kentucky [...] the roar and spray of dread Niagara [...] the solitudes where

the Indians used to roam, and from which the white man has driven everything but the red sun which lingers there [...]

Dickens reckoned to have travelled, in all, 10,000 miles in America. But that he could do it, in the space of six months and in reasonable comfort, was proof that it was not the wilderness of his dreams.

The prairies were 'too wet to be easily crossed at this season of the year', and Dickens managed only a day-trip. Instead of waving grasses, noble savages or herds of buffalo, he found 'disappointment', the 'grass not yet high', 'bare black patches on the ground', the wild flowers 'poor and scanty'. The only buffalo he saw was in the form of a 'tongue' which he ate at a picnic.[243] The one Native American individual he encountered, 'Pitchlynn, a chief of the Choctaw tribe of Indians', wore 'ordinary everyday costume' and declared his admiration for the poetry of Scott. He approached Dickens by sending him his card.[244]

The mountain heights were humbled, the silence had been broken. 'Dread Niagara' was a tourist trap, complete with visitors' book. There was no escaping his public.

Dickens was disappointed in the politics, the people, the scenery; disappointed in his belief that it would be easy to convince Americans of the need for international copyright protections for writers and in his dreams of finding either escape or inspiration.

He compiled exaggerated lists of his 'journeyings': 'We have been into the Far West – into the Bush – the Forest – the log cabin – the swamp – the Black Hollow – and out upon the open Prairies'. Writing would be easy: 'The places we have lodged in; the roads we have gone over [...] the woods, swamps, rivers, prairies, lakes, and mountains, we have crossed [...] Quires – reams – wouldn't hold them.'[245] But the book he produced, *American Notes for General Circulation* – whose title incorporates a joke about the instability of banks in the United States – wasn't, when it appeared, very long. It certainly didn't take long to write, being ready by the end of the summer and appearing in the October. The American popular response was, unsurprisingly, negative: *American Notes* was highly critical in places and criticisms from a guest are seldom welcome. The reception in Britain was, to say the least, mixed. To anyone who was reasonably well-informed on the subject of America, the book had almost nothing new to say. And it was a gift to those who did not care for tall poppies.

The *Morning Post* published a negative review, not only of *American Notes*, but of those who had reviewed it positively, characterising Dickens as barely educated, common and inartistic, at home only when describing 'The manners of the English stable yard, of the comfortable public house, of the interior of a debtor's prison, of the green rooms of minor theatres'.[246] The paper dismissed the favourable reviews as 'fulsome toadyism', suggested Dickens should be 'ashamed to be publicly described as a writer equal to Fielding and Goldsmith' and expressed the hope that the German-language newspaper *Allgemeine Zeitung* hadn't really been singing his praise, as had been reported.[247]

Another reviewer thought much of the writing effortful (noting 'an incessant straining after effect') and the project itself redundant, bemusingly so:

> what could Mr. Dickens hope to achieve after the labours of Mrs. Trollope, Fanny Kemble, Captain Basil Hall, Captain Marryat, Buckingham, *cum multis aliis* ['along with many others']? We did not want to hear any more about the cities, and towns, and villages, and corduroy roads, and railways, and steam-boats of America – nor even about her woods, and forests, and mountains, and lakes, and rivers, or the thousand-and-one times described Falls of Niagara [...][248]

It seems impossible that Dickens could have been unaware of his own lack of originality as a travel writer. Perhaps, as I have suggested, that's why he lied about the storm. Perhaps he was trying to find new inspiration that wouldn't risk exposing his secrets, or wanted to give people something to talk about that wasn't his mental health. Perhaps he imagined not only that his readers would lap up anything he cared to offer them, but also that he alone would be immune to the backlash which every other British author writing about America had met with. The writing itself can't have given him much trouble. According to Forster, the book can have amounted to little more than the stitching together of notes Dickens had already taken, and letters he had already sent back home, with a little filler.

Martin Chuzzlewit, the novel which started appearing within just a few months of *American Notes*, was, by contrast, an ambitious work, in places practically avant-garde. But while it wasn't quite like anything that Dickens had written before, it drew on old experiences as well as recent ones. He had spent six months and travelled thousands of miles looking for new material but, however hard he tried, he couldn't stop his past from breaking in.

ॐ

Martin Chuzzlewit (1842-4) has never been beloved of either readers or critics. The *Morning Post* was vicious about the first instalment: 'Few persons have better reason to deal contemptuously with the understanding of the reading multitude than Mr. Boz [...] but [...] we cannot help thinking he goes too far in this new publication.' Popular taste will soon turn away from him, opined the paper, 'but we do not see why Mr. Boz should wantonly accelerate this period by such writing as this'. It was 'abominably dull, and written so badly that even the literary society of Finsbury-square, and the parts adjacent, can scarcely fail to find out that it is written badly'.[249] Actually, the opening chapter, 'concerning the pedigree of the Chuzzlewit family', really isn't well written. It's arch, mannered. The book picks up a bit after that, but it takes a while. There are two Martin Chuzzlewits, grandfather and grandson, neither of them particularly compelling characters. The younger one falls out with the older and flounces off to the United States, but very little happens to him there, plot-wise.

The other, more interesting half of the novel resembles a detective story – a genre which is usually held to have originated only just before Dickens's book was published, in 1841, with Edgar Allen Poe's short story *The Murders in the Rue Morgue*. There's a murder in *Martin Chuzzlewit* and a competent criminal investigation, even some complicated juggling of real-life stagecoach routes and journeys, anticipating the way twentieth-century detective writers sometimes used railway timetables to construct alibis. This aspect of the novel is seldom discussed, however. Dickens's *Bleak House*, published a decade later, in 1852-3, often features on university detective fiction syllabuses, but *Martin Chuzzlewit* doesn't. It's a mystery why. And it's not the only mystery connected to this novel.

For a start, we have no idea when Dickens began working on it. The contract with Chapman & Hall was signed in September 1841, four months before he set sail for America. The next month saw him undergo his operation and he was convalescing into November, as well as struggling to finish the last weekly instalments of *Barnaby Rudge*. 'I am so thrown back,' he wrote, '[...] that it will be as much as I can do, within any reasonable regard to my health, to come out punctually every week until the end of November.'[250] December he spent making the final arrangements for the trip to America and he was there from January to June 1842, complaining that he had 'hardly time, here, to dress – undress – and go to bed [...] no time whatever for exercise [...] very little for writing'.[251]

Yet in June 1842, while Dickens was still on his way back across the Atlantic, an extract appears to have been published in a new magazine, the *Illustrated London News*: 'From the new work of Dickens, entitled the "Life and Adventures of Martin Chuzzlewit"'.[252] It's a passage of about 600 words, a lingering description of autumn leaves blowing around a Wiltshire village. It differs only very slightly from the version which was published by Chapman & Hall over six months later, on 31 December.

According to Forster, Dickens was still undecided on the title and setting far into the autumn. In September 1842, he was toying with the idea of starting his 'new book on the coast of Cornwall' and the boys' holiday the two of them afterwards took there, together with some other friends, was in the nature of a research trip. As late as November, he was apparently pondering the title 'Martin Chuzzlewig'. But if this extract had already appeared in the summer, then Forster must be mistaken.[253]

The proprietor-editor of the *Illustrated London News*, a man called Herbert Ingram, was something of a wide boy who had been heavily involved in the sale and promotion of quack medicines earlier in his career.[254] Dickens seems not to have cared for him much. Nor did Forster.[255] Perhaps this suggests a reason.

Dickens could have begun writing *Martin Chuzzlewit* during his travels around America, or even in the last couple of months of 1841, though it's difficult to see quite when he would have had the chance. It's equally difficult, on the surface, to see why he would pretend that he'd started working on it later than he really did.

In several respects, *Martin Chuzzlewit* is unusual. Many of the by-now standard Dickensian tropes are present: there's the trademark blend of pathos and comedy; a lot of the scenes are set in London; a criminal has a central role. But at points the language is noticeably different to any Dickens has used before, more elevated, with repeated quotations from Shakespeare and a decidedly Christian flavour. There are shout-outs to *The Pilgrim's Progress*, Bunyan's great text of Christian moral struggle. There are characters named Charity, Mercy, Seth and Jonas (a variation on Jonah), and references to the 'naked feet of Cain', the 'sentinels of God' and the 'Last Day'.

Even more unusual are the classical allusions, which appear in a profusion unparalleled in any of Dickens's other writings. So we have the classical epic's standard description of the sun rising ('Aurora [...] with her rosy fingers'), references to 'Diana', the Roman goddess of the hunt and of youthful virginity, to the Roman satirist Juvenal, to 'ambrosia', food of the gods. There are Latin tags (*'bis dat qui cito dat'* – roughly, 'giving quickly is a gift in itself'), mentions of the Greek philosopher Diogenes, of Midas, of 'the oracle of Apollo' and 'legions of Titans' (evoking Roman army units and a group of violent giants from Greek myth). A 'meeting' is described as having a 'Bacchanalian character' (that is, presumably, they drink lots of wine and get rowdy), the hypocritical architectural tutor Pecksniff is a 'Chorus' – who, in ancient Greek tragedy, discuss issues with the main characters. Winding alleyways are a 'labyrinth', a heap of earth over a grave a 'tumulus', breezes are 'Zephyrs', a woman's decorative belt becomes a 'zone', that is, *zona* (girdle), just like Roman goddesses wear.

Given the classical context, it looks like young Martin Chuzzlewit, who goes off to a new settlement in America, could even be a deliberate inversion of Aeneas, hero of Virgil's epic Latin poem the *Aeneid*. Aeneas is forced to leave his homeland and found a colony in another country. He has a faithful friend called Achates who is always at his side but hardly ever speaks – of whom Martin's loyal servant Mark Tapley could be seen as a comically more talkative reimagining. Aeneas is invariably described as *'pius'*, that is, he understands and acknowledges his obligations to others – to the gods, to his father, to the band of refugees whose leader he becomes. By contrast, Martin is, Dickens repeatedly tells us, 'selfish'.

Only this isn't like Dickens at all, not the Dickens we recognise, not the one who had been writing up to this point. This isn't what his readers had learned to expect, nor was it what they wanted.

Martin Chuzzlewit's oddities probably should give us pause. There's the pervasive and unprecedented classicism, the unusual religiosity, the novel's clumsy, overlong opening. Then there's what seems to be contradictory information as to the genesis, and early composition, of the novel.

We are, at this point, about to reach a hiatus in Dickens's writing life, a period when his rate of publication slows markedly. Over the course of nearly five years, between the middle of 1844 and the beginning of 1849, he would publish only one novel, *Dombey and Son*, a handful of short Christmas stories, and newspaper columns detailing some of his travels, collected together, slightly edited and expanded, as *Pictures from Italy*.

I think the most likely explanation for both the stylistic differences and the possible inconsistencies over when Dickens began the novel is that *Martin Chuzzlewit* had in fact been started earlier than 1842, maybe years before. If long enough ago, there could have been a chance that the book might have been vulnerable to legal challenge from Dickens's old publisher Bentley, who had, remember, been promised two novels which never materialised. It might even be a reworking of the novel that Dickens talked about in his early twenties. This would explain the secrecy surrounding its genesis. Dickens would hardly have wanted either his readers or his current publishers, Chapman & Hall, to discover that this 'new' novel was cobbled together from discarded drafts he'd found in his desk, with some scenes in America added to bring it up to date.

Both Dickens and his readers might have hoped for more from the American sections of the novel, given that he had spent half a year travelling in the United States and Canada. But the months of diligent searching for new inspiration hadn't been successful. Martin's time in America is, frankly, dull. The novel only starts to sing when Dickens is drawn back to the scenes and secrets of his childhood. As I've noted before, the murderer's eventual unmasking in this novel bears a marked resemblance to what had happened when the crimes of John Dickens's boss, John Slade, were exposed in Chatham in 1822.

It was starting to become apparent that Dickens couldn't keep his past out of his work completely. What he could do was deflect and distract. And he could make sure that he didn't, under any circumstances, share information that wasn't already in the public domain.

During his time in the States he received a letter from someone who had read a newspaper report suggesting that Dickens's ability to write an affecting death scene was a result of the death of his sister. The report was garbled – it was Mary Hogarth who was meant but the correspondent, who had themselves lost a sibling, felt a personal connection and wanted to condole. Dickens rejected the proffered sympathy with the bald remark that 'it was not a sister of my own, I lost': an awkward, embarrassing response.[256] And as we know, Dickens *did* have a sister of his own whom he had lost: Harriet, who had died in 1827 – only he didn't, it seems, want to risk telling the truth about her. Not openly, anyway.

With Dickens, the very act of lying, the effort at concealment, sometimes served to force the truth closer to the surface. We saw, in the previous chapter, how he was haunted, for years, by the death of his early collaborator Seymour. Whatever the official line, it's right there in his fiction. And having effectively denied Harriet's existence, it seems that he became all the more compelled to write about her – though at first he might not have been conscious of what he was doing.

A Christmas Carol, published in time for Christmas 1843, is in part a story about leaving the past behind, moving on, consciously shifting one's behaviour away from the course one has been following for years. Though Scrooge cannot undo the links in the chain which, as the ghost of his former partner Jacob Marley explains, he has already forged for himself, he can stop adding to it. He can try to change how he will be thought of in the future.

But *A Christmas Carol* illustrates vividly the difficulty that its author was going to have in escaping, how thoroughly his imagination was still chained to the images and emotions of his youth. When the Ghost of Christmas Past takes Scrooge back to the days of his childhood, we are shown him with his sister. We see her 'putting her arms' about the young Scrooge, 'and often kissing him' and calling him 'her "Dear, dear brother"'. She is called 'Fan'. A version of Fanny Dickens, it's usually suggested, only she was the oldest of the siblings, while this is 'a little girl, much younger than the boy', who has 'to stand on tiptoe to embrace him' and was, we're told, 'always a delicate creature'. Not Fanny, then, and surely not Letitia Dickens, either, who was only four years younger than Charles: this is Harriet.

Dickens told one correspondent that he found the process of creating the story emotionally overwhelming: 'Charles Dickens wept, and laughed, and wept again, and excited himself in a most extraordinary manner.'[257] He writes about himself in the third person here, almost as if he were one of his characters. And in a sense, of course, he was: brand Dickens, Instagram filters turned up. But he also describes himself as a man on the verge of spinning out of control.

This letter is dated just a few days after the birthday celebration at the Macreadys where we started, where Dickens played conjurer so brilliantly, cooking plum puddings in hats, magicking up a guinea pig. Jane Carlyle tells how the party became quite wild, with Dickens at the forefront of things; dripping with sweat, begging her to waltz with him, taking people back to his house for an after-party – 'a *royal* night they would have of it I fancy!' she says, ' – ending perhaps with a visit to the watch-house'.[258]

As Dickens sobbed over his own work, had he wondered whether his writing was wholly under his control? And as he chased a guinea pig around the drawing-room floor of the Macready house, had he begun to acknowledge just how easily the truth might get away from him?

Notes

214. The seventh edition of the *Encyclopaedia Britannica*, published in 1841, contained 'some engravings of steam engines, especially those belonging to the *Britannia* [...] and other leviathans of the deep', offering readers an insight into 'the wonderful power of that new arm to nature'. *John Bull*, 5 April 1841, page 8.

215. It seems to have been an accident waiting to happen. In January 1841, the *Naval and Military Gazette* detailed how technological shortcomings had left the *President* significantly underpowered (2 January 1841, page 7).

216. Letter to Frederick Dickens, dated 30 January 1842 or thereabouts.

217. John Forster, *The Life of Charles Dickens*, volume 1, page 268.

218. As above, pages 272–3.

219. As above, page 280.

220. *Bell's New Weekly Messenger*, 20 February 1842, page 4.

221. Letter to Charles Sumner, 13 March 1842.

222. John Forster, *The Life of Charles Dickens*, volume 1, pages 248–50.

223. As above, volume 2, pages 6–7.

224. Letter to R.H. Horne, 10 August 1848.

225. 'On Friday last as the Defiance was proceeding to town, heavily laden, in consequence of the darkness and bad state of the roads, the coach was overturned [...] Among the outside passengers was Mr. Dickens of Alphington, father of the celebrated Boz, with his youngest son, a youth 12 years of age. The former received very severe contusions, by which he has since been confined to his room. His son escaped without injury' (*Royal Cornwall Gazette*, 3 January 1840, page 4). The accident took place on Saturday 28 December 1839.

226. *The Refugee in America* is interesting for its passages dealing with slavery and secret escape routes from the south, a thrilling scene set at Niagara Falls, and for the fact that most of the character names are shamelessly pilfered from Austen novels.

227. Letter to Andrew Bell, 12 October 1841.

228. C.E. Lester, *The Glory and Shame of England*, which appeared in England in 1841, published by Bentley.

229. Letter to W.H. Wills, 6 June 1867.

230. Letter to John Tomlin, 23 February 1841.

231. Letter to Washington Irving, 28 September 1841. Irving's career – beginning with a pen name and series of magazine stories before moving on to success and fame – could almost have been the blueprint for Dickens's own.

232. Letter to Angela Burdett Coutts, 14 December 1841.

233. Letter to Thomas Mitton, 31 January 1842.

234. Letter to Albany Fonblanque, 12 March 1842.

235. Letter to Frederick Dickens, 22 March 1842; John Forster, *The Life of Charles Dickens*, volume 1, pages 274, 294 and 317.

236. John Forster, *The Life of Charles Dickens*, volume 1, page 378.

237. Letter to Samuel Ward, 21 February 1842.

238. Letter to W.C. Macready, 22 March 1842.

239. He refers to it in a number of his letters.

240. At one point, he relates, two 'Literary Ladies' are brought on purpose to be introduced to him. Letter to C.C. Felton, reproduced in *Atlantic Monthly*, XXVII (1871), page 765, dated to 14 March 1842.

241. As above.

242. Letter to Angela Burdett Coutts, 22 March 1842.

243. *American Notes for General Circulation* (1842), Chapter 13.

244. *American Notes*, Chapter 12.

245. Letter to Thomas Beard, 1 May 1842; Letter to Henry Austin, 1 May 1842, facsimile.

246. *Morning Post*, 1 November 1842, page 3.

247. Henry Fielding, mentioned above, and Oliver Goldsmith, who wrote the comic 1770s play *She Stoops to Conquer* as well as the affecting novel *The Vicar of Wakefield* (1766). The works of both men remained well thought of.

248. *Naval and Military Gazette*, 17 December 1842, page 11.

249. *Morning Post*, 4 January 1843, page 3.

250. Letter to Macvey Napier, 21 October 1841.

251. Letter to W.C. Macready, 31 January 1842.

252. See my discussion in 'A possible change to the dating of *Martin Chuzzlewit*', *Notes and Queries*, December 2020 (https://doi.org/10.1093/notesj/gjaa158).

253. John Forster, *The Life of Charles Dickens*, volume 2, pages 4 and 23.

254. According to his entry in the *Oxford Dictionary of National Biography*.

255. In a letter to Sir Joseph Paxton of 11 December 1857, Dickens refers to 'the --- Ingram'. There is a record of Forster having written, sarcastically, 'A nice man Mr Ingram!!' in December 1858.

256. Letter to Rev. R.C. Waterston, 7 February 1842.

257. Letter to C.C. Felton, 2 January 1844.

258. Letter from Jane Carlyle to Jeannie Welsh, *Letters to Her Family*, ed. L. Huxley, page 170 ff.

BREATHING SPACE (1844–7)

6

A depiction of some of the revolutionary unrest which enlivened Dickens's time in Switzerland. Skirmish on the Pont des Bergues and the Ile de Rousseau. (INTERFOTO/Alamy)

A Christmas Carol was an immediate sensation. Dickens termed it 'the greatest success [...] that this Ruffian and Rascal has ever achieved'.[259] But it inspired piracies so outrageous, even by the free-and-easy standards of the time, that within a month of its publication he had plunged into six lawsuits. And the profits were less than he had hoped. Chapman & Hall had some shortfalls to make up in their dealings with Dickens, what with the paid sabbatical, and the relative failure of both *American Notes* and *Martin Chuzzlewit*.

Dickens complained that they ended up paying him '£726 only, on a sale of 15,000 of the Carol'. By comparison, the following year's Christmas story, The Chimes, brought out with another publisher, netted him nearly twice as much.[260]

On Dickens's telling, A Christmas Carol was far less of a slog than his longer fictions, not just because of its slight word-count, but because he found it so emotionally engaging: 'I was very much affected by the little Book myself,' he writes, adding that he 'had an interest in the idea, which made me reluctant to lay it aside for a moment'.[261] This interest might have been connected with Harriet, as I have previously suggested, but another explanation for the ease with which the story appeared is that the idea was – though he never seems to have acknowledged the fact – clearly partly cribbed from his own back catalogue.

The basic plot has long been identified as a reworking of a standalone chapter of The Pickwick Papers, 'The Story of the Goblins Who Stole a Sexton', in which, one Christmas Eve night, a misanthropic grave-digger has an encounter with some supernatural beings who show him many morally beneficial visions, leaving him an 'altered man' by morning. The story is told as part of a fireside entertainment by one of Pickwick's friends, coming immediately after that same friend has sung 'A Christmas Carol'. The seasonal setting of A Christmas Carol, the feasting, the weather, the good cheer, all of this is also very Pickwickian. It was a commercially shrewd choice on Dickens's part but it was also, artistically, a step backwards.

A Christmas Carol was published on 19 December 1843. Shortly afterwards, the book A New Spirit of the Age was published. We've already talked, in the Prologue, about how astonishingly little biographical information the essay on Dickens contained, given how famous he was.

Given what we now know, it seems probable that this would have pleased and reassured him. The rest of the essay might, however, have given rise to more mixed feelings.

It's worth reading. You can find it quite easily online. Much of what it has to say is surprisingly modern, not least the suggestion that the caricature-ish impression left by some Dickensian characters might be due as much to the accompanying illustrations as to his writing. Elsewhere it's observed that his 'young lady heroines [...] have a strong tendency to be unromantically dutiful', and that the apparently central figures of his fictions often serve as little more than pivots around which the real interest of the story revolves. There's a brief side-swipe at the accuracy of the 'certain manifest exaggerations of travelling scenes' in *American Notes*, though the 'sea-faring [...] is all true enough' – supposedly. *A Christmas Carol* comes in for a good dollop of admiration, but that's undercut by a rehashing of some of the failures of Dickens's career to date: the edited memoirs of Grimaldi, published in 1838, which 'the great majority of his readers do not at all care to remember that he wrote'; his 'Farce for the theatre' (*Is She His Wife?*); and his 'Opera' *The Village Coquettes*, the libretto to which, it's claimed, could from time to time be found in the bargain bins outside book-shops, priced at 'three-pence'. The rumours about madness are brought up again, dismissed as 'absurd' but brought up nonetheless, and, as with the story about the opera scores, the intended humour doesn't draw the sting entirely.

And though this essay contained almost no personal information, it was soon borne in on Dickens that he couldn't guarantee staying in charge of the narrative forever. In spring 1844, he found himself at the centre of a story that had got away from him, cast, unexpectedly, in the role of chief villain.

৵৶

In May 1844, a man named John Walker appeared at Marylebone Police-office, charged with having obtained money under false pretences from Charles Dickens. Called as a witness, Dickens explained how he had received a begging letter from Walker, one of many unsolicited letters sent every month to his address. The family had by now moved to a new house, in Devonshire Terrace, but the address was easy to discover since Dickens published it in the newspapers whenever his wife had a baby – as she had done, again, at the beginning of the year. This particular letter proved affecting – perhaps because Walker's story of being a struggling writer touched some chord of fellow-feeling in Dickens's mind – and Dickens dispatched his brother Fred to Walker's address to check up on him, subsequently clearing the man's rent arrears as well as giving him clothes and a little ready money to be going on with. More begging letters followed. By the fifth one, Walker was threatening to murder his own children unless additional financial help was forthcoming. Then he wrote to say that his wife had died. As this last was a flat-out lie, it's hard to rouse much sympathy for the man, whatever his financial situation. Dickens seems still to have felt some, however.[262] And when the case against Walker came to court, the law treated him with surprising leniency, the magistrate declaring that 'the prisoner has, no doubt, done wrong; but here is a case of great distress' and finally electing to discharge him.[263] Several people present in the courtroom hastened to give Walker money.

The overall impression seems to have been that the whole business was, somehow, Dickens's fault, an impression which remained with him for a long time. Referring to the case six years later in an essay of 1850, Dickens wrote that he 'left the court with a comfortable sense of being universally regarded as a sort of monster'.[264] It was an unusual outcome and a world away from the police court scenes of *Oliver Twist*, presided over by the vindictive magistrate Mr Fang, in which young Oliver is tried for pickpocketing.

Possibly that's our explanation. Fang had been based, fairly obviously, on the real-life magistrate Alan Laing; the officials at the Marylebone police court might have been so keen to avoid appearing in Dickens's next novel that, knowing the author was in the courtroom – although somehow forgetting that in this case he was the victim – they chose to respond with performative clemency. Walker was tearful, apologetic and presumably must have been plausible or Dickens wouldn't have helped him in the first place. But the episode was unnerving. London police courts saw dozens of cases a day; they were usually presided over by semi-professional magistrates with some degree of legal training. You would think they'd be proof against tears and protestations, especially in a case like this, where all the evidence pointed towards the defendant's guilt. But fame, at a certain level, starts to warp everything around it. Charles Dickens, the celebrated novelist, creator of fictional objects of charity, loomed larger in the courtroom than the flesh-and-blood man who had been harassed.

The fact that within a week of the police court case, Dickens had let his house and moved – temporarily – to one in Osnaburgh Terrace may not be an instance of direct cause and effect. He'd been planning a trip to Italy since the beginning of the year, imagining how he would beaver away and on his return stymie the literary pirates by 'coming out with such a story [...] all at once – no parts'.[265] And of course, as well as involving him in legal disputes and hyping up expectations, A Christmas Carol had been a disappointment in financial terms and the Continent was generally held to be a good place to go for economising.

At the beginning of July 1844, Charles Dickens departed for Europe, bag and baggage, with his wife and five children, servants and sister-in-law Georgina, as well as a hired courier named Roche, who acted as translator, tour guide and mobile travel agent. Though he returned to England for lengthy periods over the next three years, and even became involved in the launch of a new London-based newspaper, The Daily News, Dickens spent significant portions of his time living and travelling abroad, first in Italy, and subsequently in Switzerland and France.

The court case was not the only reason he wanted to get away, but it may have provided extra impetus. Walker seems to have become dangerously fixated on Dickens; he had expressed violent ideas, and he knew where the family lived. I would almost certainly have wanted to put some distance between him and my children, too.

Whether I would have chosen, in 1844, to take them to Genoa is less certain.

By the 1840s, Genoa's days as an independent and influential sea-power were little more than a treasured memory. Napoleon Bonaparte had sacked the city (conveniently positioned in the north-west of Italy, with access to the entire western Mediterranean) in 1797 and after a few years, during which it had been permitted to continue as a puppet state, it had been annexed by France in 1805. The post-Napoleonic settlement thrashed out at the Congress of Vienna in 1814 and 1815 had prioritised the interests of the four victorious powers: Britain, Austria, Prussia and Russia. Genoa had been lumped in with the kingdom of Sardinia. Rather than being ruled by the elected doges who had led Genoa for centuries, the city was now in the thrall of foreign monarchs, reactionary, conservative ones with strong ties to Austria – the country which occupied large swathes of northern Italy.[266] Such a cavalier redivision of territories worked about as well as one might expect, which is to say it led to resentment, repression and ongoing political tensions. It's not as if any more were needed. Conservatism and radicalism, religion and reason, had been pulling the continent in different directions for years. Nationalisms, ancient and new, the growing political consciousness of the labouring classes: these were bubbling away under the surface. In 1848 a wave of revolution would spread across the continent. It didn't come out of the blue.

Dickens could hardly have been unaware of what was happening in Genoa. A number of Italian political refugees had settled in London and were taken up by his acquaintances. One was employed to teach members of the Dickens household some Italian before they left.[267] Concerns about the situation in Italy – and how Austria might respond – had been raised at the end of 1843. In spring 1844, they were renewed. *The Times* explained that 'within the Italian States the liveliest apprehensions are entertained by the minor governments', while 'the greatest activity has for some time past prevailed among the disaffected'. The paper warns of 'rash enterprizes and incoherent schemes', 'patriotism [that] bears the stamp of revolutionary passion and destructive violence' and plans for mounting 'a fresh and extensive insurrection in the Italian States'. And though (it opined) the 'undertaking would infallibly fail', the Austrian government would surely be compelled to mount a military occupation, with resultant violence and bloodshed.[268] In fact, it concluded, it would probably be better if Austria just took over the whole of Italy, properly. By May there were rumours that an insurrection was spreading rapidly in Calabria (the 'toe' of Italy) and there were political executions in 'the Roman states'.[269]

But off Dickens went, regardless, just as he had headed off to the United States two years before. He seems only to have settled on Genoa as his destination quite late on. Early in March he had been thinking of Nice; afterwards, for some time, he considered Pisa.[270] Genoa was a reasonably convenient base from which to explore the rest of Italy and was regarded as healthful, an 1844 travel guide by a medical man praising the 'dryness and elasticity of its atmosphere'.

This was held to be of particular benefit 'to those, who from irregularity of living, or from constitutional weakness, might require the assistance of a warm, pure, and invigorating atmosphere'. The area was also recommended for 'young children'.[271]

The Dickens party was a large one and travelled slowly as far as Marseilles, breaking its journey in Paris, 'the most extraordinary place in the world', enthused Charles.[272] The idea of travelling through France with five children, the oldest seven-and-a-half and the youngest not yet six months, is enough to make any parent's blood run cold.[273] Dickens wisely spent much of the road portions of the journey apart from his family on the box of the coach and, though he had, apparently, to deal with an incontinent dog whose 'bowels [...] were very open, all through the journey', may possibly be considered to have got the better end of things.[274]

From Marseilles they transferred to steamer rather than taking the picturesque Cornice road through the foothills of the Alps, puffing along the coast of France, past Cannes, Nice, Monaco and Antibes.

When they finally arrived at Genoa, Dickens's initial impressions were less than positive:

> I thought that of all the mouldy, dreary, sleepy, dirty, lagging, halting, Godforgotten towns in the wide world, it surely must be the very uttermost superlative. It seemed as if one had reached the end of all things – as if there were no more progress, motion, advancement, or improvement of any kind beyond; but here the whole scheme had stopped centuries ago, never to move on any more, but just lying down in the sun to bask there, 'till the Day of Judgment.

The place, he claimed, made him 'dreamy', 'lazy', 'rusty'. He entered a kind of hibernation: 'I should think a dormouse was in very much the same condition before he goes under the wool in his cage – or a tortoise before he buries himself.' If he was thinking, he didn't 'know what about – I haven't the least idea'.[275]

In January, Dickens had optimistically planned to write an entire novel during this sojourn in Italy. The novel did not appear. Similarly, he had been talking about 'a small successor to the little

Carol' since June, and in August had imagined that it would be finished 'about the middle of October'.[276] He didn't start work on that, either.

Instead, he sat and gazed at 'the deeply and intensely blue' Mediterranean, at 'such green – green – green – as flutters in the vineyard down below the windows [...] such lilac and such purple as float between me, and the distant hills'.[277] He spent his time swimming, planning itineraries for himself, going to Marseilles to meet his brother Fred, who came out to visit, and writing letters. He also made new friends, among them a young married woman called Augusta de la Rue, subject to what sound like fairly serious mental health issues, whom he took to mesmerising.[278]

Mesmerism was deeply fashionable in the mid-1840s, and it quickly grew to be equally deeply disapproved of. Dickens's own enthusiasm for it, maintained well into the 1860s, might be best understood as another expression of his sense of self-importance, his need to control. Given his own family history, he may also have wanted to convince himself that it was possible for character to be moulded by a variety of forces, for behaviour to be shaped by influences other than inheritance or biological destiny.

He later suggested that his wife was jealous of his mesmeric 'treatment' of Madame de la Rue; she was probably right to be. To a twenty-first-century mind, the interactions between Charles and his patient immediately suggest at the least an emotional affair. In one letter he tells Augusta that he treasured a purse she had given him, carrying it 'in a very tender place – breast pocket – left hand side – I carry you about in tenderer places still, in your own image which will never fade or change to me, come what may'.[279] Whether the relationship was at any point physical is unclear – Augusta was usually chaperoned by her husband whenever she met with Dickens – but it was, by any standards, inappropriate.

But Dickens couldn't spend all his time in intellectual hibernation or mooning about after other men's wives. And he would have been a fool if he hadn't tried to capitalise on the success of *A Christmas Carol*. He therefore reluctantly took up his pen to begin a new Christmas story in October 1844 – when he had originally hoped to have already finished it.

What came out was, if not lazy or rusty, certainly dark, confused, conflicted. *The Chimes* is a violent story, made jagged with descents into crime and street prostitution, suicide, selfishness. There's little comedy in it, precious few glints of kindness or seasonal cheer.

Like *A Christmas Carol*, *The Chimes* is set in London during the holiday season, this time on New Year's Eve, and again it features supernatural elements as well as ghostly visions of a disastrous future which turns out to be avoidable – or else a bad dream caused by eating tripe. *A Christmas Carol* is driven by the optimistic insistence that charity makes not just a difference but the right difference. Scrooge loosens the purse-strings and so everything is better and Tiny Tim doesn't die. In *The Chimes*, charity is no longer seen as an easy solution. It's a sticking plaster, and not a very effective one either; beneficial, indeed, chiefly to the giver, who, for minimal outlay, has the pleasure of imagining himself as 'the Poor Man's Friend', even their 'Father'.

The visionary terrors which menace the characters are averted by the end of the story, but it doesn't seem likely that their lives will turn out to be even moderately happy ones. The tale ends with the marriage of two young people who have little more than the clothes they stand up in but who will, all too soon, have extra mouths to feed, and won't be able to do so adequately. The reader is riled up against the characters who warn that marriage among the poor leads inevitably to unhappiness. But though they are presented as hypocritical, economically illiterate, hard-hearted, it isn't clear that they're necessarily wrong.

Probably the most famous scene in *Oliver Twist* is the one where young Oliver takes his empty bowl to the workhouse authorities to ask for 'more'. But of course at the end of that novel it turns out that he is entitled to more – to rather a lot of money, under his father's will – and so the disobedient, disruptive demand of the underclass is turned into a reasonable middle-class request. The scene in *The Chimes*, when the beleaguered, criminalised labourer Will Fern publicly calls out his landlord and one-time employer during a charitable meal, is far more disturbing. It carries with it a breath of revolution, and violent revolution at that – mob rule. A grown man, hardened by prison, is a very different prospect to a small boy, nothing like so easy to overpower physically, his presence and his arguments not so readily set aside. And Dickens shows us, in this New Year nightmare, more than one desperate man, more than one desperate woman, warns us that the clock is ticking. 'I know there is a sea of Time to rise one day,' declares one character, 'before which all who wrong us or oppress us will be swept away like leaves. I see it, on the flow!'

Liberals and conservatives alike might have found the message of *The Chimes* indigestible – assuming they could even fathom what it was. It may be, of course, that the contradictions are connected to Walker, to Dickens's own recent experience of how completely charitable efforts could fail.

But the most convincing explanation of the oddities of *The Chimes* is one I've already hinted at: writer's block.

Dickens travelled a good deal during this period. His destinations were, on the surface, standard ones, the places a rich young man might tick off when he was doing the Grand Tour. He traipsed through art galleries, climbed Mount Vesuvius, travelled over Alpine passes, visited Rome during Holy Week. But, his superciliousness about Catholicism notwithstanding, he also made pilgrimages to sites associated with his own particular saints – literary ones. There's some suggestion that Dickens wanted to rent the very house that Lord Byron had occupied when he stayed in Genoa; certainly he was quick to identify which it was, and used it as a central landmark in his descriptions of the city.[280] He visited Livorno, where Tobias Smollett, author of many of the novels which had beguiled his boyhood leisure hours, was buried. He went to see the supposed tomb of Juliet, and the real ones of Keats and Percy Bysshe Shelley. Later, in Switzerland, he settled in a house on Lake Geneva, an area crammed with spots to delight the literary tourist. Turn one way and you faced towards the setting of Rousseau's 1761 *Julie, ou La Nouvelle Heloïse*, which, though you wouldn't know reading it nowadays, was both an important step in the development of the novel and, when it first appeared, a publishing sensation. Along the shore was Coppet, home of Madame de Staël, who before her death in 1817 had been considered the first woman of letters in Europe; across the lake was the Villa Diodati, home for a time to Byron, where Mary Shelley was staying when she came up with the idea for *Frankenstein*.[281]

If Dickens had hoped that these literary pilgrimages would help his own writing, he was, for the most part, disappointed. *The Chimes* is far from his finest or most coherent work. The next of his Christmas stories, published in 1845, and called *The Cricket on the Hearth*, is remarkable chiefly for a husband's decision to accept what looks like infidelity on the part of his very much younger wife, on the basis that she has, up until now, been an excellent wife to him; also for the portrayal of a young blind woman who, due to her father's well-intended lies, has formed an entirely incorrect idea of the world around her and the people she encounters. The 1846 offering, *The Battle of Life*, is even slighter – after a big build-up about the setting, a battlefield, seen over time as its historical significance fades, it pauses around the 1740s and turns into the story of a girl who pretends to have run away with a lover in order that her fiancé should marry her sister instead.

The *Morning Post*, ever on the lookout for an opportunity to stick the knife into Dickens, dismissed each Christmas story in turn, going so far as to describe *The Cricket on the Hearth* as 'unmitigated twaddle'.[282] It remained convinced – or wanted to convince its readers – that Dickens, '[u]sed-up as a transcriber of cockney slang and Newgate dialect, and not highly appreciated as a traveller and tenth-hand retailer of stale Americanisms', was a has-been, that he had no more to offer.

It had a point. *The Chimes* is confused, *The Cricket on the Hearth* and *The Battle of Life* odd, disjointed. And they hadn't come easily. Dickens was still racing to complete *The Cricket on the Hearth* less than a month before Christmas – 'horribly hard at work with my Christmas Book'.[283] In 1846, writing *The Battle of Life*, he worried that he'd wasted ideas that required a broader canvas.[284] Dickens's letters to Forster suggest that he was struggling, suffering from a crisis of confidence ('I really do not know what this story is worth') and anxiety dreams: 'I dreamed all last week that the *Battle of Life* was a series of chambers impossible to be got to rights or got out of, through which I wandered drearily all night.'[285]

When Dickens started his travels, readers had been optimistic that he was collecting background material for a new novel and that news of it would soon start to emerge. Dickens returned to England in the summer of 1845 to await the anticipated birth of his sixth child, Alfred, and he seems to have done nothing to contradict the expectations which were building. One reporter wrote, 'I met Charles Dickens in the street the other day, looking well and stout, after his return from Italy. The subject of his forthcoming work is to be, the English abroad.'[286] Another confidently announces 'a new work from his pen [...] in which he will relate the continental adventures of two English families unable to speak French'.[287]

But time went on and no novel was forthcoming, only the increasingly indifferently written Christmas stories, and, in May 1846, the publication of another travel book, *Pictures from Italy*. Even this didn't contain a lot of new material; it was largely a collection of columns which had already been published, which seem themselves to have been based on letters written to various correspondents a year ago or more. Almost as soon as it appeared, Dickens took off again.

Having learned something from the critical response to *American Notes*, Dickens begins *Pictures from Italy* with a disclaimer. The reader, he announces, will look in vain for 'any grave examination into the government or misgovernment of any portion of the country'. Indeed, as a 'Foreigner', he claims to have chosen specifically 'to abstain from the discussion of any such questions with any order of Italians' during his time there and, in the same spirit, 'would rather not enter on the inquiry now'. He ends the book with a rolling, if deliberately vague and chronologically misty, paragraph speaking of 'years of neglect, oppression, and misrule' which Italy has undergone, the 'miserable jealousies, fomented by petty Princes' which 'have been a canker at their root of nationality, and have barbarized their language' and hopes that, as 'the wheel of Time [...] roll[s]', 'a noble people' may 'one day' arise again.

Dickens's attention was not perhaps fixed very firmly on *Pictures from Italy*. Throughout 1845 he was deeply involved in plans for the launch of a new liberal newspaper, which finally hit the newsstands on 21 January 1846 as *The Daily News*. His involvement was trumpeted in advertisements – 'The Literary Department of "The Daily News" will be under the direction of Mr. CHARLES DICKENS.'[288] Wild estimates of his probable salary circulated. The paper even went to the lengths of employing his father, John, who had been working as a journalist for about twenty years by this point, though without ever achieving any marked success. But within just a few weeks, by the middle of February, Dickens had resigned the literary editorship: 'I am again a gentleman,' he wrote. 'I have handed over the Editing of the Paper (very laborious work indeed) to Forster; and am contemplating a New Book – most probably in Numbers [i.e. in serial].'[289] By April he had 'conceived the idea of going to Switzerland for a year'. His reasons, he explained, were threefold. First, he was 'most desirous to separate myself in a marked way from the *Daily News*', having come to think of his entire connection with it as 'a mistake'. Second, he had 'a long book to write, which I could write better in retirement'. And third, he wanted 'to get up some Mountain knowledge in all the four seasons of the year, for purposes of fiction'.[290]

You may not be surprised, by now, to hear that he didn't climb many mountains, only St Bernard's Pass. Nor did he settle immediately to the promised 'long book'. Within a fortnight of his arrival in Switzerland, we find him writing to a man called Viscount Morpeth, expressing:

> an ambition for some public employment – some Commissionership, or Inspectorship, or the like, connected with any of those subjects in which I take a deep interest [...] the Education of the People, the elevation of their character, the improvement of their dwellings, their greater protection against disease and vice – or with the treatment of Criminals, or the administration of Prison Discipline, which I have long observed closely.[291]

Nothing came from this letter. Perhaps Morpeth doubted the good sense and practicality of a man who had headed off to Switzerland at this point in time.

We've already looked at why Dickens's American trip might have raised eyebrows in 1842, and why Italy might not have been considered the wisest holiday destination to choose in 1844. But Dickens's selection of Lausanne, in Switzerland, as a place of peaceful retirement was, in 1846, even more surprising than either of these – either clueless or verging on reckless.

At the end of 1845 there had been reports that a senior Swiss politician 'has been publicly insulted at the theatre, that a new revolutionary movement of the Socialists is expected; that the national guards, as supporters of the present Government cannot be depended on; and that the transport of arms and ammunition continues'.[292] Since then, not only had 'the King of the French' 'expressed some uneasiness as to the future welfare of Switzerland', but the area around Lausanne had been specifically described as 'extraordinarily interesting and strangely agitated'.[293]

Sure enough, in October 1846, the English newspapers declared that 'Civil war has burst out at Geneva between the Government and the Radical party'; that people had been called to arms, barricades built on the bridges over the River Rhône, which flows through the city; that there had been cannon set up, musket fire exchanged and, on the 7th, 'a sanguinary conflict [...] which ended in favour of the insurgents'.[294]

Dickens was staying just 25 miles away, but he took the insurgency very much in his stride. 'There has been a revolution here,' he notes, breezily, to one correspondent, 'and a few houses have been knocked about by cannon balls. With that exception everything is as it was, and in perfect peace and order.'[295] Soon we find him 'running away from a bad head ache' and in the direction of the action, choosing to go and stay 'for a week in the Hotel de l'Ecu de Geneve, wherein there is a large mirror shattered by a Cannon-Ball in the late Revolution'. Dickens expressed his 'cordial sympathy' for the revolution; described it as the work of 'free spirits, nobly generous and moderate, even in the first transports of victory [...] bent on Freedom from all tyrants'. He also expressed the belief that 'there is no country on earth but Switzerland, in which a violent change could have been effected in the Christian spirit shewn in this place, or in the same proud, independent, gallant style', and that 'Not one atom of party malice survived the smoke of the last gun'.[296]

In the event, it turned out that 'party malice' had survived, and that the October unrest was only a preliminary skirmish, with war breaking out across the country the following year.

Was Dickens uninformed when he picked out his holiday destinations? Was he unlucky or so desperate to get away that he wasn't fussy about where he went? Or was he unscrupulously, deliberately, courting danger – seeking out adventure, new stories? Hindsight is always clearer, but looking back at the times he seems to have exaggerated, or invented, exciting events (the storms, the accidents narrowly averted), remembering that *A Christmas Carol* was the solitary unquestioned triumph he had achieved in half a decade, this is possible. He had acquired, after all, a fourth son and sixth child in 1845; yet another child would appear in 1847. He had obligations.

According to Forster, it was while living in Lausanne that Dickens had realised how vital to his art London was:

> You can hardly imagine what infinite pains I take, or what extraordinary difficulty I find in getting on *fast*. Invention, thank God, seems the easiest thing in the world; and I seem to have such a preposterous sense of the ridiculous, after this long rest, as to be constantly requiring to restrain myself from launching into extravagances in the height of my enjoyment. But the difficulty of going at what I call a rapid pace, is prodigious: it is almost an impossibility. I suppose this is partly the effect of two years' ease, and partly of the absence of streets and numbers of figures. I can't express how much I want these. It seems as if they supplied something to my brain, which it cannot bear, when busy, to lose. For a week or a fortnight I can write prodigiously in a retired place [...] But the toil and labour of writing, day after day, without that magic lantern, is *immense*!![297]

And he had also, it seems, admitted to himself that he couldn't summon up inspiration simply by going to new places and seeking out new experiences. In America, in Italy, in France, in Switzerland it had been the same. No matter how pretty or dramatic the scenery, no matter how stimulating the political situation or impressive the literary connections that existed there, his creative imagination was deeply rooted somewhere else. He stopped trying to fight it.

At long last, in autumn 1846, Dickens's next novel, *Dombey and Son*, began to appear.

It was not the complete novel that he had spoken of early in 1844. Nor was it the comic tale of hapless English tourists which had been rumoured in 1845. Though we're told how the self-satisfied businessman Dombey takes his second wife to Paris, 'the delightfullest of cities', for their honeymoon, and though we visit Europe briefly during what turns out to be an abortive elopement, it doesn't appear that Dickens's own continental sojourn had provided him with much, if any, immediately usable material.

The only one of his own recent experiences which he seems to draw on directly is his sudden recall from Paris to the sickbed of his eldest son Charley early in 1847, a journey that may be reproduced in the passage where a character, almost mad with grief and fear, sees the French countryside pass by as he travels through it in a meaningless, ever-shifting kaleidoscope of 'long roads [...] ill-paved towns [...] town and country, postyards, horses, drivers, hill and valley, light and darkness, road and pavement, height and hollow, wet weather and dry'.

And though *Dombey and Son* is generally identified as a railway novel – and does indeed contain a lot of trains – that's not what we find at its centre. We find instead a sympathetic embezzler named John and Charles's dead sister. One character is even named Harriet.

Now that we know about Harriet's death, we have to reassess all the Dickens fictions which feature an older child mourning the death of a younger sibling. Take the trite but tear-jerking 'A Child's Dream of a Star', a short magazine story of 1850 in which a boy loses his little sister: suddenly it appears rather less saccharine. And since the age gap between Florence Dombey and her sickly younger brother Paul ('some six years') is the same as that between Charles and Harriet, and Florence is in her mid-teens when she is bereaved, just as Charles himself had been, *Dombey and Son* looks as if it must be, on some level, autobiographical. Florence may not be popular with readers or critics, and deservedly– she's a terrible drip of a young woman – but she's as much Dickens as David Copperfield is, and maybe, on an emotional level, more authentically so.

Rather than trying to suppress the truth about himself, Dickens began, in the late 1840s, to repackage it. If writing was the only career open to him, and if the only way he could write was to draw on his own early experiences, then he had, really, no choice. So he encouraged his readers to believe that he was sharing personal information with them – and sometimes he was – only since the public remained almost entirely ignorant about his early life, they took on the whole without being able to distinguish what was true, or based on the truth, from what wasn't. At the same time he began to work at controlling what posterity might think of him by trickling a carefully edited selection of biographical information to John Forster.

And he further confused matters by borrowing, much more freely than he had done before, from other writers.

Notes

259. Letter to C.C. Felton, 2 January 1844.
260. Letter to Thomas Mitton, 14 April 1845. According to Dickens, the profit 'on the first 20,000' of The Chimes was 'from fourteen to fifteen hundred pounds' and would have been more if the new publishers hadn't been contractually obliged to employ the old 'in the business'.
261. Letter to Charles Mackay, 19 December 1843.
262. '[...] he got off. Thank God!', Dickens wrote, in a letter of 22 May 1844.
263. Lloyd's Weekly Newspaper, 26 May 1844, page 9.
264. 'The begging letter writer', Household Words, 18 May 1850.
265. Letter to C.C. Felton, 2 January 1844.
266. This is a fair description of the first two monarchs to rule Genoa. The third, Charles Albert, was a more complicated figure. Brought up in France, and treated kindly enough by Napoleon, he had when he returned to Italy helped to foment a liberal revolution. In 1848 he would lead his armies against Austria in the First Italian War of Independence. But at the time of Dickens's visit, Charles Albert appeared as conservative as his immediate predecessors.
267. Letter to Luigi Mariotti, 1 July 1844, whose name, according to the Oxford Dictionary of National Biography, was a pseudonym used by the radical Italian nationalist Antonio Carlo Napoleone Gallenga.
268. Times, 1 April 1844, page 4.
269. The Atlas, 18 May 1844, page 2.

270. Letter to Lady Blessington, 10 March 1844; letter to Richard Monckton Milnes, 31 May 1844.

271. Henry Jones Bunnett, *A Description Historical and Topographical of Genoa* (London, 1844), pages 64–5.

272. Letter to Count D'Orsay, 7 August 1844.

273. Though the newest baby, Francis, was not included in early plans (see letter to Angus Fletcher, 24 March 1844, where Dickens mentions 'Four babbies, ranging from two years and a half old, to seven and a half'), he seems to have come along, too.

274. Letter to Daniel Maclise, 22 July 1844.

275. Letter to the Count D'Orsay, 7 August 1844.

276. Letter to Lady Holland, 10 June 1844; letter to Count D'Orsay, 7 August 1844.

277. Letter to Maclise, 22 July 1844.

278. Dickens calls it a 'sad disorder' (to Emile de la Rue, 26 December 1844). The exact nature of her problem is difficult to ascertain. It might have been what we would call schizophrenia or an anxiety disorder, perhaps OCD; this can be debilitating enough.

279. Letter to Augusta de la Rue, 27 September 1845.

280. Letter to Count D'Orsay, 7 August 1844.

281. It was, of course, during a house party at the Villa Diodati in 1816 that the assembled guests had embarked on a ghost story competition; one of the pieces to emerge ended up as *Frankenstein* (published 1818).

282. *Morning Post*, 22 December 1845, page 3.

283. Letter to T.N. Talfourd, 25 September 1846.

284. 'I am only half through my Christmas Book, for which I have a little notion that I should have been very glad indeed to have retained for a longer story, as it is necessarily very much contracted in its development in so small a space.' (Letter to Angela Burdett Coutts, 5 October 1846).

285. Quoted in John Forster, *The Life of Charles Dickens*, volume 2, pages 269–70, dated by him 18 October 1846 and 20 October 1846.

286. *Inverness Courier*, 23 July 1845, page 2.

287. A report which appeared in Irish and British newspapers in August and September of 1845 (see, for example, *Belfast Commercial Chronicle*, 27 August 1845, page 2).

288. Advertisement in the *Evening Standard*, 1 January 1846, page 1.

289. Letter to Emile de la Rue, 16 February 1846.

290. Letter to Angela Burdett Coutts, 22 April 1846.

291. Letter to Viscount Morpeth, 20 June 1846.

292. *Caledonian Mercury*, 15 January 1846, page 4. See also *Evening Chronicle*, 31 December 1845, page 3.

293. *The Era*, 12 July 1846, page 4; *Morning Chronicle*, 15 April 1846, page 3.

294. *Morning Advertiser*, 12 October 1846, page 3.

295. Letter to T.N. Talfourd, 21 October 1846.

296. Letter to W.C. Macready, 24 October 1846.

297. Quoted in John Forster, *The Life of Charles Dickens*, volume 2, page 254; perhaps August or September 1846.

HOME TRUTHS (1848–54)

7

A COURT FOR KING CHOLERA.

'A Court for King Cholera', originally published in *Punch* magazine, September 1852. (Look and Learn/George Collection/Bridgeman Images)

David Copperfield is a work of fiction, but it's one which contains an ingenious – and judicious – collection of half-truths about its creator's life. The same goes, as we have seen, for its predecessor,

Dombey and Son. And perhaps there are truthful, or half-truthful, glimpses of Dickens's life to be found in nearly all of his novels, if you go looking for them. But modern readers have been led towards reading *David Copperfield* as Forster read it; as autobiographical, the scenes in the factory especially. We've also been taught to see David's relationship with Dora as being inspired by Dickens's own memories of his youthful love for Maria Beadnell. Dickens's first readers, though unaware of what he had told Forster, were also led to read the novel as broadly autobiographical and to view the main character as a partial avatar for the author. In the preface to the book edition of 1850, Dickens wrote of 'personal confidences, and private emotions' – planting the idea that this novel offered an unprecedented insight into his own experiences and feelings.

David Copperfield serves an apprenticeship as a clerk, embarking on the training to become a specialised kind of attorney, a 'proctor' based in Doctor's Commons, which dealt with 'people's wills and people's marriages, and disputes among ships and boats'. Then he teaches himself shorthand (just like Dickens did) and starts to earn money 'reporting the debates in Parliament for a Morning Newspaper'. Acquaintances from Dickens's days as a trainee law clerk and budding reporter would have had no trouble working out whose early career formed the basis for this, though they might perhaps have struggled more with identifying a model for Dora, who doesn't resemble the real Maria Beadnell all that closely.[298] For everyone else, Dickens makes matters clearer. By the time David 'take[s] with fear and trembling to authorship', writes 'a good many trifling pieces' and embarks on a book, it must have been a remarkably obtuse reader who was failing to make the links between hero and author. David goes to Europe to recover from a period of strain, though we get to see very little of the continent, and, after a long break, he manages to embark on writing a new novel in Switzerland. To further cement the connections between himself and his creation, Dickens used the name of David's wife, Dora, for his new baby daughter, born while he was working on the story.

The novel's subplot centres on David's careless schoolfriend James Steerforth, and Steerforth's seduction of Emily, niece of David's nurse Peggotty. Having introduced Steerforth to Peggotty's family, David feels a measure of responsibility for Emily's disappearance. His attempts to atone for the situation involve him embarking on a strange sort of friendship with Emily's former friend Martha, now disgraced and prostituted. At the end of the novel he watches Martha and the penitent Emily set off for new lives in Australia. This would have been understood as connected to his own experiences, too, by readers; Dickens had got heavily involved in a halfway house intended to help women exit street prostitution and lives of petty crime. Set up by Angela Burdett Coutts, a banking heiress who put her vast fortune to charitable and philanthropic use, the halfway house – Urania Cottage – promoted the idea of emigration to the colonies as offering a second chance for its former residents.

There are as well, though, a number of elements in the novel which look as though they don't originate with Dickens.

In 1849, the old rumours about Seymour and *The Pickwick Papers* had resurfaced, in a letter from the man's widow and in a book published in America. The book also criticised Dickens's style and levelled the accusation that a scene in *David Copperfield* had been plagiarised. The author, Thomas Powell, had known Dickens, but much of what he writes is unfounded. He has Dickens meeting with Seymour the very day he killed himself, which we have no reason to believe happened. The alleged plagiarism in *David Copperfield*, from a book called *Puffer Hopkins*, doesn't seem to have much basis in fact, either – Dickens had been sent a copy of the book but the similarities are slight.[299]

Dickens braved out the allegations, allowing it to be known that Powell had left Britain under a cloud, having embezzled from his employers, attempted suicide and been confined to a lunatic asylum. Powell threatened to sue, but since Dickens was broadly correct the threat never came to anything.

Powell might have had more luck if he'd directed his readers' attention elsewhere.

While Dickens had been sunning himself in Italy and admiring the Swiss Alps, other novelists had been hard at work. The year 1847 had seen the triple publication of the Brontë sisters' novels *Jane Eyre*, *Wuthering Heights* and *Agnes Grey*. William Thackeray's *Vanity Fair* started appearing in serial form the same year. In 1848, Elizabeth Gaskell's first novel, *Mary Barton*, was published.

Mary Barton was subtitled 'A Tale of Manchester Life'. Manchester, which had grown exponentially since the beginning of the nineteenth century, was one of the biggest centres for textile manufacture in Britain, sometimes called 'Cottonopolis'.[300] Its population was large, and largely poor, with all the associated social ills you would expect. Almost the entirety of Gaskell's story takes place among working-class characters and addresses issues of inequality and labour, as well as male sexual entitlement. The heroine's father is a 'Chartist', agitating for the working class to have some say in politics; the heroine's brother died because they could not afford adequate food; her aunt, abandoned by a lover, has fallen into prostitution. Gaskell, a long-term resident of Manchester who did social work alongside her Unitarian minister husband, had a decent understanding of the realities of the place and its people and the complexity of the issues at stake. Here was stiff competition for the role of socially engaged novelist.

Nor was Gaskell the only pretender to Dickens's crown. Thackeray's *Vanity Fair* is a historical novel, set around the end of the Napoleonic Wars and after, with one of the characters dying at the Battle of Waterloo. It's a much more convincing example of the genre than Dickens's *Barnaby Rudge*. Meanwhile *Jane Eyre* succeeds, almost in passing, in doing what Dickens had been so proud of doing in *Nicholas Nickleby* – showing how awful cheap boarding schools could be, and from the more affecting point of view of a young pupil, rather than that of an adult teacher.

As well, these new novels offered engaging, provocative heroines: clever, manipulative Becky Sharp in *Vanity Fair*, doing her best in a game that has been stacked against her; stubborn, plain Jane Eyre, proof – in the end – against every would-be tyrant she encounters; Mary Barton, vain and foolish and yet able to negotiate an almost impossible moral quandary to save the man she loves. You might remember that in *A New Spirit of the Age*, Dickens's heroines were identified as a notably weak point in his fiction.

There is, in Dickens's surviving letters at least, not a single reference to *Jane Eyre*, or to the other novels Charlotte Brontë published, *Shirley* and *Villette*. Her sisters' works, *Wuthering Heights*, *Agnes Grey* and *The Tenant of Wildfell Hall*, might as well not have existed either. Gaskell sent Dickens a copy of *Mary Barton*, a gift which so far as we know he did not acknowledge, though he did recruit her to write fiction for his new magazine venture, *Household Words*, which started appearing in 1850. Thackeray he was already acquainted with, having attempted to smooth over a disagreement between him and John Forster in 1847. In January 1848, Dickens wrote to Thackeray explaining that he was 'saving up the perusal of *Vanity Fair* until I shall have done Dombey'.[301] Whether he ever got round to it isn't certain. So, too, whether his avoidance of these new works was studied or simply the result of not really knowing how to interact with his novel-writing peers.

Dickens was a brilliant novelist, one who captured the public mood and imagination as few have done before or since. But up to this point he hadn't had a lot of competition. For a number of the novelists active in the late 1830s and early 1840s, fiction was a second or third string to their bows. Benjamin Disraeli was fairly taken up with politics; Frances Trollope wrote non-fiction; Harriet Martineau's chief interest was economics. William Harrison Ainsworth was prolific but lacked Dickens's gift for shifting tone. All were older than Dickens. He had been, in comparison to them, the new kid on the block. Thackeray and Gaskell, however, were only a year or two his senior; Charlotte Brontë was four years younger. And their work was new and fresh.

Thackeray was confident not only that Dickens had read *Vanity Fair* but that he must have seen its superiorities and wished to emulate them. Writing in 1849, Thackeray suggested that *David Copperfield* had been 'improved by taking a lesson from *Vanity Fair*'.[302] At the end of *Vanity Fair*, a pretty woman kills a man; just what happens in *Bleak House*, Dickens's next novel.

Charlotte Brontë and Elizabeth Gaskell might have wondered whether Dickens was taking hints from them, too.

Like *Jane Eyre*, *David Copperfield* is written in the first person; *Bleak House* partly so. Previously all of Dickens's novels had been written from the point of view of an omniscient narrator. Jane Eyre is a neglected little girl brought up by an aunt. She is shown lavishing childish affection on her dolly, going to school and later being employed to work in a house some distance away. She becomes engaged to her much older employer but the marriage doesn't take place. Eventually she meets her hitherto unknown relations. Ditto (and ditto and ditto) Esther, the heroine of *Bleak House*.

In *Bleak House*, as in *Mary Barton*, the solution of a murder is unfolded alongside family secrets; in both novels the heroine embarks on a journey to uncover the truth. The set-up for Gaskell's story, of a beautiful working-class girl courted by both a man of her own class and a rich but dishonourable lover, also bears a striking resemblance to the subplot in *David Copperfield* in which the rich Steerforth seduces Emily away from her working-class fiancé. Both girls are employed as seamstresses, one for a dressmaker, one at a haberdashery – admittedly one of the few jobs, aside from service, which was open to young and uneducated women. Gaskell also offers a sympathetic portrait of a woman in prostitution, an alcoholic, damaged and brutalised, but capable of generous impulses, and motivated by a desire to prevent others from following in her footsteps; a more complex figure than *Oliver Twist*'s Nancy, she might perhaps have contributed to Emily's friend Martha in *David Copperfield*.

Whatever these similarities prove, they do suggest that neither *David Copperfield* nor *Bleak House* is as original as is sometimes claimed.

❧

Dickens was on his mettle, making up for lost time.

The public had liked the idea that he was kind, generous, a friend of the oppressed. Deviating from that – as he had done by taking Walker to court in 1844 – hadn't met with positive results. And so in 1847 he had begun his involvement with Urania Cottage. This wasn't just for show, though. His letters indicate how much effort he devoted to it, over years, concerning himself with sanitation and staff, meeting with prospective candidates, wearing a disciplinary hat when necessary. This was a demanding role, and he received no payment for it. He even took to wandering into the back-streets and slums and docks of London, looking for likely candidates for the halfway house.

He invited people to visit him at his holiday lodgings in the Kent seaside resort of Broadstairs and to go on walking tours with him. He found time to write and publish another Christmas story; a much better one this time, *The Haunted Man*. 'Adroit', said *The*

Morning Herald, 'uniquely felicitous'. Dickens was, it averred, 'the great exponent of the charities of life – the high priest of the household gods'.[303]

It was perhaps to shore up this reputation further that he started organising a series of play performances, the profits to be given to a man named Leigh Hunt. Hunt was a well-known figure on the literary scene, a dabbler in poetry, journalism, drama, theology, biography and fiction. A generation older than Dickens, he had been a friend of Keats and the Shelleys, and at one point of Byron. Dickens got in touch with all his old writing friends, and some new ones, to persuade them to take part.

And in 1850 he started a magazine, *Household Words*, which had his name at the top of every page. The magazine's title obviously played on his connections with the domestic, but it was the nineteenth-century version of a musician setting up their own label, an actress her production company; it sent a message that he didn't need anyone else, he could do it on his own.

The sharp elbows Dickens had employed to such good effect when starting out were back. The press was, for a wonder, positive – in the main. Finally, work was going well.

Other aspects of his life were not.

એ⸲

Charles's sister Fanny, whose health had long been declining, died in autumn 1848, her disabled son not long surviving her. The same year Frederick Dickens made a marriage of which Charles strenuously disapproved. The two had been close and Charles had clearly viewed him as someone on whom he could rely implicitly, picking him to look after the children when he went to America in preference to his own parents or parents-in-law. But as Fred began piling up debts – and expecting them to be paid off by his wealthy big brother – their relationship began rapidly to deteriorate.

So too did other relationships. At the tail end of 1847, Charles and Catherine had been travelling by train between Edinburgh and Glasgow when Catherine was 'taken very ill' – 'a miscarriage, in short, coming on, suddenly, in the railway carriage', Dickens explained to his brother Alfred.[304] The ugliness of the sentence suggests that the incident had been upsetting to witness, though it was doubtless considerably more upsetting and frightening to experience.

Catherine conceived again about four months later. Within less than a year of the birth of that child, Henry, she was expecting another. Married for fourteen years, she had been pregnant for over half of that time. She was often unwell, sometimes dangerously so, and her labours were slow and difficult; it's likely that she also suffered to some degree from post-natal depression. But the babies kept coming. And though Dickens was fond of his older children, the appearance of the younger ones was met, on the evidence of his own letters, with a lack of enthusiasm which became more strongly marked with each new arrival. 'Kate is all right again,' he writes, after her delivery early in 1844, 'and so, they tell me, is the Baby. But I decline (on principle) to look at the latter object.'[305] That was only baby number five.

Several of Dickens's real-life children shared their names with his fictional ones. But Dora, the ninth, born in 1850, was the only one deliberately named for one of her father's characters, Dora Spenlow, the young 'child-wife' of David Copperfield, so ill-equipped for real life that after a short and unsuccessful struggle she leaves it.[306] Dickens was hard at work on the denouement of the novel when the baby arrived – so preoccupied with it, indeed, that he left for Broadstairs the very day that she was born.[307] And once in Broadstairs, he promptly set about killing off his newest child's namesake. He does talk elsewhere about murdering characters when he was working on death scenes, but it's disconcerting to find him remarking, in a letter to his post-partum wife, that 'I have still Dora to kill – I mean the Copperfield Dora'.[308] How baby Dora's mother felt reading this, or having it read to her – blood seeping from between her legs, milk starting to weep from her breasts again – we can only imagine, just as we can only imagine how she reacted to the letter her husband sent the day after she'd given birth, expressing his delight that he had 'left her so well', during a period when sepsis and death remained very real possibilities for recently delivered women, telling her in one breath to 'Take every care of yourself' and in the next not to 'let them coddle you'.[309]

In February 1851, six-month-old Dora was taken ill, suddenly, and so seriously that a dinner guest performed an emergency baptism. A few days later, when the child was, in her father's own words, 'very ill [...] not out of danger', Dickens kept a date to go to the theatre with a friend.[310] The following week he left for a work trip to Paris, now deemed sufficiently calm to visit after the political earthquakes which had shaken the city in 1848.[311] By the middle of February Dora was seemingly well again; Dickens states in a letter to his wife how 'delighted' he was 'to have such good accounts of all at home'.[312]

Yet, just over three weeks later, we find him writing to a medical man in Malvern, proposing that Catherine should go to him for treatment.[313] What was wrong with her? And when did it become apparent?

It's unclear what form the illness took. Her case is 'a nervous one' he says, in his letter to the man in Malvern, 'and of a peculiar kind'. She had already seen a doctor named Southwood Smith, who worked at the London Fever Hospital, and who had 'particularly requested' that Dickens 'mention' something which 'render[s] great caution necessary'. What that something might have been, the letter doesn't say; nor does it offer much by way of clues. Dickens explains that he will 'forebear to describe it [...] until I have the pleasure of seeing you'. Yet writing to a female friend the following day, Dickens says that his wife 'has an alarming disposition of blood to the head, attended with giddiness and dimness of sight'.[314] To his brother-in-law Henry Austin, he adds the details that Catherine has 'alarming confusion and nervousness at times'.[315] Why couldn't he tell the doctor this? Or is it that he's lying?

On Thursday 13 March, Charles took Catherine the 120 miles to Great Malvern, a spa town in the Welsh Marches where he had arranged private lodgings in a house called Knotsford Lodge. Catherine's maid Annie – who had been made Dora's godmother the night the baby had been taken so ill – was already there. Georgina Hogarth was present for at least some of the time. Charles himself spent much of the next month in Malvern, travelling back and forth to London by train, but their presence attracted surprisingly little press attention. Though the *Worcester Chronicle* notes that among the arrivals at Malvern is one 'Chas. Dickens, Esq.', the idea that this might be *the* Charles Dickens doesn't seem to have registered.[316] It was not until early April that the press picked up the story, and it was still being reported when, in fact, all the family had returned to London.[317]

During that time they suffered not one but two bereavements.

We'll come back later on to look at what might have been wrong with Catherine because I'm going to suggest that this sojourn at Malvern may have been part of a serious ongoing health problem, one which puts everything that comes afterwards – and quite a lot of what came before – in a different light.

Let's focus for the moment on John Dickens.

Charles's relationship with his father was clearly a difficult one. It's noticeable that, though he included two of his mother's names among those he gave to his children, as well the names of his grandmother, his sister and some of his brothers, various aunts, uncles, in-laws, literary acquaintances and dead authors, not one of his children was given his father's name, John, or any variation on it. And he had seven sons. Nineteenth-century naming conventions were not as rigidly patriarchal as we sometimes think; it's difficult, however, to see this as anything other than a deliberate, calculated snub.

Faced with the prospect of losing his father, he struggled with what were obviously some very complicated emotions.

John Dickens, gravely ill, was obliged to undergo what his son called 'the most terrible operation known in surgery' and 'without chloroform', the new wonder-anaesthetic.[318] Male readers may wish to skip to the next paragraph here. The operation involved cutting into John Dickens's penis while he was fully conscious in order to release a urethral constriction. This is usually caused either by injury or chronic inflammation and chiefly appears in modern medical contexts as a complication of gonorrhoea and chlamydia.[319] It can, however, also occur in cases of prolonged or repeated urinary tract infection, which without either good sanitation or antibiotics would have been much more common.

Charles describes the room afterwards as being 'a slaughter-house of blood'. It was to Catherine that he wrote ('My Dearest Kate'), telling her how 'greatly hurried and shocked' he was, how the doctors had 'thought it impossible my father could live many hours', sharing medical talk of 'mortification [i.e. infection] and delirium', continuing 'danger'. Charles was horribly shaken, unable to 'write plainly', experiencing again an old pain in his left side ('I feel as if I had been struck there by a leaden bludgeon').[320]

Then he went back to Malvern. John Dickens lingered for the better part of a week before he died.

It happens that the 1851 census return captures the day of his death, in his doctor's house in Keppel Street. He passed away on the night of the 30th/31st; his name does not appear. John's wife – his widow – Elizabeth remained with him, supported by her only surviving daughter, Letitia, and three of her four surviving sons. Alfred and Augustus were there. Charles was there, though only by chance. Frederick Dickens alone was absent.

The census also tells us that Catherine Dickens was still in Great Malvern with her sister Georgina, and her maid, Annie. Charley, the eldest son, was at Eton; Walter, his younger brother, at prep school. The other children – seven of them altogether, the youngest baby Dora, the oldest twelve-year-old Mamie – were in the house in Devonshire Terrace, with the cook, the aptly named Harriett Ovens, a 'nurse' (nanny), Mary Burttell, and a wet-nurse called Mary Gurtland. All three adults are listed as 'unmarried'; Mary Gurtland, then, had presumably fallen pregnant outside wedlock, and had either lost her baby or been obliged to live separately from it. Dickens paid for everything, but it is noticeable how much female labour was required to maintain the lifestyle he had chosen; that two women were needed to look after his wife, and another two to care for his young children.

The services of the wet-nurse could soon be dispensed with, though, because in the middle of April 1851, a fortnight after her grandfather, Dora suddenly died.

If Dickens's long indulgence in grief for his dead sister-in-law Mary Hogarth strikes a false note for us, then we are confirmed in our impression by how differently he reacted to this dizzying double blow. 'I have been in trouble,' he wrote, with uncharacteristic understatement:

> My wife has been, and is, far from well. Frederick caused me great vexation and expence. My poor father's death caused me much distress – and more expence – but of that, in such a case, I say nothing. I came to London last Monday to preside at a public dinner – played with little Dora my youngest child

before I went – and was told, when I left the chair, that she had died in a moment. I am quite myself again, but I have undergone a good deal.[321]

He had indeed undergone a good deal. On this occasion we might be glimpsing Charles Dickens the man rather than the famous writer with one eye always on the public and posterity. The addressee, Thomas Mitton, was for a long time his solicitor and their friendship dated back to Dickens's teens.[322] This is, I think, a raw paragraph. Certainly it's tasteless in its references to money, and clumsy.

But think of poor Catherine. Her mysterious illness meant she had been absent from her daughter for an eighth of Dora's short life. Rather than break the news in person, or letting her know the truth, Charles sent a letter telling his wife that the baby was very ill, sent it via the hand of John Forster, and let Catherine travel all the way home, hoping against hope that she would find the child alive. Perhaps he was, as he claims, motivated by care for her health, but this is cruel.

When members of Dickens's family fell ill, he engaged top-flight doctors to care for them. He was punctilious in ensuring that his children spent their summers away from London, chiefly in order to avoid a terrifying new disease, cholera, which had only arrived in Britain in the 1830s. During the cholera epidemic of 1848–9, he had removed his household to the more distant and isolated Isle of Wight for the summer, rather than taking them to Broadstairs, as he usually did. Like most illnesses at the time, cholera was thought to be communicated via what was called mephitic vapour, produced by rotting organic matter (human waste, dead bodies, rubbish) – an idea very little developed, in essentials, from the Ancient Greek notion of *miasma*. It wasn't until 1854 that it was realised that the disease could become water-borne. What was known, however, was that cholera was no respecter of class, and that when it reared its head the safest course of action was to move away from centres of population and to maintain good levels of hygiene. Dickens always took pains with household cleanliness, insisting on having a water-closet in the hired villa in Genoa and, on the Isle of Wight, installing a 'shower bath' under a waterfall.[323]

And yet he was forever going off into just the sort of insalubrious places that were supposedly filled with mephitic vapours in order to interview prospective candidates for the halfway house. He sometimes accompanied a police inspector through the seedier parts of the city.[324] He went to prisons, walked the streets at night, sometimes stopping to chat to the women working them.[325] According to the medical thinking of the time, his behaviour was wildly cavalier.

So far as Victorian science was aware, Charles breathed in dangerous 'vapours' every time he visited the docks or the slums, whenever he followed his tame police officer down alleyways and into drinking dens. He must, in actual fact, have been exposed to far more infections and diseases than he would otherwise have encountered. And even if he stripped off his outdoor clothes when he got back and scrubbed himself with carbolic soap, he wouldn't entirely mitigate the risk of transporting infection into his home. Wet-nurses were often required to follow strict rules to keep their milk of high quality, but as we now know, there are risks associated with breast-feeding. Alcohol and drugs taken by the woman can affect the baby. Skin diseases and even infections like herpes and syphilis can also sometimes be passed on. Dickens wouldn't, of course, have been aware of all these potential dangers, but given what everyone believed about infection and the way it was transmitted, I wonder whether he can have been entirely easy in his own mind, how he could have been sure that the baby's death was not, on some level, his fault.

He, who had been to all appearances so blasé about Dora's dangerous illness in February was, in April, completely overset by her death. He asked his brother-in-law Henry Austin how to go about buying a burial plot for them all. There's no sign, here, of the obsession over Mary Hogarth's grave which had consumed him a decade earlier. Indeed, the indication is that he still saw his marriage as being for life and beyond: 'I wish to buy a piece of ground where we may lay the child, and be laid ourselves one day.'[326]

In 1852, he began publishing instalments of a new novel, *Bleak House*, which is obsessed with cleanliness, disease and infection.

Bleak House opens, famously, in 'mud' and 'fog', with an extraordinary passage which takes us now 'up the river', now 'down', glancing one moment at 'green aits and meadows'[327] and the next at 'tiers of shipping and [...] waterside pollutions', skipping from the 'Essex marshes' to the 'Kentish heights', from big ships to small, drifting inside to 'fireside' or 'close cabin' and seamlessly out again. We are shifted rapidly through time, proffered an image of 'a Megalosaurus, forty feet long or so, waddling like an elephantine lizard up Holborn Hill', then prodded with references to 'umbrellas', 'gas' lamps and a hot air 'balloon'. Children grow up and, within the space of a sentence, grow old and die. 'Soot' falls like 'snowflakes' in 'mourning', fog is below, as well as above. The scenes are dirty, they are mephitic. Graveyards, a dead father, a dead baby; they're all present.

Both the letter to Mitton and elements of *Bleak House* do seem like genuine emotional responses. But in between them there appeared a peculiar publication – self-conscious and arch.

As well as being a year of losses for the Dickens family, 1851 saw the appearance of a cookery book entitled *What Shall We Have for Dinner?* by one 'Lady Maria Clutterbuck'. It was described as the second edition, but no one has discovered any trace of a first and we'd be well-advised to take much concerning this particular publication with a pinch of salt.

The book met with a favourable enough review in the *Morning Advertiser*, was the object of a small joke in *Punch* and went through several editions. It was written under an obvious *nom de plume*, that of a character from a play which, earlier in the year, had been performed at a house party at which Charles and Catherine Dickens were present. The preface imitated Dickens's prose style. It was published by Bradbury & Evans, the publishing house with which Dickens had been collaborating for several years in one way or another. One or two recent critics have floated the idea that the compiler was Catherine Dickens, because Lady Maria Clutterbuck was the role she had been meant to play.[328] Though she was, by June 1851 – just weeks after Dora's death – pregnant again, this doesn't preclude her having worked on the text.[329] It's a lovely idea, but it leaves us with the question of why Catherine would have chosen to identify herself with such a silly character, and of why the book wasn't published – or at least advertised – under the much more marketable name of 'Mrs Charles Dickens'.

Modern concepts of the mid-nineteenth-century attitude to female authors have been unduly coloured by the Brontë sisters and George Eliot, who had reasons of their own for concealing their identities. Plenty of women published under their own names; it wasn't seen as shameful, particularly if they were married. If Catherine had collected the recipes together, why would Dickens bother to conceal the fact? Eliza Acton's *Modern Cookery*, published in 1845, might not have enjoyed the runaway success which Mrs Beeton's cookery book would in 1861, but it had still done well; this volume, centred on entertaining, was a useful addition to it. As likely, perhaps, is the suspicion which seems to have been current at the time – that *he* was the author, 'that Lady Maria Clutterbuck is no other than Mr. Charles Dickens!'[330] The evidence is purely circumstantial, either way, but it does sound like the kind of project Dickens might have embarked on, frivolously, as a distraction from his grief or as a house-party joke. Or, perhaps, as an exploration of how the public would react if the Charles Dickens brand took a shift towards more traditionally female subjects; if, after a book narrated by a man, *David Copperfield*, he published one partially narrated by a woman.

Dickens's lifestyle was, as we have seen, dependent on the labour of multiple women.

Yet he did acknowledge domestic labour as labour, at least in his writing. In October 1848, after finally finishing *Dombey and Son*, Dickens had ventured on a fifth Christmas story, *The Haunted Man*.[331] This is set in London, in a college that seems to have migrated into the city from Oxford or Cambridge. The central character is an academic, a chemist, older, single, childless, embittered by past unhappiness; Scrooge, but kinder. As the title suggests, and as had been the case with *A Christmas Carol* and *The Chimes*, there is a supernatural element, a phantom somehow linked to the chemist, which confers forgetfulness on everyone it comes into contact with. It is the housekeeper who succeeds in vanquishing – or neutralising – the amnesia-inducing powers of the story's supernatural menace. There is heroism in her daily small-scale efforts – the tidied floor, the making of a curtain, the scrubbing. The little things are not as small as they appear.

Dickens had touched on the importance of domestic labour in *David Copperfield*, with the entirely impractical Dora. He returned to it again, and with more sustained attention, in *Bleak House*. The fog which shrouds the opening of the novel drifts away, to return from time to time in the form of 'mist', 'fumes', 'vapour' and 'smoke'. The mud and dirt remain omnipresent. We focus on a central figure, at first glance an underwhelming one, Esther Summerson, whose origins are shrouded in obscurity. From her boarding school, the novel takes her first to London and then to Bleak House, the home of Mr John Jarndyce, to act as housekeeper to him and companion to his young ward Ada. Here she occupies herself in gentle charitable endeavour and with housework, 'bustle and business', 'accounts', 'rearrangements of drawers and presses [i.e. cupboards]'. Feminist critics have complained long and loud about Esther Summerson. She enjoys her domestic work too much, says one. She is passive-aggressive, says another. But this surely misses Dickens's point.

If Esther is always expressing her disbelief that anyone could be interested in her, or admire her, or fear that she might inveigle their son into marriage, repeatedly detailing her astonishment that she should be thought worthy of time or attention, then it's entirely natural. Her earliest memories are of being told that she was her mother's 'disgrace', was 'degraded', 'different from other children'; as an adult she understands that she is not only a bastard, but one whose parents appear to have wanted nothing whatsoever to do with her. Of course she's needy, of course she has an insatiable thirst for reassurance, despite being both young and beautiful and domestically and emotionally competent. The woman who raised her told her that her only choice was 'Submission, self-denial, diligent work', and so little Esther decided to be 'industrious, con-tented, and kind-hearted', 'to do some good to some one', with the pardonably self-interested aim of trying to 'win some love to myself if I could'. It's the self-interest that saves her, as a character. She has actively chosen to pursue the feminine arts; her expressions of humility are only partly truthful. When she's self-deprecating, she wants to be contradicted. She likes her efforts to be appreciated. And those efforts aren't just good in themselves, they're intrinsi-cally connected to the central theme of the novel – the importance of putting (and keeping) one's house in order, of cleanliness, of control.

We have the housekeeper Mrs Rouncewell, generally believed to have been modelled on Dickens's paternal grandmother, who had been employed for decades in a similar role. When we first encounter Charley, the orphan who becomes Esther's maid, she is working as a laundress, although she's hardly tall enough to reach over the washing-tub. Esther's friend Caddy Jellyby is raised in a slovenly, chaotic home, ignored, along with her siblings, by a mother obsessed with distant charitable endeavours. The street-child Jo doesn't just beg under the guise of brushing the crossing for pedestrians, he actually cleans as well as he can, sweeps corners even when there is no small coin forthcoming for his efforts. All are struggling to control their environments; several to compensate for the domestic ineptitude or failures of their parents, or of the state. Charley is an orphan, desperate to keep her younger siblings out of the workhouse. Caddy's mother is clearly criticised for the state of the house (the food inedible, the children feral, carpets torn, dirt in every corner) but Caddy's father isn't allowed to get off scot-free. Inactivity is morally wrong. So, too, is the 'rapacious benevolence' of the philanthropists who spend all their time raising money for faraway charities while ignoring what needs to be done on their own doorstep – both literally and figuratively.

All you can do is to keep sweeping, keep cleaning, try to wrest order from disorder, try to keep your own space clean and safe. But even then, you might easily fail.

Jo picks up an infection in a London 'berryin ground'. Getting him a hospital bed will be slow and difficult, so the charitably inclined folk at Bleak House decide to take him in – although they prudently house him in an outbuilding. The caution makes no difference. Jo passes the infection on to Esther's maid Charley. Charley then infects Esther. Although it's left unspecified in the novel, most commentators and adaptors understand the illness to be smallpox. One character recoils on seeing Esther's face after her recovery, which suggests she is left with some pitting and scarring. Smallpox was a public health priority when the novel was written. The state started offering free smallpox vaccination in 1840, and it was made compulsory (in theory, at least) for all children born after August 1853. Some protection from smallpox had been available in England since the 1720s via the cruder practice of variolation. That no one took basic, elementary steps to protect Esther's health is perhaps intended as an indication of how neglected her childhood was.

The balancing act Dickens achieves in *Bleak House* is astonishing. Here are his recent bereavements, here too his bitter resentment of his father – the novel's fathers are, almost without exception, dead losses even before Dickens kills them off, which he does with abandon. Esther is given his own controlling and sanitising tendencies, his desire to influence how people react to him, the charitable wanderings as well. Esther even brings infection into the household. But mixed in with what is personal we find liberal borrowings from other writers, an interest in the domestic certain to play well with his audience and, sprinkled over the top, public health messaging and pious exhortations about the fate of the poor and the real meaning of charity. He even includes a character recognisably modelled on Leigh Hunt, the literary man he had raised money for; he came close to admitting as much.[332]

Dickens really does seem, at this point in his career, to be confident in his ability to handle material drawn from his own life while managing to manipulate exactly how his readers will understand and respond to it. How else should we see his delicate dancing around the truth of his own experiences in *David Copperfield*? The careful doling out of information to Forster? By making some of the connections between real life and his fictions so obvious, he invited his audience to make more on their own – both at the time, and in the future.

Later readers, primed by the biographical readings Forster makes of some of the other novels, have tended, with *Bleak House*, to focus on the figure of Mrs Rouncewell, a housekeeper in a stately home (as Dickens's grandmother was), who has two sons (as she had). A number of people have wondered whether Mrs Rouncewell's story might not be family history – or at least family myth – whether the revelation, in the novel, that the fictional housekeeper had a baby by her aristocratic employer suggests that Dickens's grandmother did the same in real life. Is this the reason, they (sometimes) continue, that one of her sons was given a leg up with the job in the Navy Pay Office, when the other one wasn't? Does this explain why John Dickens thought the world owed him a living?

Well, maybe. What I think is far more likely is that Dickens wanted us to wonder; that Mrs Rouncewell's story is a nugget carefully positioned for us to find in the future – yet another of his distractions.

What we see, in the early 1850s, is Dickens energised, his writer's block vanished. Perhaps the explanation lies in his relief at having found a way to write about personal matters while protecting his brand, the comforting knowledge that Forster was already primed with a selective version of his life which, while not contradicting what was already known, guided people away from all the really sensitive topics. Perhaps, strange as it seems, bereavement released him. After all, now that John Dickens was dead, the risk that the old scandal would be dragged up was far smaller. It is suggestive that it was in 1851, almost as soon as John Dickens was out of the way, that his son started to relax about the subject of Chatham.[333] The competition offered by Thackeray, Gaskell and Charlotte Brontë may have proved stimulating.

His new magazine, *Household Words*, started appearing in March 1850 and *David Copperfield* was finished six months later. In January 1851, he started *A Child's History of England*, published serially between 1851 and 1853, and collected into volumes at the end of each year.

In parts this is very funny, but it's not really suitable for children. Some of the language is robust. Henry VIII is described as a 'Royal pig', and the Stuarts as 'a public nuisance'. Dickens even refers – and not in all that roundabout a way – to rumours that James I engaged in same-sex relationships ('He used to loll on the necks of his favourite courtiers, and slobber their faces, and kiss and pinch their cheeks; and the greatest favourite he ever had, used to sign himself in his letters to his royal master, His Majesty's "dog and slave"').[334]

While *A Child's History* was underway, Dickens started on *Bleak House*, which was published between January 1852 and the middle of 1853. In addition, there's the cookery book, assuming that it is wholly or partly his work. In 1854, he published another novel, *Hard Times*. He started the annual Christmas stories again, although as collaborative ventures. This isn't far off being a return to his early publication rate, back when he first became 'the inimitable Boz'.

His personal life, however, was not improving.

Charles had shown more concern for his wife during her illness than he had done for years previously. Whatever was wrong with her, he took it seriously; there was no telling her to buck up as there had been after she'd given birth to Dora. Dora's death seems to have drawn her parents closer together – for a time. They moved house – to Tavistock Square – and embarked on a flurry of improvements. They conceived their final child, Edward. Yet not long after Edward's arrival we see an opening up of emotional distance between his parents.

In 1853, Dickens spent six months in Europe; the first half of that time at Boulogne with his family and a house guest, his great friend the writer Wilkie Collins, the second indulging himself in 'bachelor wanderings' with Collins and the painter Augustus Egg.[335] The phrase 'bachelor wanderings' is Dickens's own, but perhaps his wife, having now produced ten children, waved him off with her blessing. When a woman had neither reliable contraception methods nor a considerate husband, two decades of married bliss might have been about as much as she could take.

At the same time, there's something rather sad in Dickens's preference for the company of his new friends, who were not only unmarried and footloose, but who also seem to have been selected to give him a delightful sense of his own superiority. Egg was only four years Dickens's junior, but was plagued by ill health and, though he had shown promise as an artist, recognition was slow to arrive. Collins, not yet out of his twenties, was still finding his feet as a writer – his *Antonina*, dealing with the fall of Rome, had been published in 1850, and a modern novel, *Basil*, in 1852. Dickens was older, more famous, richer – though he didn't foot any more than what he considered his fair share of the bill, keeping strict accounts.[336]

He wrote to his wife from Strasbourg, from Lausanne, from Chamonix, Milan, Genoa, Rome, Florence, Venice. His letters are full of other people, instructions, complaints that her replies have gone astray, or that her handwriting on the envelope is illegible. One letter is, he states, 'merely [...] business', giving his proposed itinerary. He refers to meeting the de la Rues again, the couple with whom he had become so oddly involved in 1844 when he started mesmerising the wife, Augusta. He does not, however, set his own wife at ease concerning them. His letters to Georgina and to his philanthropist friend Angela Burdett Coutts are, though less frequent, more relaxed and descriptive; funnier. Letters sent to his wife on previous trips away had been kinder, more intimate. There is a discernible difference between the tone of this correspondence and the way he was communicating with her in 1851. She has become, almost without exception, 'Catherine', rather than the affectionate 'Kate'.

The relationship between Charles and Catherine had never rested on the firmest of foundations. Charles's emotional fidelity to his wife was at best fitful. He could be, at times, breathtakingly selfish – 1837, the year when Catherine gave birth in January, miscarried in May and was, by December, six months into another pregnancy, while enduring her husband making a vast parade of his grief for *her* sister, is one of the low points, albeit not the lowest. The marriage had survived all of this, though; it had weathered the storms of workaholism, rumour, depression, pregnancy loss, career setbacks, hostility from America, and the financial burden of Charles's father. But clearly it was now in serious trouble.

Grief is hard. It doesn't become easier if the person you are mourning was – say – a parent who failed you on numerous occasions, whom you resented, passionately, and perhaps justifiably. If anything it's more painful, more complicated. And losing a child has driven apart many couples far more devoted than Mr and Mrs Dickens ever were.

This second long trip around Europe didn't coincide with a writing hiatus as the first one had done. A few weeks after Dickens returned, he set off to the northern industrial town of Preston, to observe the strike by cotton workers. He travelled by train – a prominent stop in the old coaching days, the town became a hub in the railway age, and by 1854 had eight separate lines running into or through it. He remained there only two days, wandering about the town and attending meetings associated with the strikers. His visit inspired a new story, which was published in his own *Household Words*: *Hard Times* (1854).

Hard Times is a grim book, not just in its depiction of the factories, but in its view of human nature. The novel's anti-hero, the educational theorist Thomas Gradgrind, sees his theories blasted, while his children turn out to have been profoundly wounded by their rigorous, utilitarian upbringing. The strikers are ignorant and easily led. The masters are selfish and self-satisfied. Religion, temperance, even education – all, in this novel, turn out to be almost completely pointless. Love is fled from, or rejected.

The story is set in 'Coketown', which, from its murmurings of industrial unrest and numerous train tracks, seems to be based on Preston. Much of the book consists of characters taking train journeys, with relatively few street or factory scenes – indicative of how little time Dickens had spent in the place. Preston was enjoying fifteen minutes of fame in the spring of 1854. The day before the first number of *Hard Times* hit the newsstands, the *New York Tribune* had published an article about the strike by Preston cotton hands, which was then entering its sixth month. It was written by Karl Marx.

Critics often remark on this juxtaposition, usually not in Dickens's favour. Nor does his book always come out well when compared with another industrial novel, Elizabeth Gaskell's *North and South* (the serialisation of which followed immediately on the heels of *Hard Times* in *Household Words*). *North and South* is undoubtedly the better-realised work. It's clear that Dickens didn't really understand the issues, the people or the environment that he was trying to write about. Gaskell, living in Manchester, engaged in social work, had a much better grasp of all these essentials and, though her story is over-egged, with half a dozen deaths, fortunes appearing and disappearing, a riot and a brother on the run, her extensive real-life knowledge ensures that it remains grounded in a way that Dickens's is not.

Hard Times is an outlier among Dickens's work, and perhaps a misfire as well. Half the length of *David Copperfield* or *Bleak House*, it is short for a Victorian novel, by Dickens's own standards very short, and it is the only one of his novels not to visit London (though one or two of the characters do so). Despite its brevity, it's crammed with disconnected themes and issues. As well as the industrial sections, there's a critique of utilitarian education. Elsewhere, environmental concerns are foregrounded; the setting described as 'a town of […] brick that would have been red if the smoke and ashes had allowed it [...] of machinery and tall chimneys, out of which interminable serpents of smoke trailed themselves for ever and ever' with a 'black canal, and a river that ran purple with evil-smelling dye'. In the surrounding countryside, meanwhile, the fences are 'rotten', the fields soiled with heaps of coal and made dangerous by 'deserted works' and 'old pits'. One abandoned mine shaft claims the life of a factory worker who, while walking through green fields, tumbles into 'a black ragged chasm hidden by the thick grass' – a fate which might hark back to events in Dickens's childhood. More than one inhabitant of Chatham had vanished into wells around the period that the Dickens family were living there. The novel also features a circus, with the circus girl Sissy Jupe an important character; this seems like a reworking of the theatrical troupe who appear in *Nicholas Nickleby*, or the travelling waxwork show which temporarily offers shelter to Nell in *The Old Curiosity Shop*.

Dickens also bemoans the fate of a hard-working man married to an alcoholic wife, one who had 'disgraced herseln everyways, bitter and bad'. Despite this, divorce is totally out of reach for him, in part for financial reasons and in part because, though aware of her behaviour, he has taken her back. This was known in legal terminology as 'condonation', and basically reset the clock on a marriage.[337] The first readers of *Hard Times* might have been led to ponder the potential repercussions of the condonation rule. In one scene in the novel it becomes apparent that the wife in question is suffering from syphilis. She has 'wounds', one described as a 'sore', and we are told that when her unfortunate husband catches sight of the label on the medicine bottle by her bed, 'he turned of a deadly hue, and a sudden horror seemed to fall upon him'.[338]

The poor hard-working man and his alcoholic wife have been married for 'eighteen years' – precisely the length of time Dickens had been married to his own wife when he wrote and published this passage. If it is a coincidence, it's a hell of an unfortunate one. If it isn't, what is Dickens trying to communicate, and to whom? Is this another example of him attempting to control what posterity might think of him?

And yet (and yet) perhaps the truth forces its way up, again, as we've seen it do before. It's in this book that Dickens creates a character whose tales of his own hard childhood are exaggerated, manipulative, self-congratulatory lies. The repellent Bounderby is introduced as 'a rich man: banker, merchant, manufacturer, and what not' and one 'who could never sufficiently vaunt himself a self-made man. A man who was always proclaiming, through that brassy speaking-trumpet voice of his, his old ignorance and his old poverty.' He claims that his mother 'bolted', and that he was left to the indifferent care of a grandmother, 'the wickedest and the worst old woman that ever lived', who would steal his shoes and 'sell 'em for drink', who could 'lie in her bed and drink her four-teen glasses of liquor before breakfast!' These assertions, repeated again and again, are revealed to be pure fiction. Bounderby's parents, though not rich, took care to 'pinch a bit that he might write and cipher beautiful' and later on apprenticed him. His mother ran 'a little vil-lage shop' and, rather than deserting him, used to come and 'take a proud peep' at her son, after he was grown. The grandmother, far from drunkenly abusing her grandson, died before he was even born.

Dickens hadn't quite gone so far as Bounderby in his little chats with Forster. But by encouraging Forster to believe implicitly in the tragic tale of his boyhood and by missing out certain crucial details – like Harriet – he had ensured that any available sympathy would be directed towards him and not his parents.

By this point, given what we've learned about Dickens, we shouldn't need a warning. But Bounderby is one, if it's needed: you shouldn't always believe the stories people tell you about themselves.

Notes

298. Maria was a year older than Dickens, had several siblings and a mother still living. Her father resided in Lombard Street in the City of London. Dora is a motherless only child, clearly younger than David, and lives in Norwood.
299. Letter to Cornelius Mathews, 28 December 1842.
300. A name that can be found as early as 1830 (*Berkshire Chronicle*, 29 May 1830, page 4), but which came into common use during the 1850s and 1860s.
301. *The Letters and Private Papers of W. M. Thackeray*, ed. G.N. Ray, Vol. II, page 336.

302. *The Letters and Private Papers of W. M. Thackeray*, ed. G.N. Ray, Vol. II, page 531.

303. *Morning Herald*, 18 December 1848, page 5.

304. Letter to Alfred Dickens, New Year's Day 1848.

305. Letter to T.J. Thompson, 15 February 1844.

306. Dickens specifically states that she was 'called Dora, in remembrance of Copperfield' (letter to Mrs Sigourney, 24 May 1851).

307. See letter to W.H. Wills, 16 August 1850, in which Dickens announces his intention to head to Broadstairs that very afternoon, the day of the birth.

308. Letter to Catherine Dickens, 21 August 1850.

309. Letter to Catherine Dickens, 17 August 1850.

310. Letter to Mrs John Leech, 3 February 1851.

311. Louis Phillippe was overthrown in February 1848, a popular insurrection followed in June of that year and Napoleon Bonaparte's nephew was made president in December. The Republic was still in place during this visit by Dickens in 1851, but was replaced the following year by an empire when Bonaparte mounted a coup.

312. Letter to Catherine Dickens, 12 (in fact 13) February 1851.

313. Letter to Dr James Wilson, 8 March 1851.

314. Letter to Mrs Richard Watson, 9 March 1851.

315. Letter to Henry Austin, 12 March 1851.

316. *Worcestershire Chronicle*, 19 March 1851, page 4.

317. 'Mr. Charles Dickens and his family are at present staying at Great Malvern, undergoing the "water cure".' *Liverpool Mail*, 5 April 1851, page 3. The same report was still circulating two weeks later (for example, *Nottingham Review*, 18 April 1851, page 7).

318. Chloroform was used in at least one of Catherine's confinements. See letter to William Empson, 21 January 1849; 'Her confinement was almost as bad a one as its predecessor, but Chloroform did wonders, and she knew nothing of it.'

319. Stefan Tritschler et al., 'Urethral stricture: etiology, investigation and treatments', *Deutsche Ärtzeblatt International*, Vol. 110, No. 13 (March 2013), pages 220–26.

320. Letter to Catherine Dickens, 25 March 1851.

321. Letter to Thomas Mitton, 19 April 1851.

322. Mitton had been a clerk in the same lawyer's office as the young

Dickens and their families may have known each other before this period.

323. Letter to Thomas Beard, 18 July 1849.

324. In a letter of May 1851, he describes 'Inspector Field' as 'one of my Night-Guides'. Letter to the Duke of Devonshire, 9 May 1851.

325. 'In the course of my nightly wanderings into strange places, I have spoken to several women and girls, who are very thankful, but make a fatal and decisive confusion between emigration and transportation.' Letter to Angela Burdett Coutts, 12 April 1850.

326. Letter to Henry Austin, 15 April 1851.

327. 'Ait' is a variant of 'eyot', meaning a small island in a river. There is a Chiswick Eyot on the Thames Boat Race course.

328. Susan M. Rossi-Wilcox, *Dinner for Dickens: The Culinary History of Mrs. Charles Dickens' Menu Books* (2005).

329. The youngest of the Dickens's children, Edward, was born in March 1852.

330. *Elgin Courier*, 23 April 1852, page 4.

331. 'I wonder what will come of the Christmas book! I have entered on the first stage of its composition this morning, which is, sitting frowning horribly at a quire of paper'. Letter to Mrs Richard Watson, 5 October 1848.

332. 'I suppose he is the most exact portrait that was ever painted in words! ... It is an absolute reproduction of a real man.' Letter to Mrs Richard Watson, 21 September 1853.

333. The essay 'One Man in a Dockyard', published in *Household Words* in September 1851, describes Chatham Dockyard, though we have to wait until a much later essay, 'Chatham Dockyard', published in 1863, for an explicit acknowledgement that Dickens had known the place as a child.

334. The confusing repetition of 'he' and 'his' seems to be deliberate.

335. Letter to W.F. de Cerjat, 20 December 1852.

336. Letter to Wilkie Collins, 16 December 1853.

337. It was condonation which prevented George Henry Lewes, George Eliot's partner, from divorcing his wife, though she had given birth to children fathered by her lover.

338. The alarming medicine bottle appears to be a substance which can be applied topically but will certainly prove fatal if drunk: perhaps a preparation containing mercury or arsenic, both of which were prescribed for the treatment of syphilis sores.

ENTER RUMOUR (1855–62)

8

A *carte de visite* of Frances, Maria, and Ellen
Ternan. (History and Art Collection/Alamy)

To celebrate his 43rd birthday on 7 February 1855, Dickens went walking across the north Kent marshes with a friend – from Gravesend, on the River Thames, towards Rochester, on the Medway, a journey of about seven miles. It was cold. The previous week had seen heavy snowfall and out in the open country the thaw had not set in. The main road, with the way cleared, and the snow piled up on either side, had been turned into a glassy corridor, walls of ice and frozen wheel-ruts crunching into slush under his boots as he went. Once he was clear of Gravesend, there were hardly any houses to be seen, only one or two, lonely in that landscape, and looking back, the snow and the wide grey river, the white blanket on the marshes intersected by the dark lines of dyke and ditch. In one of those houses, in the tiny village of Chalk, he and Catherine had spent their honeymoon and had lived for several months after the birth of their first child. That child was now eighteen, and struggling to decide on a career.

Two miles further on, he would have come to higher ground – Gads Hill, a pub, a handful of houses clustered around it, the closest, immediately opposite, being built of red brick, large but not too large; plain, solid.

This 'very house' had been, Dickens explained in a breathless letter written just two days after his birthday, 'literally "a dream of my childhood"'.[339] Possibly it had been, though for little legs it's quite a distance from Chatham, four miles by the most direct route. The children of the early nineteenth century were, I'm sure, better walkers than many of today's children are, but it's difficult to believe young Charles can have often passed the house on foot. The turnpike road ran right past the door, however, so it's likely that he had seen it several times before. Another attraction was something he would mention a lot later on; Gads Hill features in Shakespeare's *Henry IV Part 1* – it's where Prince Hal and his friends mount a 'hilarious' prank, getting Falstaff to rob travellers, and then attacking him and taking the money. The house was for sale.

That same day, two days after Dickens turned 43, he received a letter from Maria Beadnell, now Maria Winter, the woman with whom he had fancied himself in love two decades before. In a novel the coincidence would be meaningful, each reminder of the past intensifying the other, making it seem more significant. In real life, too, it's possible that her letter would, two years, even a week earlier, have received a different response.

Instead, Dickens wrote back to her, telling her how 'Three or four and twenty years vanished like a dream' when he recognised the handwriting on the envelope, and how he had 'opened it with the touch of my young friend David Copperfield when he was in love' and read 'with perfect delight'. Until, that was, he encountered a reference to Maria's children (she had two, both girls), whereupon 'the three or four and twenty years began to rearrange themselves in a long procession between me and the changeless Past'.

His letter moves from remembered intimacy to jokes about how much time has gone by, and decorous plans for dinner together with their respective spouses. Then it skips back again. Dickens was about to leave on a trip to France and recalled how, years before, his 'whole Being' had been 'blighted, by the Angel of my soul being sent there to finish her education'. In the final paragraph the past seems about to overwhelm him once more: 'I cannot end my answer to you lightly. The associations my memory has with you, make your letter more – I want a word – invest it with a more immediate address to me – than such a letter could have from anybody else.'[340]

Less than a week later, he wrote to Maria again from Paris, a more serious and far more selfish letter. His imagination had carried him away again – that, or his love of controlling how others viewed him. This time there are no jokes, no mention of his wife or Maria's husband. Dickens is too busy crafting a version of the past in which he has always been 'faithful', 'devoted', 'innocent', 'ardent', suffering from a 'heartache' which, once renewed, seems hardly to have stopped in all the years since the pair were separated.[341] Mary? Augusta? Catherine? Who are they again?

How serious the relationship had been all those years before, how heartfelt, is, as we have seen, very difficult to ascertain.

Maria doesn't seem to have preoccupied Dickens's thoughts to the exclusion of all others even in the 1830s – at least two other young women appear in his letters at the time, and both seem to have evoked strong emotions. We might doubt whether, nearly a quarter of a century later, he could remember what he had felt for her at all. He works hard to sell the idea, though. Maria 'may' (he thinks) have recognised 'in one of my books a faithful reflection of the passion I had for you, and [...] seen in little bits of "Dora" touches of your old self sometimes'. Dora Spenlow, David Copperfield's vapid love interest, completes her fashionable education in France – as Maria had done – though otherwise there are no obvious resemblances between the two. If Maria recognised anything else of herself, she must have been unusually lacking in self-conceit.

As well as imagining Maria's past experience of reading his novel, Dickens also sketches out a version of her future, in which he is still firmly ensconced as a prominent character, as he imagines how her daughter and grandchildren will be told all about him. He feels, he says, 'a stirring of the old fancies'.[342]

There was, evidently, something else stirring as well.

The next letter, written the following week, seems to be working up to an extramarital liaison. There's no need for anxiety about sending letters to him, he assures her; 'I could be nowhere addressed with stricter privacy or in more absolute confidence than at my own house.' Come on Sunday, he writes, between three and four, when '[i]t is almost a positive certainty that there will be no one here but I'. Or he'll meet her on the street, as if by chance, only they must be careful, 'knowing what odd coincidences take place in streets, when they are not wanted to happen'. At one point he even seems to suggest disguising himself ('you may expect to encounter a stranger whom you may suspect to be the right person if he wears a moustache').[343] He also brought her and her older daughter jewellery ('little ornaments') back from Paris.[344]

The sequel to the encounter is usually considered to have been the disappointing discovery that Maria, who'd not long had baby number two, had got fat, a crime for which she was duly punished by being turned into Flora in *Little Dorrit* (1855–7), the long-ago love of the main male character Arthur Clennam. Flora is silly, girlish still, though she has long ceased to be a girl. Returning from more than twenty years in China, Arthur finds not only that she talks too much ('such a chatterer', he calls her), but that she is obese, alcoholic and (to put it politely) desperate for the warmth and connection of physical contact, however it comes.

What actually happened between the real-life pair, we don't know. In June 1855, Dickens is addressing her as 'My Dear Maria', and expressing anxiety over a letter of his which had gone missing. In February 1856, halfway through a long stay in Paris with his family, when he has begun writing *Little Dorrit*, he sends Maria a chilly missive, but one which is clearly designed to be seen by her husband, too. 'My Dear Mrs. Winter,' it begins, formally, 'It comes into my head that I have never acknowledged the little letter you wrote me on receipt of my books' and so he is, he explains, sending 'this short note'.[345] In August 1858, he writes to say that he can't see her in Liverpool, explaining that he has 'so much business to transact at times, and have to keep myself so quiet at other times, and have so many people to give directions to, and make arrangements with (four travel with me), that I see no one'.[346] In November of the same year, he writes to condole with her on a financial reverse her family had suffered.[347] Soon afterward, her daughter sends him a 'pretty book-marker'.[348]

It seems perfectly possible that there was an affair and that it only dwindled away when Dickens fell for someone else – which, as we'll see, it's generally agreed he did in 1857. In this case, the unkind caricature of Flora might be better understood as a blind, a distraction. The letters and the arrangements to meet seem all rather practised, as if Dickens might have done this sort of thing before, maybe even more than once.

The version Dickens told his friend Forster, though, was both innocent and high-minded. He admits only to a quiet 'formal call with his wife', and to being inspired to write about Maria for a second time – with 'comic humour' but 'kindly' intentions.[349] He could not, he said, forget that it was his long-ago love for her which had inspired him to better himself. Perhaps this had even been true, once upon a time. Maria had been an almost totemic object for him and, for a time, a muse. As a young man, Dickens had written poems with acrostics on her name; long, impassioned letters smuggled to her via a friend, Henry Kolle, who later married her sister. Whatever other career motivations had accrued in the years since, you can see how Maria's attempt to revive their relationship might have been emotionally destabilising, might have seemed poised to unravel the narratives Dickens had constructed for himself. 'No one,' Forster reports him as saying, 'can imagine in the most distant degree what pain the recollection gave me in *Copperfield*.' The idea of seeing Maria again 'loosens my hold upon myself'.[350]

It appears to have loosened his hold upon his writing as well.

David Copperfield and *Bleak House* are among his finest works and remain deservedly popular today. *Hard Times* isn't a particularly convincing industrial novel, but it has a coherent plot. *Little Dorrit* does not.

The novel flits from setting to setting. It's stuffed with so much unconnected material that Dickens is obliged to fall back on contrivance, coincidence and hastily knotted loose ends to try to bring it into any sort of unity. There's a ridiculously complicated codicil to a will, by which the testator leaves money to his nephew's mistress's career-mentor's brother's youngest daughter.

The 'Little Dorrit' of the title is Amy Dorrit, youngest daughter of a gentleman imprisoned for a debt he cannot repay. She was born and raised in the Marshalsea, evidently during the 1810s and 1820s. This is the very place where John Dickens had been confined in 1824. She is, arguably, another of Dickens's female self-portraits. But she lacks savour; as too does the nominal hero, Arthur Clennam. There's a wasted subplot about Arthur's true parentage which, rich in religious repression, replete with suggestions of a secret marriage and bigamy, a stolen child and a mother locked up in a private madhouse, is more than enough to sustain an entire novel. Here it's squashed into just a few pages close to the end of the story and is, so far as we can gather, never even revealed to the individual it most concerns. What seems to happen is that Amy, whom Arthur eventually marries, decides to conceal it from him, but the text is so dense and imprecise at this point that it's difficult to be certain – just as we remain unclear about who was married to whom, how long Arthur's birth mother was incarcerated and whether she was really mad.

These are missed opportunities. Arthur, at the end of the novel, becomes an appendage, Dickens writing of 'Little Dorrit and her husband'. The two vanish into the crowd and – due to some absent pronouns in the concluding paragraph – pass implicitly together into 'a modest life of usefulness and happiness' in which they 'give a mother's care' to Amy's nieces and nephews as well as to their own children and act as 'a tender nurse' to Amy's ne'er-do-well brother. Subsumed, feminised – Arthur Clennam is an odd kind of hero.

Even the temporal setting of *Little Dorrit* is odd.

The first date to be mentioned explicitly in the novel is 'the thirty-first of December, One thousand eight hundred and eighty-six' – that's 31 December *1886*, more than thirty years after it was published. The date is part of an epitaph that a minor character, the young, fanciful John Chivery, is imagining for himself and the rest of it enables us to work out that the current narrative time is 1826. It's one of the most exact datings in any of Dickens's fictions and we are told that 'At that time' there were 'no small steam-boats on the river, no landing places but slippery wooden stairs and foot-causeways, no railroad on the opposite bank [...] nothing moving on the stream but waterman's wherries and coal-lighters'. Yet this is historically incorrect. Steamboats were on the river by the middle of the 1820s. Indeed, one character, a rent collector called Pancks, is compared repeatedly to a 'Tug', or a 'little labouring steam-engine', 'steam[ing] out of his little dock'. At one point, the same comparison appears to be repeated, not just in the narrative but inside the head of Arthur, who imagines Pancks as a 'little coaly steam-tug' towing away 'an unwieldy ship in the Thames river'. It's truly terrible historical novel writing.

We could view this – like the character of Bounderby – as an unconscious admission, on Dickens's part, of his ongoing obsession with how he might be viewed in the future, and of a recurrence of his old anxiety about the wisdom of drawing on early memories when there was so much about his early life that he was, still, unwilling to share with the public.

Equally, though, the oddities might be simply an indication of how much Dickens had on his mind in the mid- to late 1850s – a house to buy (the purchase was time-consuming), the return of Maria and, perhaps, a liaison with her, a marriage moving into its death throes, his older children emerging into young adulthood, the never-ending job of editing his magazine *Household Words*, grief for his father and daughter, grief over the wrong turnings that so many of his relationships seemed to have taken. He had now fallen out with not one but two of his brothers. Fred had temporarily separated from his wife in 1854 and in 1857 the couple parted ways again. Augustus, meanwhile, abandoned his wife, who had lost her sight, and moved to America where he lived with another woman. Dickens was left to clean up the mess and make arrangements for his blind, abandoned sister-in-law. His mother, Elizabeth, was beginning the inexorable slide into dementia.

And now another preoccupation joined these.

Enter Ellen Ternan.

Less a cause of marital trouble than – like Maria Beadnell, like the holidays with young buck Wilkie Collins – a symptom of it.

The biographer Claire Tomalin calls Ellen 'the invisible woman' and though the affair was not in fact a very well-kept secret, Ellen herself is quite a shadowy figure. She was just eighteen when she supposedly first met Dickens; younger than his two eldest children, twenty-seven years younger than he was himself. She was one of three sisters, third-generation theatrical performers on their mother's side. Their father Thomas had been an actor too, and for a time his brother had been one as well; the girls spent their childhoods in and out of theatres and had a large theatrical acquaintance, including one of Dickens's closest friends, the actor William Macready.

Macready had stood godfather to Dickens's second daughter Katie, and had kept an eye on the Dickens children when their parents were in America in 1842.[351] He had also acted with both of Ellen's parents in *Othello* and played Macbeth to Mrs Ternan's Lady Macbeth. After a disastrous theatrical business investment, Mr Ternan vanished into an asylum, dying in 1846, and leaving his three pre-pubescent daughters, Fanny, Maria and Ellen, fatherless.[352] Even before Mr Ternan died, Macready showed an interest in the family: 'After the play sent for Mrs. Ternan, and asked to see her little gifted girl, who, I saw, was in the theatre – a very sweet child,' he writes in his diary.[353] This was Fanny, the eldest, who had already built up a fair reputation as a child performer.[354] When Mrs Ternan was widowed, Macready sent her ten pounds, urging her to consider it as a gift to 'her little girl. Poor thing!'[355] In November

1846, he was rehearsing Shylock against Mrs Ternan's Portia in
The Merchant of Venice; her recital of 'the beautiful speech on mercy'
moved him, he recorded, as did the sight of 'her three little girls'
whom she brought to see him.[356] Dickens usually made a point of
attending Macready's performances, but he would have missed this
one, which took place while he was living in Switzerland. It seems
probable that Macready continued to put work the Ternans' way.[357]

Charles Dickens and the Ternans knew quite a few of the same
people. They moved in some of the same circles. Dickens states in
one letter that he had seen Maria Ternan 'on the stage' when she
was 'a little child', though not where or when he did so.[358] He had a
number of possible opportunities of seeing Maria's sisters perform,
too, although far more for Fanny – praised from early on as 'one of
the prettiest of precocious performers' and much in demand – than
for Ellen, the youngest and, by general assent, least gifted of the sisters.[359] The girls played 'breeches' parts, at least on occasion. These,
in which youthful actresses took the roles of young men or boys, were
extremely popular, in part because, to be crude, the audience could
cop an eyeful. When an adaptation of Dickens's own *Barnaby Rudge*
was staged in 1841, the part of Barnaby, a character with profound
learning disabilities, was played as a breeches role by an actress. In a
letter written to Dickens after seeing her perform, the artist Daniel
Maclise dwelt lecherously on 'the wild attractions of her legs [...] the
small waist [...] the woman bust – the tunic reaching exactly where
we wish it'.[360] Ellen played the male role of Hippomenes in *Atalanta*,
in April 1857: her costume is likely to have been revealing.[361]

Perhaps to discourage unsavoury suspicions from their readers,
a number of biographers have tended to ignore or hurry over the
earlier possible connections between the Ternans and Dickens.[362]
A common implication is that a first meeting took place only in
August 1857 when one of Dickens's amateur theatrical projects
spiralled in scale and ambition, necessitating the engagement of
professional actresses – partly because of lingering qualms about
'decent' women appearing on the public stage, and partly because
untrained female voices would struggle to fill an 'immense' performance space which had been arranged for the piece in Manchester.[363]

The play was *The Frozen Deep*, written by Wilkie Collins and
much-edited and stage-managed by Dickens. Both men performed

in it. Focusing on the rescue of a group of polar explorers who have been despaired of, the play's storyline was clearly inspired by the determined public unwillingness to accept the probable fate of John Franklin's Arctic expedition of 1845. Franklin and his men were still missing after having set out to find the fabled Northwest Passage. Search missions had failed; an official report had already concluded that the crew had been reduced to cannibalism before dying. Though there's quite a large body of scholarship investigating Dickens's fascination with the eating of human flesh, an article in *Household Words* inveighed against the suggestion that Franklin's crew could ever have done so, throwing in some not-at-all-casual racism against Inuit communities for good measure.[364] In case the play's backdrop of polar exploration and privation should prove insufficiently engaging, the plot includes a tragic love triangle and adventurous journeying by the heroine.

Maria and Ellen Ternan both appeared in the Manchester production, as did their mother. Dickens's character, Richard Wardour, has little to do with Ellen's Lucy Crayford; Richard is in love with Clara Burnham, played by Maria. There's an intense, climactic scene between the pair. Dickens describes Maria in a letter as 'a very gentle and good little girl', with 'a very good little pale face'; he also explains how, on the stage, her tears rolled 'into his mouth, down his beard, all over his rags – down his arms as he held her by the hair'.[365] Charles's eldest daughter Mamie had previously taken this role in the smaller-scale performances, but still, the description raises a frisson or two of unease.

Dickens had finished *Little Dorrit* in the spring of 1857. *The Frozen Deep* had filled his days through the summer. The end of August found him bored and dissatisfied; full of, in his own words, 'grim despair and restlessness of this subsidence from excitement' – depression returning again, perhaps (that 'grim' seems heartfelt).[366] He suggested a working holiday to Wilkie Collins; a northern walking tour to include Doncaster, where Maria and Ellen Ternan were going to be performing.[367] Collins sprained his ankle badly, drastically cutting down the actual walking. They managed nevertheless to reach Doncaster, and the holiday was written up as *The Lazy Tour of Two Idle Apprentices* (1857), comically fictionalised.

This part of Dickens's life looks familiar: a successful man growing older, dissatisfied that his wife has the temerity to do the same; a chance encounter with a younger woman; infatuation; and, as powerful, a mourning for lost youth, turns not taken. Thus, a whole life, a family, a quarter of a century of shared history go up in flames. We might be inclined to view the matter, not with favour, but perhaps with rueful recognition.

Let's pause, though, before assuming we know for certain what was going on.

Dickens apparently wrote to Forster twice just before he left for the walking tour, both letters making the assertion that he had married the wrong woman, but without so much as touching on the possibility of separation. 'Poor Catherine and I are not made for each other, and there is no help for it [...] nothing on earth could make her understand me, or suit us to each other. Her temperament will not go with mine.' '[...] for her sake as well as mine, the wish will force itself upon me that something might be done. I know too well it is impossible. There is the fact, and that is all one can say.'[368]

Meanwhile, in a letter to another friend, written while in Doncaster, he relates that he is 'going to take the little – riddle – into the country this morning'.[369] It was reported in the newspapers that he had 'viewed the ruins of Roche Abbey and enjoyed a walk in its beautiful grounds', also that he had 'frequented the Theatre Royal' – which was where the Ternan sisters were appearing.[370]

The little 'riddle' is usually presumed to be Ellen, and probably is. Though it was Maria who Dickens had written about so admiringly, we know him well enough by now to know that he made a habit of pulling the wool over people's eyes. But we've also seen how, in some part of Dickens's mind, sisters came in sets – look at his attitudes to Catherine, Mary and Georgina Hogarth. Was his attention already fixed on Ellen this early on? She may not have been a very good actress, he might have been more impressed by Maria's performance, but from photographs Ellen looks pretty, and early photography seldom flattered.

In October 1857, Dickens started sleeping separately from his wife. He arranged for 'a small iron bedstead' to be delivered to his London house and placed in his dressing room, and for the connecting door to Catherine's room to be blocked up.[371] Reading between the lines of later letters, it seems likely this decision was the immediate result of a terrible argument between husband and wife – such a bad one that he banged out of the house in the small hours of the morning and marched the 30 miles to Gads Hill.[372] Catherine had given birth to her first baby at twenty-one and, though she suffered more than one miscarriage, continued to conceive without any difficulty until she was 36. After that there were, so far as we're aware, no more pregnancies. Female fertility does start to decline of course, but it's unusual for it to decline so much quite so early. In the absence of any other evidence, it's reasonable to make the assumption that, though the Dickenses may have continued to share a bed, they had not been intimate for several years.

At the beginning of September, writing to Forster, Dickens had stated that the problems in his marriage resulted from incompatibility, not any failing or vice on the part of his wife. Towards the end of October, he was merrily lambasting her in a letter to his old friends the de la Rues: 'She has been excruciatingly jealous of, and has obtained positive proofs of my being on the most confidential terms with, at least Fifteen Thousand Women of various conditions in life, every condition in life, since we left Genoa.'[373] This is his wife, the woman who loved him before he was famous, who had given him ten children. And she had perfectly good reasons to be jealous. Think of Augusta de la Rue and Maria Winter *née* Beadnell.

Here Dickens is in December 1857, months after the performance, still going on and on about Maria Ternan and the thrill of acting with her – Ellen has a minor appearance as an uninteresting bystander, simply Maria's 'sister':

> when she came on to me in the Morning at Manchester, I said, 'Why my dear, how cold your hand is, and what a tremble you are in! This won't do at night.' [...] She had to take my head up as I was dying, and to put it in her lap, and give me her face to hold between my two hands. All of which I shewed her elaborately [...] When we came to that point at night, her tears fell down my face, down my beard (excuse my mentioning that hateful appendage), down my ragged dress – poured all over

me like Rain, so that it was as much as I could do to speak for them. I whispered to her, 'My dear child, it will be over in two minutes. Pray compose yourself.' [...] And if you had seen the poor little thing, when the Curtain fell, put in a chair behind it – with her mother and sister taking care of her – and your humble servant drying her eyes and administering Sherry (in Rags so horrible that they would scarcely hold together) [...] you would have remembered it for a long, long time.[374]

1857 turned into 1858, and whatever Dickens's feelings about the Ternan girls, his attitude towards his wife showed no sign of softening.

He was 'inexpressibly vexed' to find that she had written to Angela Burdett Coutts about a brother who had lost his job: 'I hope,' he writes coldly, 'you will forgive her more freely and readily than I do.'[375] The 'present circumstances at home' were clearly not good. He spoke of his marriage now to Forster as 'a dismal failure' and had begun to plan a series of readings which would take him away.[376]

If we are to believe Dickens – and, as ever, I'm not sure that we can – he had not yet received any satisfaction from whichever of the Ternan girls it was he was interested in: 'The Doncaster unhappiness remains so strong upon me that I can't write, and (waking) can't rest, one minute. I have never known a moment's peace or content, since the last night of the Frozen Deep. I do suppose that there never was a Man so seized and rended by one Spirit'.[377]

On 2 April, the 22nd anniversary of Charles and Catherine's wedding passed unmarked, as it appears to have done for several years past. We find no references to celebratory dinners, such as they had made a tradition of up until the early 1850s. The following month Dickens began to inform friends and acquaintances that he and Catherine were to separate; to most people's understanding, it appeared that they had already been separated for some time.

Dickens can't resist setting out his own version of events. His 'married life' has been 'a blighted and wasted life', he tells Angela Burdett Coutts. Catherine's children don't love her and never have. She has 'fallen into the most miserable weaknesses and jealousies';

her own mother 'could not live with her'; 'her mind has, at times, been certainly confused'. Generally he seems quite cheerful, however: 'I have come for a time to the office, to leave her Mother free to do what she can at home, towards the getting of her away to some happier mode of existence if possible. They all know that I will do anything for her comfort, and spend anything upon her.'

This letter is dated 9 May. On 19 May, he writes to Burdett Coutts again. He is not cheerful. He's furious: 'If you have seen Mrs. Dickens in company with her wicked mother, I can not enter – no, not even with you – upon any question that was discussed in that woman's presence.'[378]

❧

The gossip mills had started working overtime.

Charles Dickens had eloped from his family with an actress. It was said there were *two* actresses. Or, alternately, his wife had left him because he was sleeping with her sister Georgina. Some newspapers spoke of mere 'incompatibility'.[379] Others referred to accusations that Dickens had engaged in 'gross profligacy' – this indicating something a good deal more outrageous than a man taking a mistress, particularly a mistress who had been raised up from babyhood in the *demi-monde* of the theatre.[380] It's a phrase you find associated with behaviour which shaded from immorality into illegality, or which shocked, or offended deeply against social norms, in particular sexual conduct – repeated and blatant infidelity, married men frequenting brothels and bringing infection home, fathers prostituting their own daughters.

Some of this is down to the particular historical context. Though there were ways of effecting formal marital separation, divorce had, for a long time, been a rich man's game. Liberals had been agitating for reform; Dickens had done so himself in 1854 in *Hard Times*, you'll remember, with a subplot about a factory worker tied to a monstrous, serially unfaithful syphilitic wife. And in January 1858, just a few months before the scandal broke, the Matrimonial Causes Act had come into law. This not only transferred jurisdiction from the ecclesiastical to the civil courts but also made divorce cheaper and easier to obtain, though more so for men

– who needed only to demonstrate their wife's adultery – than for women, who had to prove not just infidelity, but effectively some form of criminal behaviour as well: serious violence, illegal sexual practices, incest or cruelty.

What seems to have happened is that Dickens's personal marital trouble became, in 1858, a focus for wider cultural anxieties about the new Matrimonial Causes Act. Half of literary London must have been speculating as to whether Mrs Dickens might be able to obtain a divorce and, if so, on what grounds.

Given that Dickens's wife had a sister who lived with them, and given how very oddly he had previously behaved over the death of another of his wife's sisters, there probably would have been the odd whispered rumour about him and Georgina anyway when the separation became public knowledge. But when Georgina made the decision not only to support her brother-in-law rather than her own flesh and blood, but also to carry on living in his house, effectively unchaperoned, the whispers started multiplying. And they never really went away. There were still insinuations about the nature of their relationship in some of the critical reporting of the terms of Dickens's will a dozen years later.

In 1858, Georgina was 31; not quite on the shelf, yet seemingly uninterested in marriage or children or a career or anything of her own. Her elder sister Catherine had the status attached to being a married woman; her younger sister Helen had trained as a singer. Georgina had, for half her life, been facilitating someone else's, as Dickens's 'little right hand'.[381] There was money, there was travel, there were exciting people coming round to dinner, but she hovered close to being a servant – an Esther Summerson deprived of either a plot or a happy ending. In the 1861 census she is actually described as 'Servant Housekeeper'.

Georgina had known Dickens since she was a little girl and had lived largely in his household from the age of fifteen. That she chose to stay with him when the Dickens's marriage foundered, despite the damage to her reputation and to her relationship with her own family, indicates how important he had grown to her, how important she believed him to be and that she trusted his judgement over that of her parents.

But throughout the summer and autumn of 1858, Dickens seemingly kept making matters worse.

He devoted the front page of his own magazine *Household Words* to the topic of his separation and the rumours which surrounded it; a self-exculpatory piece. Many newspapers reprinted it – indeed, it was released to a number of larger London publications several days in advance[382] – but some took the opportunity to mock him for imagining that the population at large either knew, or cared, about his private life, suggesting that by responding to the rumours he had succeeded only in attracting more attention and in making himself look guiltier. 'We would urge him,' suggested one paper, '[…] to send forth no more mysterious protests – and to suggest no more inquiries into matters of sacred privacy.'[383] Another pointed out that the statement 'so far from satisfying' curiosity or quashing the story, 'gives a latitude to the construction which those who know the facts would never dream of' – that is, the terms in which it is couched are so opaque that they're likely to give rise to new, different and perhaps even more salacious rumours.[384] Dickens's statement refers to 'misrepresentations, most grossly false, most monstrous and most cruel' which involved not only him 'but innocent persons dear to my heart, and innocent persons of whom I have no knowledge, if, indeed they have any existence'. More and more publications began gleefully to insert clues as to the identity of the women said to be involved, even as they reported everyone's denials that there was any basis to the scandal. Of course they did. Who wouldn't want to know more, after being fed such tantalising morsels of information?

There could hardly have been a series of events more calculated to bring out Dickens's urge to control what the public saw and thought and felt about him than those surrounding the break-up of his marriage. And even before the press had got hold of the story, he had put contingency plans into action. He coerced his mother-in-law and his youngest sister-in-law, Helen, into signing a statement expressing their official belief in his innocence. Dated 29th May 1858, it was clearly designed to be circulated:

> It having been stated to us that, in reference to the differences which have resulted in the separation of Mr. and Mrs. Charles

Dickens certain statements have been circulated that such differences are occasioned by circumstances deeply affecting the moral character of Mr. Dickens and compromising the reputation and good name of others, we solemnly declare that we now disbelieve such statements. We know that they are not believed by Mrs. Dickens, and we pledge ourselves on all occasions to contradict them as entirely destitute of foundation.

In fact the rumours – so far as they related to actresses – appear to have been pretty accurate. Sections of the press, particularly in Ireland, went so far as to bandy names about, explaining that 'Miss Ternan, a handsome and accomplished actress of the Haymarket Theatre [...] is the lady whose name has been unwarrantably mixed up in the calumnious reports about Mr Dickens' – that is, Ellen.[385] We also hear about Catherine Dickens being obliged to write a letter which was read to the staff of the theatre where Ellen was working, expressing her perfect belief in the young lady's virtue.[386] Elsewhere, though, there is some apparent confusion about *which* of the three Misses Ternan were involved. It was to Fanny that a distant cousin wrote, having heard gossip as far afield as America. She obviously informed Dickens of the letter, because he replied to the cousin stating that he was 'blamelessly and openly' Fanny's 'friend', and only her friend, and including dark mutterings about 'wild misrepresentation and amazing falsehood'.[387] Some reports, otherwise nearly identically worded, replace the 'Miss T—' with a 'Miss M—', which may indicate that gossip encompassed the middle sister, Maria, as well.[388] This, as we've seen, not without some basis.

The scandal did die down for a few weeks – giving way to the even more lurid marital problems of Dickens's friend and fellow-novelist Edward Bulwer-Lytton, who had arranged for *his* wife to be confined to a lunatic asylum, to such public outrage that she was quickly released – but it was stirred up again at the end of August, when a letter written by Dickens some months earlier made its way into the American newspapers.[389] Dickens called this the 'violated letter', but it appears to be one he had sent to his speaking agent Arthur Smith, then in the United States drumming up interest for a tour, with the express intention of having him circulate it there.[390] Dickens had complained in the past about the

American press's love of scandal; the publication of the letter can hardly have come as a total shock to him.

Full of praise for Georgina and for a nameless but 'spotless' and entirely 'virtuous' 'young lady', the letter talks of Catherine Dickens only in terms of her inadequacies, the 'peculiarity of her mind' and her 'mental disorder'. But just as some sections of the British press had doubted Dickens's word before, so they doubted it again now. And this time they responded, not just with queries as to the wisdom or tastefulness of Dickens's conduct, but with cold, sometimes furious, condemnation. 'There is,' wrote the *Irishman*, 'a studied endeavour to throw the whole blame of the estrangement on Mrs Dickens; and an equal marked attempt to make it appear that [...] he, and he alone, is the aggrieved party.'[391] His behaviour was 'outrageously impertinent', blustered the *Leeds Times*, 'wantonly cruel' (perhaps enough, the phrasing seems to suggest, to justify his wife obtaining a divorce). He was wandering far from 'common sense, and manliness, and self-respect'. It made right-thinking people think less of him, for surely 'a man with a particle of generous feeling would scorn to drag before the public the fault and infirmities (real or imaginary) of his wife'.[392] Nor did many believe Dickens's assertion that there had been no affair. Even supportive sections of the press became bolder about mentioning names.[393]

Plenty of people will claim, confidently, that Dickens, already besotted, thought only of protecting Ellen's reputation. Others, less romantically, will suggest he was more preoccupied with preserving his own. Yet neither take is entirely borne out by what he did. Getting your estranged wife to write a letter defending a young actress with whom your name has been connected is only going to focus gossip more intensely; much wiser to say nothing. The rules of Victorian morality were not as rigid as is sometimes claimed and Dickens taking an actress as his mistress was at best a minor story, especially if he didn't call attention to it. Being involved with more than one of the Ternan sisters would have been considered extremely distasteful, but it was the allegation that he had pursued a sexual relationship with his wife's sister under his wife's nose – with his unmarried daughters in the house – that was so immensely damaging to everyone concerned, including Dickens.

He issued press releases and made people write letters and sign statements. For some reason, however, he avoided the easy, obvious solution to the worst rumours, those focused on his sister-in-law. If he had just sent Georgina back to her parents or arranged for her to spend some time with them, or with Catherine, the story would have died. By this point Dickens had been famous for a quarter of a century and had been consciously managing his reputation for nearly as long. He wasn't new to rumours and media storms. How did he get it so wrong?

Love, perhaps. But if Charles was using Georgina to distract from his affair with Ellen, it was a poor choice. No one could even agree on which of the Ternan sisters he was involved with. And they were, according to Victorian morality at least, fair game. Georgina wasn't. Under English law it was impossible for Charles to marry her, even if he was divorced or widowed. He had no way of ever making good the damage that was being done to her reputation.

There is another possibility, though: that Dickens's behaviour, once the scandal broke, was neither the blinkered obsessiveness of a selfishly infatuated middle-aged man, nor the flailing about of a clueless, arrogant one, but that it was instead a deliberate attempt to conceal the truth behind fluttering veils of competing rumour about his actresses (in the plural) and his sister-in-law. We might be reminded of how, twenty years before, he had responded to reports about his mental health by throwing extra rumours into the ring, by adding more fuel to the fire.

But what was the truth?

The eldest of the Dickens children, Charley, by now officially an adult, left his father's house to live with his mother. All agreed, Dickens assured the newspapers, all planned. It seems very doubtful. After spending some time in the East, on business, Charley returned to England and married, though without his father's approval – or presence at the ceremony. His bride, Bessie Evans, was the daughter of one of Dickens's former publishers, Bradbury & Evans, with whom Dickens had fallen out, but still, refusing to attend your own child's wedding isn't something that can just be forgiven and forgotten. Father and son later reconciled, but the relationship was rocky for a while.

Catherine's mother supported her. Mark Lemon, co-founder of *Punch* and a friend of Dickens since 1843, advocated for Catherine during the separation – and Dickens barely spoke to him for the next decade. Charles's sister, Letitia, managed to remain on reasonable terms with both parties, but it's noticeable that she received nothing at all in her brother's will when he died. Sections of the press insisted on seeing Catherine as the wronged party. There were clearly those who believed there was more to the story than Dickens was prepared to admit in public. The mountaineer and author Albert Smith – brother of Dickens's speaking agent Arthur, the man who had leaked the letter attacking Catherine to the American press – welcomed Catherine's sister Helen as a guest in his house. Dickens was furious.[394] He had been furious, too, to find that Angela Burdett Coutts was still speaking to Catherine, insinuating that she had been taken in: 'As to Mrs. Dickens's "simplicity" in speaking of me and my doings, O my dear Miss Coutts do I not know that the weak hand that never could help or serve my name in the least, has struck at it – in conjunction with the wickedest people.'[395] His fury doesn't seem to have convinced Burdett Coutts, though. For years her correspondence with Dickens had been extensive and friendly, ranging over many topics besides their shared interest in the halfway house. Now it dwindled to a trickle.

Given that the Hogarth family had already signed their statements, and that the Ternan women had been identified in the press, you have to wonder why there was any need for Dickens to keep on reiterating himself with such angry energy.

Whatever Catherine or the Hogarths accused him of, it must have been credible and it must have been serious – much more serious than a mere affair with Ellen could ever have been. But at the same time the Hogarths wouldn't – surely – have wanted to destroy the reputation of Georgina Hogarth by encouraging the story that she had entered into a sexual relationship with her own sister's husband.

So what was it, exactly, that Dickens was afraid they would tell people?

⋙⋘

The house at Gads Hill – the house which had been the 'dream' of Dickens's childhood – was now his own. He had discovered that it was for sale the week that Maria Beadnell came back into his life, had bought it and had embarked on repairs early in 1857, as he was finishing *Little Dorrit*. It was there that he retreated when the scandal broke; there that he made his home after he sold the remaining lease on the house in London; there that he burned armfuls of his papers in a bonfire, in autumn 1860; and there that he spent many of the most tranquil intervals of the years that remained to him.

But though Dickens spoke about Gads Hill as his country house, sang the praises of its rural scenery, delighted in telling correspondents that the neighbourhood featured in Shakespeare's *Henry IV*, it was far from being as bucolic and restful as he implied. He presents it as surrounded by 'blessed woods and fields' and 'green lanes', with a 'little rustic alehouse' over the way. The house has, he explains, 'the distant Thames in front; the Medway, with Rochester and its old Castle and Cathedral, on one side'.[396] Rochester and the Medway are actually a touch further away than he implies here; two-and-a-half miles and, due to the lie of the land, not visible.

There are acres of almost empty marshland near Gads Hill, but the house itself sits on what was then the main road between London and Dover, close to a railway station, only a few miles from the river port of Gravesend, and the public pleasure-gardens of Rosherville which were for decades a huge draw to visitors from London, host to concerts, theatres and drinking establishments as well as a landscaped park and a zoo.[397] In spite of the railway line, there was still a lot of traffic along the road, both vehicular and pedestrian. Travellers tended to stop at the 'little rustic inn' to rest by the wayside or drink. Among those who did so, according to newspaper reports, were thieves, counterfeiters and travelling performers with dancing bears.[398] In 1859, a man stole hay from Dickens's haystack.[399] Dickens explains that he had got into the habit of keeping 'big dogs' to defend him from 'Tramps and Prowlers', even of taking them with him when he drove out alone.[400] Volunteers, and troops stationed locally, marched in the neighbourhood or met there.[401] The week before Christmas 1860, a war game took place on the marshes, based on 'the existence of a large invading force posted in the vicinity of Rochester, midway between the city and Gravesend, and threatening the garrison and arsenal at Chatham'.[402] So not so peaceful, after all.

Nor was Gads Hill the best refuge from scandal and rumour or the most obvious place for Dickens to escape from his past.

Turn left out of the gates of Gads Hill and the next village you come to is Chalk, in which was the house where Dickens had spent his honeymoon and lived in again for several months when his eldest child was a small baby. One story relates that he often stood in the road, staring at it.[403] Dickens's 1859 Christmas collaboration, *The Haunted House*, tells of a building reputedly filled with phantoms. One is a mischievous servant playing tricks, but others are real, while one character is menaced by visions of his own past selves. The parallels with his own life at the time seem suggestive.

Not quite three miles in the other direction from Gads Hill is Rochester, with which Ellen Ternan had a number of links. For one thing, she'd been born there, in 1839.[404] For another, her uncle William Ternan lived for many years on Rochester High Street with his wife Catherine (*née* Heyman or Hyman) and their children. Catherine's brother also lived on the High Street, with his family.

The Tiernan brothers had come to England from Dublin, abandoning the more obviously Irish spelling of their surname along the way, together with their Catholicism.[405] A sense of familial loyalty and belonging remained, for both drew on family names for their children, but it's noticeable that they avoided the ethnically recognisable ones. There were no Bridgets or Patricks, no Michaels or Terences.

William's eldest daughter was named after Thomas's wife, who may well have been her godmother (they were both 'Frances Eleanor').[406] In March 1850, we can locate 'Mrs and the Misses Ternan' at 'the Rochester Theatre'.[407] In January 1851, they appeared there again, in a semi-amateur performance 'under the patronage of the Cobham troop of West Kent Yeomanry Cavalry'. The mother played 'Julie de Mortimer' in 'that most beautiful play of Sir E. Bulwer-Lytton's, entitled *Richelieu*'. Meanwhile, the girls performed a 'dance between the play and farce' and were 'encored'.[408] There was also a comic piece in which 'H. Haymen delight[ed] the audience' – this is probably Henry Haymen, William Ternan's nephew by marriage. In the 1851 census, both Ellen and her sister Maria were listed as members of their uncle's household on Rochester

High Street, as 'nieces', not visitors. This suggests that, though they also appear on their mother's census return for lodgings in St Clement Dane's, on the Strand in London, Rochester was their main home.

Dickens had bought the house at Gads Hill with the idea of occasionally renting it out. Choosing to move there, and to make it his home and his base, meant that he was placing himself in a neighbourhood where plenty of people were not only aware of who Ellen was, but might well recognise her.

Ellen's uncle and cousins were still living locally – indeed the 1861 census shows some of them living even closer to Gads Hill, on the outskirts of Strood. Such proximity might have proved convenient, of course. And perhaps not just for clandestine meetings between Dickens and Ellen. It's in this household that we find a plausible candidate for their child.

The existence of this child was stated as fact in a 1939 book entitled *Dickens and Daughter*, written by Gladys Storey, who cultivated a friendship with Dickens's youngest surviving daughter Katie when the latter was growing older. The information that Dickens and Ellen had a son who died is supposed to have come from Katie herself. It has been suggested elsewhere that this son was born in 1862 or 1863, possibly in France, as there are references in correspondence to Dickens making frequent brief trips there. Extensive research has thus far failed to locate him.

Before we go any further, I should say that I am very much aware of the case of Felix Aylmer and it's only fair to make you aware too. Aylmer was an actor who, in 1959, published a short book entitled *Dickens Incognito*. In it, he suggested that Charles Dickens had regularly made use of the surname of Tringham both for practicalities, such as paying taxes in the household in which he had ensconced Ellen, and to conceal the identity of their illegitimate child. Aylmer had discovered the existence of a Francis Charles Tringham, born in Lambeth in 1867 to Francis Thomas Tringham and Elizabeth Stanley, and made some wild leaps of logic to arrive at the conclusion that here were Dickens, Ellen and their son. We now know that if Dickens had built up an alter ego as Francis Thomas Tringham, then he'd started doing so in 1836, when Francis was baptised, and maintained it after his own death.

There's no earthly reason to believe that there's a connection, just some people who actually were called Tringham.

It's a cautionary tale, however, and so let's remain cautious in what follows.

In January 1862, newspapers reported the birth of a son to a Mrs Cleveland, a widow living in Strood. The baby had arrived, apparently, on the 7th of the month.

Mrs Cleveland was William Ternan's daughter Frances – one of Ellen's cousins. In August 1857, she had married a sailor called Charles Cleveland. He must presumably have left her a few weeks pregnant when, in February 1858, he set off with his ship – one of the few sailing ships then remaining in the service, HMS *Calypso* – for a tour of duty in the Pacific.[409] The birth of a son, also Charles, was announced as having taken place on 29 October that year.[410]

Charles Cleveland senior remained in the Pacific until February 1861, when he was invalided home.[411] His official record lists his service with the *Calypso* as ending on 12 April 1861 and, since the ship herself didn't return to England until January 1862, this is probably also the date of his return to Britain.[412] By the middle of August 1861, he was dead.[413] The following month his will was proved, leaving everything to his widow.[414] Five months later, early in January 1862, came the announcement of the birth of a second Cleveland son, this one called Howard. Assuming the baby was born on or close to his due date, he would have to have been conceived pretty much immediately on his father's return. Perhaps he was born early. Perhaps Mr Cleveland – though ill enough to be invalided home halfway across the globe, and, indeed, ill enough to die, though only in his early forties – took up his conjugal rights with alacrity on his return. But given the circumstances, it would have been the easiest thing in the world to have placed a little cuckoo in the Cleveland nest.

Is there any supporting evidence? Well, there's an intriguing letter from Dickens to a Mr Vaughan, dated 13 September 1861, in which he 'presents his Compliments to Mr. Vaughan and begs to thank Mr. Vaughan for his interesting and gratifying communication', which is rather suggestive language.[415] As well, on 3 January 1862, Dickens encloses a cheque for £10 in a letter to Georgina Hogarth with a cryptic observation about 'dates' and a wish that 'it may not be too late'.[416] This might – possibly – be read as a careful reference to engaging the services of a doctor for the period when Ellen might be likely to go into labour. And the very next day Dickens appears to have made a sudden, unanticipated dash back to Kent in between reading engagements.

We have two letters by Dickens dated from Cheltenham on Saturday 4 January. In one of them he mentions that 'at 6 o'clock' he is going on from Cheltenham to Plymouth.[417] And sure enough we have a letter dated Sunday 5 January from the Royal Hotel at Plymouth.[418] But we also have a letter to Wilkie Collins which Dickens seems to have written at some point between these. It has, for a date, the confusing 'Sunday January Fourth 1862', perhaps suggesting it was written so late on the night of the 4th it properly belonged to the next morning; this time the address is given as Gads Hill.

Maybe Dickens was using spare notepaper that he'd brought from home. In that case, though, why not write the correct address on it? That seems to have been what he usually did.

Dickens has long been a favourite of forgers but there's never been any suggestion that this letter is a forgery. If Dickens rushed home to Kent unplanned and was there on the 4th and early part of the 5th, then it strengthens considerably the theory that the baby whose birthdate was given as the 7th and whose mother was publicly identified as Ellen's widowed cousin might have been his, the baby we've been trying to find for so long.

The announcement of Howard Cleveland's birth appeared in a dozen newspapers, in rather marked contrast to that of his older brother, which seems to have been inserted only in two. At the end of February 1862, Dickens swapped his house at Gads Hill for one in London for three months.[419] Later that year he started making the visits to France which have intrigued so many of his biographers. Perhaps, we might think, he may have been laying a false trail.

Towards the middle of the 1860s, little Howard Cleveland's grandfather William Ternan moved to Theobald Square – the buildings situated just off the middle of Rochester High Street which are nowadays almshouses and known as La Providence or the French Hospital.[420] The 1871 census finds Howard Cleveland living there too, together with his mother and uncle, at No. 20. Later the family moved to Hampshire, settling first in Portsea and then in Southsea. Mrs Cleveland died as a result of an accident in 1882.[421] Her brother Richard remained living there, however, and was joined by his surviving sisters, Catherine and Mary. The theatrical Ternans ended up close by. Maria, who died in 1904, is buried in Highland Road Cemetery, while in 1911 we can find Frances and Ellen living just round the corner from Catherine Ternan.[422] Howard Cleveland had entered the navy in 1878, and rose from being a clerk to a paymaster.[423]

If he was Charles and Ellen's son, Ellen would have been able to gain news of him and his wife and children, and perhaps to see him, fairly easily and without occasioning any comment. It would be fitting, too, that his job was so similar to that of John Dickens and Charles Barrow.

There is a significant caveat to include at this point, which is that Katie Dickens supposedly stated that her half-brother had died in infancy, while Howard Cleveland outlived her, surviving until 1942. The story comes to us at several removes, however. And the other Cleveland boy, Charles, did die fairly young, in 1886 when he was in his late twenties. Having survived several years at sea in the merchant navy, he drowned after diving into a harbour to retrieve his hat.[424]

Perhaps, then, Dickens and Ellen did have a son who survived, and Dickens managed to set his child up with an unassailably respectable identity and carefully establish homes for him first in Strood and then in Rochester, close enough that the boy could be met with from time to time in secret or as if by chance. And perhaps he did move Ellen away somewhere – maybe France – to recuperate and regain her figure, maybe to be treated for a medical issue which had arisen, maybe, partly, to mislead future biographers.

But he wasn't always so careful.

I've talked before about how oddly, and disingenuously, Dickens writes about Chatham, and about his own connection with the town. In one essay which appeared in 1860, Dickens pretends to have just visited his childhood home – a blend of Rochester and Chatham, which he designates as 'Dullborough' – for the first time in years. 'The first discovery I made, was, that the Station had swallowed up the playing-field,' he declares, and 'Of course the town had shrunk fearfully, since I was a child there.' All nonsense. Earlier I suggested that Dickens may have wished to conceal his links with Chatham because of concerns as to the extent of his father's involvement in the fraud which had taken place in the pay office there in the early 1820s. But with his father's death in 1851 that motive had weakened. It's possible that the strangeness in these later essays may be connected with Ellen, that some of the local recollections, especially the ones focusing on Rochester, might belong not to Dickens but to her. There are several points during his connection with her where his fiction seems to be drawing on her experiences in the area rather than his own. She was pretty and he was rich, but perhaps this, too, was part of the attraction each held for the other.

Great Expectations (1860–61) is set almost on the doorstep of Dickens's home at Gads Hill, opening in a marshland churchyard, where the terrified Pip meets the escaped convict Magwitch – with life-altering consequences for them both. The story follows Pip from his home at the village forge to the shuttered house of the reclusive Miss Havisham, where, as she intends, he breaks his heart over her cold, beautiful ward Estella. Afterwards, when he has been informed of his mysterious 'great expectations', we go to London, where Pip is to be educated as a gentleman. Some of the story is set in the 1820s, when Dickens and his family lived in Chatham; he would have seen the convicts and the prison hulks as a child, and heard the gun go off to report escaped prisoners, just as Pip does. Part way through the novel, Pip's sister, with whom he has lived since he was a baby, is attacked. She can walk, but is left with her 'hearing [...] greatly impaired; her memory also; and her speech [...] unintelligible'. She requires an attendant always by her. It's sometimes argued that this is intended for a portrait of Dickens's mother, who, suffering from dementia, had been unable to comprehend her son Alfred's death in 1860, and whom Dickens had placed under the watchful eyes of Alfred's widow – thus killing two birds with one stone, since she had not been left well provided for.

Another common interpretation is that Ellen is the inspiration for Estella, with Dickens as Pip. A number of commentators have also seen Ellen in pretty Lucie Manette of *A Tale of Two Cities* (1859), in Bella Wilfer, the piquant but money-obsessed joint heroine of *Our Mutual Friend* (1865), and in the 'tigerish' Helena Landless, who appears in *The Mystery of Edwin Drood* (1870).[425]

But actually there are stronger similarities to be found between Pip and Ellen. Pip, like Ellen, is born in the 'marsh country' around the two estuaries. He has a quasi-uncle named Pumblechook, a 'corn and seedsman' who lives on what is clearly Rochester High Street. Ellen had two, both of whom had lived in Rochester, on the High Street – her aunt's brother, William Haymen, and her own uncle, who was, among other things, a dealer in 'patent manure'.[426] Periodically through his late adolescence and early adulthood, Pip returns to Kent to visit his relatives; so did Ellen, while Dickens, having left the area at the age of ten (or perhaps eleven or twelve) didn't, so far as we know, come back to it until he was grown up. *Great Expectations* features a terrifying scene in a lime kiln; William Haymen had interests as a 'lime burner and lime merchant'.[427] The novel is, as well, quite noticeably more thespian than either its predecessor or successor (respectively, *A Tale of Two Cities* and *Our Mutual Friend*), with references to the theatre and to actors and pantomime, a scene backstage, and more than one performance being described at length.

And if the absurd, puffed-up Pumblechook resembles, in certain respects, Mr Haymen, so too does the equally absurd, puffed-up auctioneer Mr Sapsea in *The Mystery of Edwin Drood*. Mr Sapsea lives on the High Street of Cloisterham – which corresponds so closely to the centre of Rochester that you can follow the characters round the streets and identify the exact houses they live in. Mr Haymen lived on the High Street, too, and he had a wife who'd died in 1847; she is buried in the precincts of Rochester Cathedral together with her mother-in-law, making her a possible inspiration for the dead Mrs Sapsea, whose cathedral tomb seems to have been set to play an important role in unravelling the central mystery.[428]

I suggested earlier that even if Dickens was reluctant to enlarge on the faith and background of his Lamert relations, the positive depictions of Jewish characters in *Our Mutual Friend* and, possibly, in *A Tale of Two Cities* might offer another version of his feelings about them, a softening, perhaps a changed under-standing of whatever it was that had happened in the 1820s.

But the goodness of Mr Riah and of the Jewish family who offer refuge and employment to a friendless, vulnerable young woman and the portrayal of Miss Pross, in *A Tale of Two Cities*, might also owe something to Ellen's relations, to her experiences. The Haymens – Ellen's aunt Catherine, Catherine's brother – seem to have belonged to a family which had only recently converted from the Jewish faith.[429] From the records of their baptisms we can identify their parents as Solomon Hyman and Keturah (otherwise Catherine) Patten, who married in London in 1799.[430] There is a 'Sol^n: Hyman' living in Rochester in 1798, renting from an Ebenzer Tull.[431]

Ellen and her family must have registered some of these links. Others in the area might well have done so, too; seen in them, if not an admission of an affair, then an invitation to remember what Dickens – and Ellen Ternan – had been accused of.

In another essay, published in 1860, Dickens returns to his Dullborough 'memories' again to relate a story he had supposedly been told as a child, a variation on Bluebeard in which a murderous husband woos twin sisters, marries one, and cooks her in a pie. Her twin, discovering the truth, marries him, and lets him cook her, too – only she has taken poison beforehand, and he dies.[432] If we want to identify autobiographical significance to this, should we attach it Dickens's wife and her sister, or sisters, or to the Ternan girls? It was Maria Ternan whom Dickens embraced on the stage and Fanny Ternan whom he sent to study music in Florence, complete with letters of introduction in which he expressed the 'warmest interest' in her family.[433] Perhaps rumour had been accurate in linking his name with all three.

But let's just concentrate for a moment on quite how astonishing it is that Dickens was choosing to publish this story in 1860 – positively inviting readers to recall one of the most damaging rumours that had been circulating in 1858, that which had centred on a possible illicit sexual relationship with his sister-in-law Georgina. He did it again the following year in the 1861 Christmas collaboration *Tom Tiddler's Ground*, writing about a maid who, left in charge of a small child while the rest of the household are out at a wedding, takes off herself, explaining that she's had news that her 'brother-in-law has been took unexpected bad' and that she is 'much attached to him'. He also wrote to a theatre producer in 1861, recommending Maria Ternan as an addition to an acting company. In the letter, he states that he takes 'a strong interest in herself and her family'.[434]

This all sits rather oddly alongside the argument that the secret Dickens was concealing, the revelation he feared being made public, was to do with Ellen. Nor – it seems – can he have been all that bothered by the rumours about Georgina.

It's common for critics to point out that Dickens's later novels are preoccupied with exposure and double lives – to a degree unusual even for Victorian fiction, which sometimes seems not to deal in any other currency. Charles Darnay, in *A Tale of Two Cities* (1859) sheds his past as an aristocrat in pre-Revolutionary France like a snakeskin. Both he and John Harmon, in *Our Mutual Friend* (1864–5), marry their wives under false identities; Harmon, in particular, gaslights his wife mightily, supposedly in order to test her character. Each man has, inexplicably, a double – Darnay's is the lawyer Sydney Carton, who goes to the guillotine for him because he loves Mrs Darnay; Harmon's is a man who, fished dead out of the Thames, is misidentified as him. The truth will out, though. Chance encounters on the street, dogged pursuit, witness testimony, expose it and them. It's not unreasonable to think that we're meant to see autobiographical elements to these two novels. Each deceptive man, after all, has one of his author's names (Charles and John), and shares the initial of another (D for Darnay and Dickens, H for Harmon and Huffam – though this last was a name the author rarely used).[435] Darnay is unjustly convicted by a jury incensed against him by evidence of the sins other members of his family have committed; while the novel was being published, Charles's brother Frederick was in the divorce courts, his adultery having been made public.[436] Since another of Charles's brothers, Augustus, had abandoned his wife and run off to America, where he was raising a second family, the optics were not ideal for the Dickens brothers.

Readings usually connect these later novels to Dickens's fear that his affair with Ellen might be revealed. The detective work of Claire Tomalin and others has made a convincing case for Dickens having used a false name for paperwork connected with the houses in which he set Ellen up and for his telling lies about where he was and who he was with, presumably to free himself up to spend stolen afternoons or weekends with her. We'll see him doing this in later chapters. But stories about the affair had already made their way into the public domain. And by living at Gads Hill, in the self-same local community as Ellen's extended network of family connections, by borrowing aspects of Ellen's experience for his fiction, he was tempting fate, enlarging the pool of people who might know both of them by sight or see them together, who could connect them.

As has been pointed out numerous times since the 1860s, *A Tale of Two Cities*, published in just six months in 1859 to pro-mote Dickens's new magazine project, *All The Year Round*, closely resembles a play called *The Dead Heart*. This also has a French Revolutionary setting, an innocent man confined to prison for years, a young aristocrat pursued for the sins of an older relation and a rejected lover who saves a man from the guillotine by tak-ing his place. There are differences: the play takes place entirely in France, which Dickens's novel does not; the innocent prisoner and the self-sacrificing lover are the same man, rather than two separate characters as in Dickens; it is the heroine's son, rather than her husband, who is saved, and she is a far more interesting figure than Dickens's Lucie Manette. But the similarities were so marked that, when the play first appeared, its author, a man called Watts Phillips, was accused of plagiarism and the management of the theatre was forced to make repeated assertions that it was an original piece.[437] This was unfair, because there were witnesses who stated that the play predated Dickens's novel, and it's even plausible that Dickens knew of it.[438] Since several of the elements which look like they might be drawn from Dickens's own experi-ences also feature in *The Dead Heart*, perhaps we ought to exercise a modicum of caution.

What might be more significant, what might edge us closer to a different truth, is Dickens's parallel tendency, at this point in his career, to conceal secrets from the characters themselves, even ones which, according to generic norms, ought to mark the denouement of their stories. Dickens had grown up reading authors like Henry Fielding, whose novels more than once play on the common romance plot of the apparently parentless orphan or poverty-stricken young person establishing their true identity. He had played on it himself, in *Oliver Twist*, *Nicholas Nickleby* and *Bleak House*. In *Little Dorrit* he inverted the standard pattern; Arthur Clennam, who has spent 40 years thinking himself the product of a rigid, relentlessly respectable family, turns out to be illegitimate. And the revelation is squashed in hurriedly, almost at the end of the novel, with Dickens apparently condoning his heroine's decision to conceal the truth from her husband. A very similar concealment takes place towards the end of *Great Expectations*, when Pip discovers the real family origins of Estella, the mysteriously sourced 'orphan' whose true identity is unknown even to the woman who adopted her: he tells her father, but he doesn't tell Estella, or her biological mother, who turns out to still be alive. Even at the time, there were commentators who expressed perplexity at this.[439]

Concealing truths from spouses, from the children of a marriage; if we want to pursue autobiographical readings, then this might relate not just to Howard Cleveland but to Dickens's wife and legitimate children as well.

Just a few weeks before Dickens began work on *Great Expectations* – at around the time he published the odd Bluebeard-style story about the twin sisters – he built a bonfire in the field next to his house and, in his own words, 'burnt [...] the accumulated letters and papers of twenty years'.[440] Ellen was then only 21. Whatever he was so set on concealing, from himself, from his wife and children, from his future biographers, it can't have been only to do with her.

We're approaching the final years of Dickens's life but there's a lot still to fit in. There are other accusations of plagiarism to consider. There are losses. There's Dickens's failing health, a train accident he's involved in which led to what looks like post-traumatic stress disorder (PTSD). There's the thousands of miles of train travel he nevertheless put himself through, the hundreds of public readings. There are more lies – concealments, evasions, flat-out fibs.

And if, as it seems, he may have had a secret that wasn't to do with Ellen or with Georgina, what was it?

Notes

339. Letter to W.H. Wills, 9 February 1855.

340. Letter to Mrs Winter, 10 February 1855.

341. Letter to Mrs Winter, 15 February 1855.

342. Letter to Maria Winter, 15 February 1855.

343. Letter to Maria Winter, 22 February 1855.

344. Letter to Maria Winter, 24 February 1855.

345. Letter to Mrs Winter, 5 February 1856.

346. Letter to Mrs Winter, 16 August 1858.

347. Letter to Mrs Winter, 13 November 1858.

348. Letter to Miss Ella Maria Winter, 15 December 1858.

349. John Forster, *The Life of Charles Dickens*, volume 1, page 73.

350. As above.

351. Letter to W.C. Macready, 31 January 1842.

352. A number of newspaper reports maintained the polite fiction that he had been suffering from depression and had died at his brother's house in Kent; Tomalin identifies his place of death as a London mental asylum and the cause as being general paralysis (or paresis) of the insane, associated with late-stage syphilis.

353. *The diaries of William Charles Macready, 1833–1851*, ed. William Toynbee (New York, G.P. Putnam's, 1912), 3 December 1845, page 313.

354. *York Herald*, 3 May 1845, page 4.

355. *The diaries of William Charles Macready*, 21 October 1846, page 347.

356. As above, 4 November 1846, page 348.

357. By the end of November, Ellen Ternan was appearing as 'The Child Orestes' in a Dublin revival of *Iphigenia*, along with her mother, who played Orestes' mother Clytemnestra, and an actress called Helen Faucit in the main role (*Dublin Weekly Register*, 5 December 1846, page 7). Faucit had frequently worked with Macready, and there were rumours that she had been his mistress.

358. Letter to Angela Burdett Coutts, 5 September 1857.

359. *Carlisle Journal*, 19 August 1843, page 3. Reproduced from the *Standard*.

360. Letter from Daniel Maclise to Charles Dickens, 16 July 1841.

361. *Globe*, 14 April 1857, page 4.

362. Not so Brian Ruck, who suggests that Dickens may have been involved with Mrs Ternan in the late 1830s, and that Ellen was their daughter. While of course not impossible, this doesn't seem to me particularly plausible; the admission of a fleeting youthful affair with a married actress, safely in the past, would not have been that damaging to the Dickens brand, certainly less damaging than the belief, widely held by contemporaries, that Ellen had become his mistress – which also, of course, injured Ellen's reputation and marriage prospects. However, see Ruck's article, 'Illegitimacy in Dickens, and the riddle of Ellen Ternan', *The Dickensian*, Winter 2022, page 319 ff. The novelist Cora Harrison has made the same suggestion.

363. Letter to Wilkie Collins, 2 August 1857.

364. *Household Words*, 2 December 1854, opening article (1 ff.). The – barely implicit – accusation is that Franklin's crew had been murdered by some of the 'Esquimaux' with whom they came into contact.

365. Letter to Angela Burdett Coutts, 5 September 1857.

366. Letter to Wilkie Collins, 29 August 1857.

367. A fact which was advertised in *The Era*, a London paper, on 6 September (page 11).

368. Quoted in John Forster, *The Life of Charles Dickens*, volume 3, pages 162–3, and according to him dated early September 1857. A reference to hop-picking in the second, seemingly related letter, seems to confirm the season, though not necessarily the date.

369. Letter to W.H. Wills, 20 September 1857.

370. *Sheffield Independent*, 26 September 1857, page 6.

371. Letter to Mrs Cornelius, 11 October 1857. She was Catherine's maid and had been Dora's godmother.

372. In letter to Mrs Richard Watson of 7 December 1857 he describes the walk as having taken place 'Six or eight weeks ago' and himself as being 'very much put-out'.

373. Letter to Emile de la Rue, 23 October 1857.

374. Letter to Mrs Richard Watson, 7 December 1857.

375. Letter to Angela Burdett Coutts, 2 February 1858.

376. John Forster, *The Life of Charles Dickens*, volume 3, page 173.

377. Letter to Wilkie Collins, 21 March 1858.

378. Letter to Angela Burdett Coutts, 19 May 1858.

379. See *Dumfries and Galloway Standard*, 9 June 1858, page 4;
     Cumberland and Westmorland Advertiser, and Penrith Literary Chronicle,
     22 June 1858, page 2. The provincial press – particularly those
     newspapers based in Ireland and Scotland – tend to be more
     critical.
380. 'The accusation [...] has been one of gross profligacy,' noted the
     London *Sun* (7 June 1858, page 1), before printing Dickens's
     statement denying any wrongdoing. The wording of this report
     was widely reproduced in other newspapers.
381. Letter to W.H. Wills, 21 October 1855.
382. Clearly this was a carefully arranged and synchronised press
     release. 'We willingly comply with the request of Mr. Charles
     Dickens,' states the *Morning Herald* (7 June 1858, page 6). 'We are
     requested to anticipate the publication of the following article,'
     writes the *Evening Mail* (7 June 1858, page 7). The statement
     appeared on 7 June in multiple newspapers, including *The Times*,
     the *London Evening Standard*, the *Morning Post*, the *Globe*, the *Sun*,
     the *Morning Chronicle* and the *Morning Advertiser*. It was not printed
     in Dickens's own magazine until several days later. See 'Personal',
     Household Words, 12 June 1858, page 1.
383. *Fife Herald*, 24 June 1858, page 2.
384. *The Era*, 13 June 1858, page 9.
385. *Downpatrick Recorder*, 19 June 1858, page 4.
386. 'Mrs. Dickens [...] has addressed a letter to the Haymarket com-
     pany, which was publicly read in the green room of the theatre, in
     which she expressed her regret that the name of a member of the
     company should have been mentioned disparagingly in connection
     with her husband; and that she was satisfied there was no ground
     whatever for it' (*Cork Examiner*, 16 June 1858, page 1, reprinted
     from *Belfast News Letter*).
387. Letter to Richard Spofford, 15 July 1858.
388. See, for example, *Belfast News-Letter*, 11 June 1858, page 2;
     Saunders's News-Letter, 12 June 1858, page 2; *Greenock Telegraph and
     Clyde Shipping Gazette*, 10 July 1858, page 4.
389. The so-called 'violated letter' which appeared in the *New York
     Tribune* in August 1858.
390. Letter to Arthur Smith, 25 May 1858; 'You have not only my full
     permission to show this, but I beg you to show, to any one who

wishes to do me right, or to any one who may have been misled into doing me wrong.' No manuscript; transcript only.

391. *The Irishman*, 11 September 1858, page 7.

392. *Leeds Times*, 11 September 1858, page 8; reprinted elsewhere.

393. 'There are a few sentences exculpating a young lady (Miss Ternan or Miss Sedgwick?) whose name had been mentioned, very grossly, with that of Dickens', *Chester Chronicle*, 9 October 1858, page 6.

394. Letter to Albert Smith 14 February 1860.

395. Letter to Angela Burdett Coutts, 23 August 1858.

396. Letter to W.W.F. de Cerjat, 7 July 1858.

397. Dickens refers to Rosherville on several occasions in his letters.

398. *Maidstone Journal and Kentish Advertiser*, 1 March 1869, page 6; *Kentish Gazette* 24 August 1869, page 6.

399. *South Eastern Gazette*, 4 January 1859, page 5.

400. Letter to W.W.F. de Cerjat, 7 July 1858.

401. *Maidstone Journal and Kentish Advertiser*, 5 February 1861, page 8.

402. *South Eastern Gazette*, 25 December 1860, page 6.

403. Related in William R. Hughes, *A Week's Tramp in Dickens-Land* (Chapman & Hall, 1891). The anecdote was reprinted from Frederic Kitton's *A Supplement to Charles Dickens by Pen and Pencil* (1890), apparently originating with one 'E. Laman Blanchard' who lived for 'seventeen years' at Rosherville, just the other side of Gravesend, and who 'on repeated occasions [...] had the good fortune to encounter the great novelist [...] Generally, by a curious coincidence, we passed each other [...] on the outskirts of the village of Chalk, where a picturesque lane branched off toward Shorne and Cobham. Here the brisk walk of Charles Dickens always slackened, and he never failed to glance meditatively for a few moments at the windows of a corner house on the southern side of the road [...] It was in that house he had lived immediately after his marriage' (page 393).

404. 'Mar.3, at Rochester, Mrs. Ternan, of the Theatre Royal, Drury Lane, of a daughter', *Dover Telegraph and Cinq Ports General Advertiser*, 9 March 1839, page 8.

405. Thomas and William's parents were Michael Tiernan and Susanna Lawless, who married in St Paul's (or Arran Quay) in Dublin on 25 September 1785. Susanna appears to have been the daughter of Michael and Bridget Lawless, baptised in Dublin in 1761.

From references in newspapers and trade directories, it appears that Michael Tiernan also had children from a previous marriage, including two sons named Patrick and Terence.

406. Thomas had a Frances, a Maria, an Ellen and a Thomas; William had a Frances, a William, a Mary, a Catherine and a Thomas.

407. *Lloyd's Weekly Newspaper*, 10 March 1850, page 10.

408. *South Eastern Gazette*, 14 January 1851, page 5.

409. According to *Lloyd's List*, HMS *Calypso* set out from Portsmouth on 15 February (17 February 1858, page 1).

410. *Morning Herald*, 3 November 1858, page 8.

411. See a report of the voyage which appeared in the *London Evening Standard*, 13 January 1862, page 6.

412. See *London Evening Standard*, 8 January 1862, page 3 and National Archives, ADM 196/21/169, service record for Charles Augustus Cleveland.

413. *Maidstone Journal and Kentish Advertiser*, 20 August 1861, page 4.

414. National Probate Calendar, 1861, page 142, accessed via Ancestry.

415. Letter to Mr Vaughan, 13 September 1861.

416. Letter to Georgina Hogarth, 3 January 1862.

417. Letter to Letitia Austin, 4 January 1862.

418. Letter to W.H. Wills, 5 January 1862.

419. Letter to Edward Yates, 25 February 1862.

420. His name and address is given in poll registers taken during the 1860s.

421. *Hampshire Advertiser*, 29 March 1882, page 2. Mrs Cleveland apparently used a 'bath chair', a wheelchair, which was struck by a laundry van (*Portsmouth Evening News*, 24 January 1882, page 2).

422. Eleanor Trollope, Ellen Lawless Wharton Robinson, and Gladys Eleanor Wharton Robinson are listed, in the 1911 census, as living in 27 Victoria Grove, Southsea. Catherine Ternan lived at 27 Albert Grove, Southsea.

423. Howard Cleveland's service record, National Archives ADM 196/80/87.

424. See the UK register of Births, Marriages and Deaths at Sea, 1844–1890 (National Archives, BT 157, Piece 08 (1886–1887)).

425. See for example Hugh Kingsmill, *The Sentimental Journey: A life of Charles Dickens* (1934); Ada Nisbet, *Charles Dickens and Ellen Ternan* (1952); Christopher Hibbert, *The Making of Charles Dickens* (1967).

426. *South Eastern Gazette*, 26 February 1839, page 1.

427. London *Sun*, 26 September 1849, page 12.

428. See https://www.gravestonephotos.com/public/gravedetails.php?-grave=436197; Catherine Haymen and Mary Elizabeth Haymen are laid to rest in the burial ground of St Nicholas' Church which abuts the cathedral. The difference between the cathedral burial ground and that of the church is not very clear to a layperson.

429. The name appears variously as Hyman, Hayman, Heyman and Hayman.

430. Marriage record of Keturah Patten and Solomon Hyman, at St George's Hanover Square, 1799. Baptism records of Catherine Hyman, daughter of Solomon and Keturah, St Nicholas in Rochester, 5 December 1803 and William Patten Hyman, son of Solomon and Catherine, baptised St Margaret in Rochester, 11 January 1805. Accessed through Find My Past (https://cityark.medway.gov.uk/wwwopacx/wwwopac.ashx?command=getcontent&server=files&value=P306-01-08.pdf); Medway Archives P306/1/8, P305/1/6.

431. Land Tax Redemptions, 1798, Vol. 2, 338, accessed via Ancestry.

432. 'Nurses' Stories', *All the Year Round*, 8 September 1860.

433. Letter to Mrs Trollope, 20 September 1858.

434. Letter to Benjamin Webster, 9 September 1861.

435. The name is occasionally written as 'Huffham'.

436. See *London Express*, 27 July 1859, page 4.

437. See, for example, *Morning Chronicle*, 11 November 1859, page 3, where the play is described as a 'very remarkable melodrama, purporting to be original' and Watts Phillips as 'a clever adaptor, even if he is not the genuine originator'.

438. See Watts Phillips to the Editor of the *New York Times*, 3 December 1860, printed in the newspaper on 25 December; Carl R. Dolmetsch, 'Dickens and the Dead Heart', *Dickensian*, Vol. 55 (January 1959), page 179.

439. 'Estella's story is meagre in the extreme. It was hardly worth while to find a mother for her [...] if mother and daughter were not even to be made acquainted with each other.' *Leeds Times*, 21 September 1861, page 6.

440. Letter to W.H. Wills, 4 September 1860.

GREATEST HITS (1863–9)

9

Charles Dickens relieving the sufferers at the fatal railway accident, near Staplehurst, originally published in *Penny Magazine Illustrated*, 24 June 1865. (British Library Board. All Rights Reserved. Bridgeman Images)

Great Expectations was generally very well received, but there were damning observations mixed with the praise.

'*Great Expectations* has given every one a shock of agreeable surprise,' announced an Edinburgh-based newspaper. *Hard Times*, it says, 'almost fell dead from the press', while *Little Dorrit* was 'so tedious as to be almost unreadable'. As for *A Tale of Two Cities*, though 'the attempt was very ambitious', it 'almost entirely failed'.[441] Meanwhile, another literary critic observed that:

> Some dozen years ago it would have been superfluous to analyse a story, published periodically and just completed, by Mr. Charles Dickens. All the world would have read it as it came out; it would have been an affront to his readers if a reviewer had ventured to assume their ignorance. But the great days of Pickwick and Nickleby and Oliver Twist have long ago melted into the past: their freshness had been dimmed, not only by time and later novelties, but by their author's own endless repetitions of them.[442]

This review remarks that the novel contains 'the full measure of Mr Dickens' usual faults' and ends by concluding that it's 'a fair average sample of his present manner, much below his greatest works, but a good deal better than his worst'. Even the positive reviews trumpeted what they saw as a return to Dickens's old style. Clearly it was impossible for him to keep everyone happy.

Between 1836 and 1844, in the white heat of his early career, Dickens finished six full-length novels, several works of non-fiction, and the first two of five sole-authored Christmas stories. After something of a hiatus, during which he produced only one full-length novel, he began publishing more regularly again from the end of the 1840s, though with gaps. *David Copperfield* (1849–50) was followed in 1852–3 by *Bleak House*, with *Hard Times* appearing in 1854 and *Little Dorrit* running from late 1855 to 1857. But then came – in whatever order – Ellen, the separation from Catherine and a return to uncertainty about how well he could control the narrative of his own life. Fiction took a back seat again. *A Tale of Two Cities* (1859) had borne uncomfortable similarities to the play *The Dead Heart*. After *Great Expectations* the publication gaps open up again, wider than before; there are nearly three years between the end of the serialisation of Great Expectations and the beginning of the serialisation of Our Mutual Friend, and then another four-and-a-half before The Mystery of Edwin Drood.

There were personal reasons to explain Dickens's relative lack of productivity. In addition to his 'old load' of anxiety came a new one – or that is was what he started explaining to correspondents: Georgina was ill. A heart complaint, Dickens writes, potentially impacting her lungs and spine.[443] Some commentators think this was invented to explain his visits to Ellen. It is admittedly somewhat unusual to find someone with a serious heart problem surviving to a healthy old age – Georgina lived to be 90, not dying until 1917.

In 1863 came two deaths, though, those of Dickens's mother and his son Walter. The news about Walter reached Dickens in February 1864, the week he turned 52, the week Walter ought to have turned 23. Walter had been in India, serving in the army since he was sixteen – he had got into debt, had become unwell and hoped to return home. Instead he was buried in a graveyard in Calcutta.

Though Walter had been ill, his death was sudden, due to 'aneurism of the aorta' – a fact omitted from the short reports and death notices which appeared in the press and, indeed, deliberately kept from many members of the family. As Dickens wrote to Angela Burdett Coutts: 'The immediate cause of his death, his sisters and Charley and I, keep to ourselves; both because his Aunt has the same disorder, and because we observe strong traces of it in one of his brothers.'[444]

This seems rather an odd decision. Dickens is clearly suggesting in this letter that there was a familial heart weakness on the Hogarth side – known about in two members and already strongly suspected in another. Though he doesn't say so, most people would jump to the conclusion that it was this same family heart problem which had caused the sudden death of Mary Hogarth a quarter of a century before. Heredity in disease was not perfectly understood, but people knew it existed. Even if Dickens took the decision not to alarm his five younger children, one might expect to read that he was careful to safeguard their health as far as possible, perhaps steering them away from physically demanding occupations or long journeys overseas. Not a bit of it.

Out of those five, only one, Henry, even remained in England. Perhaps he was the one whose health was thought to be weak – though, again, he lived to a ripe old age, dying in 1933 after a successful and demanding legal career. Francis was, at the time Dickens wrote this letter, already on his way to India to serve in the Bengal Mounted Police, which he proceeded to do, afterwards becoming a Canadian Mountie. In 1865, Alfred was sent out to Australia, where he was joined a few years later by the baby of the family, Edward. Sydney, not yet seventeen, was already in the navy; a hard life. His father left him there.

Occasionally Dickens jokes about forgetting how many children he had. 'I have [...] considered whether there are any more children, and I don't think there are. If I should remember two or three others presently, I will mention them in a postscript.'[445] He obviously had favourites – his surviving daughters, Mamie and Katie, the high-achieving Henry and, to a lesser extent, his eldest child, Charley. The others he seems to have found both disappointing and burdensome. He couldn't get rid of them fast enough or send them too far away. He would pay their debts, but it's hard to shake the notion that half the reason they got into debt was because they wanted, desperately, to have some of their father's attention.

Dickens devoted a substantial amount of his time to large-scale commercial touring in the late 1860s and perhaps one reason was that his relationships even with his favourite children seem by this point to have been conducted almost exclusively through the medium of money. It also might have offered a welcome break from having to produce new material.

જેન્છ

In 1844, *A Christmas Carol* had come easily to Dickens's pen. Its seasonal successors, by and large, had not. He complained repeatedly about how much of a struggle the Christmas stories were to begin and to finish, but they were incredibly popular, and so on he soldiered. By the 1850s, he was increasingly reliant on the aid of collaborators to meet the public appetite for them. In some years, he co-wrote seasonal offerings with just his buddy Wilkie Collins, largely yarns of peril on the sea, shipwreck, piracy and treasure: *The Wreck of the Golden Mary* and *The Perils of Certain English Prisoners* in 1856 and 1857, *A Message from the Sea* in 1860. In others, he would come up with a framework for a loosely linked series of short stories, usually write the introduction and conclusion, and a section or two himself, and work the other contributions together as a special 'Christmas number' of first *Household Words* and later *All the Year Round*.

These Christmas numbers weren't a James Patterson-style scenario; the other authors were named, their individual contributions identified in the newspapers. Dickens must have used only a light editorial touch, too, because it's usually easy to recognise which sections were written by, say, Wilkie Collins or Elizabeth Gaskell, simply from the style. Other collaborators included Wilkie's brother Charles Collins, who had become Dickens's son-in-law by marrying Katie Dickens; the journalists George Sala and Elizabeth Lynn Linton; the popular poetess Adelaide Proctor; and Hesba Stretton, a religious children's writer.

Stories like *The Seven Poor Travellers* (1854), *The Holly-Tree Inn* (1855), *A House to Let* (1858), *The Haunted House* (1859) and *Tom Tiddler's Ground* (1861) are of this portmanteau style, with multiple chapters by multiple authors. So, too, are *Mrs Lirriper's Lodgings* and its sequel *Mrs Lirriper's Legacy* (1863 and 1864), *Dr. Marigold's Prescriptions* (1865) and *Mugby Junction* (1866). The collaborations may have kept Dickens's stress levels down, but artistically speaking they weren't very good for him. Most of them make for peculiar reading nowadays. You can find lots of cheap editions which either exclude the parts of the texts written by other authors, or fail to identify them as such, either revealing how little Dickens was really contributing to some of the Christmas numbers or showing how uneven the overall effect could be, how abrupt the tonal shifts. Even more apparent when the 'Inimitable' is rubbing shoulders so closely with other writers are his own oddities and weaknesses, his tics and habits.

Dickens seems to have half-suspected that the story collections were having a negative effect on his writing. *Our Mutual Friend*, begun in 1864, is filled with collections and collectors.

The novel opens with a corpse being dragged out of the Thames by 'Gaffer' Hexam, and his improbably good-looking daughter Lizzie. It is supposedly that of John Harmon, who is meant to be coming home to claim his dead father's fortune, founded on heaps of rubbish gathered from the city and then sifted for resale – 'Coal-dust, vegetable-dust, bone-dust, crockery dust, rough dust'. Lizzie's father collects drowned bodies from the river and empties their pockets; his home is wallpapered with printed descriptions of the dead, circulated in often-futile attempts at identification. The illiterate Mr Boffin collects books and pays someone to read them to him. The *nouveau riche* Veneerings collect disparate acquaintances for their dinner parties, the grotesque Mr Venus body parts – babies kept in jars, under spirits; skeleton hands. The story itself is an odd collection of scenes and ideas. One early review described it as having 'many threads' – a 'distinctive peculiarity' for a Dickens novel, it was suggested.[446]

The whole book, indeed, is reminiscent of a greatest hits compilation, or of one of Mr Venus' articulated skeletons, assembled from bits and pieces of Dickens's own back catalogue – and, it's been suggested, the work of other people as well.[447] A strange corner of London (a house amid the dust-heaps) offers an arresting setting for the story. A will affects the course of many lives. A child dies. A murderer is discovered. Social mobility causes psychological harm as well as widening opportunities. There is Dickens's usual inclusion of a character with a disability (here the sharp 'doll's dress-maker' Fanny Cleaver or, as she calls herself, Jenny Wren), his fascination with the River Thames, his long-standing fondness for fairy-tale imagery.

The novelist Henry James dismissed *Our Mutual Friend* as 'lacking in inspiration'. '*Bleak House* was forced,' he wrote, '*Little Dorrit* was labored; the present work is dug out as with a spade and pick-axe.' The characters were 'mechanical', James complained, while the portrayal of Jenny Wren particularly riled him: 'This young lady is the type of a certain class of characters of which Mr. Dickens has made a speciality, and with which he has been accustomed to draw alternate smiles and tears, according as he pressed one spring or another. But this is very cheap merriment and very cheap pathos.'[448]

There's a good chance, we know, that for Dickens the pathos may have been real and personal, not mechanical in the least. But for critics, it was old.

Though other reviews were mostly positive, readers were less convinced. Following an initial burst of enthusiasm for the first instalments, sales tailed off. One newspaper reviewer of the novel claimed that Dickens had developed 'unpleasant tricks', transmogrifying into a 'pretentious, puling sentimentalist'.[449] He hadn't, though; he was doing what he'd been doing for years. One difference might be that *Our Mutual Friend* was published more slowly than Dickens's two previous novels had been, in monthly pamphlets as opposed to weekly, in his own magazine. Perhaps the story, with its many 'threads', was just too complicated for readers to sustain interest in over a long publication period. Perhaps, without the forward momentum of weekly episodes, there was time and space to see the flaws.

Dickens's contributions to the 1865 Christmas number, *Dr. Marigold*, also came in for criticism – a measured, thoughtful criticism, difficult to shrug off, and touching on some of the same problems identified by James. 'It is unfortunate,' pronounced the *Pall Mall Gazette*, '[...] that cynical readers, after laughing at his humour, are very apt to yawn at his pathos.' To create emotion by means of 'a dying child' and afterwards 'a deaf and dumb girl' may be effective, the piece suggests, but it's a 'very old chord', a hackneyed, creaking 'device'. The reviewer also objects that it is impossible to believe in the central character, a peddler, a 'rough fellow knocked about by a rough way of life' who 'somehow or other is always talking sentiment' and 'preaches Mr. Dickens's simple doctrine'.[450]

The number sold extremely well, however – possibly because, that year, the public had very nearly lost Dickens forever.

We've seen that Dickens had a tendency to exaggerate for effect. Crossing the Atlantic by steamer in 1842 he had endured danger, unparalleled storms, while his fellow travellers had a much less exciting voyage. He consistently selected high-risk destinations, on the verge of civil war, though if he was deliberately searching for danger he didn't find it. All the evidence suggests, though, that on 9 June 1865 he really did have a dramatically close brush with death.

Dickens was on his way from the coastal town of Folkestone towards London on the 'fast tidal train' which met the cross-Channel steamers. Along a straight stretch of track, the Kent countryside would have passed him in a sunny blur of apple orchards and hop fields, the trees a deep summer green, the fine whitish dust of the chalky substrate drifting in the air. Then – flashing past – a danger signal – and almost before the driver could react to it or the passengers register that anything was amiss, the rails simply vanished. Failures in communication had led a team of rail engineers to mis-time their maintenance work, with disastrous results. The engine was flung forward across the gap in the tracks, while 'seven or eight' coaches, hurled into a ditch below, became a mass of splintered, buckled wood and metal. Rescuers, when they arrived, found only the engine and the first and last carriages still more or less upright. The coaches in the ditch were 'twisted, flattened, and turned upon their sides' and there was initial uncertainty as to whether the victims had been killed straight away or had been smothered to death in the mud.[451] According to reports, there were over 100 people travelling on the train. Looking at the photographic panorama of the scene that exists, it's amazing that only ten of them died, and no more than a handful more reported injuries.

In most respects Dickens was lucky. He had been sitting in the first carriage – the one which had remained attached to the engine – and was able to climb out. He was even able to rescue his bundle of manuscript papers – part of *Our Mutual Friend*. His name appeared in newspaper reports, mostly flatteringly, as a brave rescuer of the injured.[452]

But in one respect he wasn't so lucky. He had given more than one person the impression that he was going to take a short holiday at home during this very period. 'I settle down in these parts early in June,' he wrote, in a letter dated from his house at Gads Hill. In another he explained that he had engagements for 4 and 5 June, and would then be 'going home'.[453] The crash revealed to both of his correspondents – and they were, respectively, a war reporter for *The Times*, and Sir Edwin Landseer, the painter – that he had been 50 miles away from Gads Hill, on the coast.

It's possible, though not certain, that, as the biographer Claire Tomalin and others have argued, Dickens had actually been across the Channel, in Condette, near Boulogne, where he was in the habit of holidaying. It's possible, too, that Ellen Ternan was travelling on the train, though, as with the idea that her mother was also present and involved in the accident, that Ellen may have been living in France for some time, that she was injured in the crash, we remain in the realm of plausible suggestion rather than fact.

We have letters in which Dickens, writing of the accident, talks about 'two ladies', 'an old one and a young one' who were his 'fellow passengers'.[454] Ellen and her mother, perhaps. However, in the 'Postscript, in lieu of preface' which usually appears in modern editions of *Our Mutual Friend*, Dickens refers to some of the novel's characters having been 'on the South Eastern railway with me, in a terribly destructive accident', and to having climbed back in 'to extricate' them. It's possible, then, that he's making a similar joke in the letters. Lists of those injured appeared in the newspapers, including a reference to one 'lady, name unascertained' who 'was taken to Guy's Hospital'.[455] It's been suggested this is Ellen and at first everything looks quite promising because in later reports the woman's name is given as Ann Pattinson or Patterson or Ann Epps, and her age as 26 – the same age as Ellen was.[456] But there was an Ann Epps who, in 1864, had been admitted to a workhouse in London, 'destitute', 'deserted by husband' and 'pregnant'. Her age is listed as 26, and she was said to be connected to the town of Maidstone, about nine miles from Staplehurst.[457] It's not unlikely that she might have been on the train, or that she might have gone back and forth between two surnames.

Certainty keeps eluding us. The references to Ellen as 'the Patient' in some of Dickens's subsequent letters might have a different explanation. Dickens was very fond of assigning nicknames.

Another suggestion is that Dickens, dreading publicity, carefully avoided giving evidence at the inquest that followed the crash, that it was part of the years-long programme of sustained deception designed to maintain Ellen's reputation and his own. He apparently told people at the crash site who he was, though; his name appears in some of the earliest reports. And he wrote, under his own name, to the station-master at Charing Cross, explaining that a 'lady who was in the carriage with me in the terrible accident on Friday, lost, [...] a gold watch-chain with a smaller gold watch chain attached, a bundle of charms, a gold watch-key, and a gold seal engraved "Ellen'" – a loss which seems to indicate that Ellen may well have been present.[458] It could be the case, though, that he was wearing the tangle of chains and seals himself. He did, in his will, leave a watch – a 'gold repeater' – and 'the chains and seals, and all appendages I have worn with it' to his friend Forster. Either way, the letter would have been prime blackmail material; its existence surely weakens further the hypothesis that his priority was to conceal his affair with Ellen at all costs. Perhaps, as I suggested previously, Ellen wasn't the most important, or the most secret, of his secrets.

Dickens may not have been well enough to attend the inquest. He had been – by his own account and that of others – quite calm in the immediate aftermath of the crash, and had retrieved his manuscript from the carriage and given aid to other passengers. But in the days that followed it he found himself unable to write legibly. He experienced fits of shaking and noticeable changes in his voice, perhaps temporary vocal cord paralysis related to whiplash, perhaps the result of sustaining a head injury.[459]

The shaking stopped, his voice returned, but psychological effects persisted for years. He had to give up carriage driving altogether and, as we'll see in a minute, started displaying symptoms of PTSD. He did at least get one good story out of the experience, though.

The Signalman, a creepy tale set on a lonely railway, is one of Dickens's very best short fictions. Written in 1866, the year after the accident, it is for that reason difficult to read outside the context of Staplehurst. It was praised at the time as a 'weird wild romance', 'one of the most thrilling ghost stories Mr. Dickens has ever conceived'.[460] The story is less high-octane than this description suggests, and in fact consists chiefly of two men having a conversation in a railway cutting on an isolated stretch of the track. Only one death takes place during the story – that of the signalman himself, though we are told of a 'memorable accident' which occurred a year earlier, and also of the death of a young woman – and it's never made clear whether anything supernatural has taken place, nor what that might have been. Yet for all its simplicity it possesses a certain coiled horror, and there are folds of ambiguity which, as a reader, you have no wish to open out fully. We might wonder what the narrator is even doing on this steep-sided cutting, whether he is perhaps a ghost, unknowingly doing the haunting himself.

The Signalman might, with some effort on Dickens's part, have been worked up into a superb standalone Christmas ghost story. Instead it was bundled in with *Mugby Junction*, the title given to the 1866 Christmas edition of *All the Year Round*. Despite praise for *The Signalman*, the collection as a whole was judged to be 'full of what we may call character-hyperbole'. Though the 'opening description' of the railway station was praised, Dickens's comic section, 'The Boy at Mugby', was dismissed as 'caricature', even though it was apparently inspired by his own real-life experience.[461] However good *The Signalman* was, then, its effect was partly spoiled for some readers. The brief respite from the critics' lashings offered by Dickens's brush with death was over.

Critical tastes were shifting; so, too, were ideas about intellectual property. Dickens ought to have been pleased. For decades he'd been the victim of literary piracies, unauthorised retellings, plays which galloped ahead of his serial stories. He'd been involved in law cases; his campaigning for stronger international copyright protections had helped to turn the American press against him in the 1840s.

Yet he was not always that respectful of other people's published work himself. There were the possible, very broad borrowings from Charlotte Brontë and Elizabeth Gaskell. At one point he clearly helped himself to a ghost story Gaskell had told in his hearing, which offered just the climax he wanted. The story is *To Be Read at Dusk*, published in a magazine called *The Keepsake* at the end of 1851. It's set at an inn in the Alps, the narrator listening as a group of tour guides discuss the supernatural tales they have collected on their journeys across Europe. One story tells of a man who sees a fetch, a ghostly double which presages not his own death but that of his identical twin. Another – the one taken from Gaskell – focuses on a woman who is terrified by a face which appears to her in a dream, and is still more terrified to meet the real-life possessor of it afterwards. She vanishes from her room, seemingly abducted by him, and the pair are never traced. When Gaskell objected to the theft, Dickens sent her a coaxing letter, addressing her as 'Scheherazade' (the character in *The Thousand and One Nights* who saves herself from her murderous husband by telling stories) and assuring her that no one read *The Keepsake* anyway. He did not, however, apologise.[462]

As time went on, the pilfering started to become more obvious. Increasingly discernible, too, is an undertone of disapproval of it in the press, and a greater willingness to bring the matter to the attention of the public. I mentioned before that the parallels between *A Tale of Two Cities* and Watts Phillips' play *The Dead Heart* were noticed and commented on. Dickens and Phillips had made their peace but the play continued to be staged throughout the 1860s and still tended to be reviewed with particularly lengthy plot summaries, some of which even mentioned Dickens by name.

In *Our Mutual Friend*, Dickens borrowed from two authors, both of them known to him.[463] One was R.H. Horne, the editor of *A New Spirit of the Age*, who in 1850 had published a short story in *Household Words* called *Dust; or Ugliness Redeemed*.[464] Set among dust-heaps, this featured a man rescued from drowning by someone named 'Gaffer Doubleyear', an important legal document and a character with a wooden leg, all of which may look rather familiar. The other author was James Sheridan Knowles, who had died in 1862. Knowles's play *The Hunchback*, which has several points of correspondence with Dickens's novel, was performed regularly through the 1860s, going through a wave of popularity during 1865 and afterwards – that is, after the similarities between it and *Our Mutual Friend* had become apparent. These were obvious, but probably too broad to be subject to any legal proceedings. Still, we do find a few juxtapositions of Dickens's name with that of Knowles in newspapers of the period, which might indicate that there had been murmurings, and on one occasion their names are coupled together for seemingly no reason at all.[465]

In the spring of 1866, the old accusation about Robert Seymour and *The Pickwick Papers* resurfaced yet again. This time, though, Dickens was sufficiently stung by it to pen a lengthy letter to the *Athenæum* – and sufficiently anxious about it that he wrote again a week later to correct some minor detail.[466] In December 1866, a reprint of a book called *Sketches by Seymour* was published, containing almost 200 of the dead artist's illustrations, and prefaced by a new 'Life' which, while it took leave to doubt the accuracy of the Seymour family's version of events, still gave it plenty of space and oxygen. It had been 30 years since Seymour's death in his garden in Islington, and suicides and summerhouses had largely vanished from Dickens's fiction, but here was the ghost returned again.

In autumn 1867, a new piece by Watts Phillips, called *Nobody's Child*, was staged, to great popular acclaim. Set in Cornwall, it featured a character falling into a ravine ('a marvel of scenic art', according to the advertisements), a woman rescuing her lover with some unexpected abseiling skills, a missing will and an uncle. This was just a touch unfortunate for Dickens and Wilkie Collins. Their play – and novel – *No Thoroughfare* was first staged and published just a couple of months later, during the Christmas season of 1867. And though it was set mostly in London and Switzerland, not Cornwall, it also features an orphan (a foundling, truly 'Nobody's Child'), a will, an evil uncle, a ravine and a brave abseiling fiancée. There may have been less in this set of resemblances than at first appears. It's not unusual nowadays for two films or plays with similar premises to pop up simultaneously but independently, and there was, in the 1860s, something of a craze in theatres for setting scenes in ravines and crevasses. The borrowing – if there had been any – might easily have been done by Collins rather than Dickens. But it still had the potential to create bad publicity.

Even if the coincidences were innocent, what did it say about Dickens as a writer if, of the handful of fictional works that he had managed to produce in the previous decade, two of them were so similar to stories that a hack like Watts Phillips had come up with? How successful an author was he, when for years he had to call on collaborators for the Christmas stories? If character and voice were beginning to fail him too, if they no longer convinced, if his sentiment no longer moved his more discerning readers, what was left?

In the middle of the 1850s, Dickens had decided to start monetising some of his public appearances. He even sent his tour manager, Arthur Smith, to make preliminary enquiries about appearing in America, though between the demands of *Great Expectations*, begun in 1860, his busy personal life and the outbreak of the American

Civil War in 1861, the plans came to nothing. Other, shorter reading tours did take place at home, however; it was during one of these that it appears he might suddenly have dashed back to Kent to attend the birth of Ellen's baby. But with the premature death of Smith, the touring was allowed to slide almost completely. Though 1862 and 1863 were years in which Dickens produced very little of his own writing, he performed only a handful of readings in London and Paris – the Parisian ones for charity.

It wasn't until 1866, after the completion of *Our Mutual Friend* – in the wake of increasingly unsubtle insinuations that he had plagiarised other authors and after the Seymour story had been revived – that Dickens returned to large-scale commercial touring. And he returned to it with a vengeance. Of the three years between April 1866 and April 1869, he was touring for more than half the time, twenty months.

On the face of things, it's an extraordinary decision. Not only did it restrict further Dickens's already limited time with Ellen, it involved him in hours of train travel when, after Staplehurst, travelling by almost any means was torture to him.

'My escape,' he wrote, three years after the accident,

> is not to be obliterated from my nervous system. To this hour I have sudden vague rushes of terror, even when riding in a Hansom Cab, which are perfectly unreasonable, but quite insurmountable. I used to make nothing of driving a pair of horses habitually through the most crowded parts of London. I cannot now drive, with comfort to myself, on the country roads here; and I doubt if I could ride at all in the saddle.[467]

There was at this point a growing public belief that train accidents were becoming both more frequent and worse, a belief that can hardly have helped to ease Dickens's fears.[468] On one occasion in January 1867, he abandoned a train part-way through his journey, so convinced was he that it was about to come off the track. He wrote an impassioned letter to *The Times* warning 'the public [...] against the morning express train on the Midland railway between Leicester and Bedford'. The engine had, he said, been driven with 'reckless fury' and the carriages shaken by 'violent rocking', resulting in 'general alarm' among the passengers. Despite his extensive experience of train travel, he claimed to 'have never been so shaken and flung about as in this train, and [...] in such obvious danger'.[469] A debate followed in the letters pages about just how bad the driving, and the shaking, had been – one fellow commuter claiming that he had noticed nothing amiss and had peacefully read one of Dickens's novels the whole way.[470] The railway company blamed the weather (*plus ça change*), while one provincial paper printed some unsympathetic doggerel in which 'Charles Dickens', 'an Editor | And author of renown' is shown 'roar[ing]' 'from the window' of the train and, at Bedford, deciding to 'Skeedadle'. It ends with a jeer: 'When next he tries the fast express | May we be there to see.'[471]

So overwhelming were the panic attacks, when they came, that Dickens was sometimes unable to do anything to help himself and had to be dosed by others. 'My Reading-Secretary [...] knows so well when one of these odd momentary seizures comes upon me in a Railway Carriage,' Dickens wrote, 'that he instantly produces a dram of brandy, which rallies the blood to the heart and generally prevails.'[472]

Dickens had deliberately put himself in risky situations in the 1840s, travelling first to Italy and then to Switzerland when there were widespread concerns that civil war was threatening in both countries. Early in 1867 he travelled to Ireland despite fears that a Fenian (Irish nationalist) uprising was about to take place there. George Dolby, who had taken over as his tour manager, writes of having to let the police search their packing cases on the quayside, and of finding Dublin 'alive with constabulary and soldiery'.[473] Later that year Dickens went back to the United States. It was another bold choice. Even a quarter of a century after his first trip there, its unfortunate repercussions had not died away entirely. The American Civil War had only ended in 1865, while US-based Fenian groups enjoyed widespread support, sufficient to enable them to mount occasional small-scale incursions into Canadian territory. And it isn't as if Dickens was ignorant of this. Before he set out for the States he drew up a memorandum for W.H. Wills, co-editor of *All the Year Round*, instructing him 'that no reference, however slight, is to be made to America in any article whatever, unless by myself. Remember that the same remark applies to the subject of the Fenians.' The States was also home to a woman who claimed to be Dickens's sister-in-law, the widow of his brother Augustus. She had in fact been a mistress, Augustus having abandoned his real wife in England. Dickens must have known, though, that the American press might take the opportunity to get at him and, perhaps, to bring up the rumours which had circulated about his depraved behaviour towards his own wife.

Some of Dickens's oldest and closest friends were opposed to his returning to America – including Forster, who didn't really approve of the touring – but he brushed their concerns and cautions aside. Writing to Wills, Dickens asserted that he was stronger than he had been on his previous visit, when – as he recalled – he'd just 'had a painful surgical operation performed', more patient, less irritable. 'I don't want money,' he says. But almost the whole of the letter is about money, about his conviction that 'the receipts would be very much larger than your Estimate', that the tour would give 'an immense impulse' to the new edition of his back catalogue, the 'immense consideration' of getting a large lump sum 'in a heap so soon', 'of making a very great addition to one's capital in half a year', another 'immense consideration'. He repeats himself intentionally, he says, because 'there *should* be something large, to set against the objections'. It is the sheer scale of possible profit which moves him so much, a solid mass to weigh in the balance against the burdens of his family – 'my wife's income to pay – a very expensive position to hold – and my boys with a curse of limpness on them'.[474]

This was only the half of it. There was also Ellen to be paid for, and possibly her son, too. Dickens's mother was no longer with them, but as well as the real Mrs Augustus Dickens, Dickens had been left to support another sister-in-law, Alfred's widow, and her children. His only surviving brother, Frederick, lived on a pittance of a pension, and spent most of that on alimony and alcohol. The two were by now effectively estranged. Charles didn't even attend Fred's funeral in October 1868. He kept an appointment with the dentist instead, sending his eldest son, Charley, to represent him.

There was Mamie, his unmarried daughter, still dependent on him. Katie was married but her husband was in delicate health. The

Dickens sons were expensive. Henry, the sixth of the seven brothers, was about to start at Cambridge. The youngest, Edward, was still at home. All the others seem to have expected their father to pay for them. Pleas from them, letters from their dissatisfied creditors, came in from all over the world. Walter had 'always been in debt', his father said, during the whole of his time in India.[475] Even Charley, married, the father of several children, had got into financial trouble over a paper-making business. Dickens had warned him about it, but had ended up bailing him out.

Whatever his other faults, Dickens was neither penny-pinching nor ungenerous. He liked wine, cigars, plants for his garden. He spent lavishly on Gads Hill and rented town houses in London for the winter and spring. When young Henry Dickens went up to Cambridge University in 1868, he did so with an annual allowance of £250 – the equivalent of something like £20,000 today – and that didn't even have to cover alcohol.[476] Dickens also paid for Mamie to hunt – which suggests that he was not, at any rate, too concerned about *her* heart.

The costs mounted up.

This is another reason why we find Charles Dickens hurtling around Britain and Ireland on train after train, shivering with terror and knocking back the brandy. It's why, the month after he turned 56, he could be found making his way to Albany, NY, along a flooded valley, though the rails were under inches of dirty water, and flotsam had to be pushed out of the way.[477] He spent months on tour in the United States in 1867 and 1868, pinballing between Boston and New York, Philadelphia and Baltimore, travelling to Connecticut, Rhode Island, Massachusetts and Maine, and to various towns and cities in New York State – Albany, Buffalo, Rochester, Syracuse – with a brief foray as far south as Washington DC.

Dolby was a competent and hard-working tour manager, but Dickens needed him to be. The ticket touts descended. The winter of 1867–8 was bitter, even by North American standards, with heavy snow, and Dickens spent the majority of his visit nursing what he called 'the true American catarrh', which sounds as if it started as a bad cold and developed into quite a serious sinus infection.[478] He had never enjoyed robust good health. Now he began to experience periods of lameness, which he put down variously to frostbite, to 'erysipelas' (a skin infection similar to cellulitis), to 'pressure on a bone', perhaps to gout.[479] Sometimes he was unable even to get an ordinary boot on, forced instead to wear what he dismissed as a 'leathern bucket made for the purpose'.[480] Yet still he read and still he travelled; he drove sleighs and set up walking races in the snow, trod the city streets and crossed the vertiginous bridge that had been built at Niagara Falls, shook hands, felt up ballet dancers, and kept going despite hotel fires and floods.[481]

By the time he was nearing the end of the American tour, his diet apparently consisted of the following:

> At seven in the morning, in bed, a tumbler of new cream and two tablespoonsful of rum. At twelve, a sherry cobbler [i.e. with sugar, lemon and ice added] and a biscuit. At three (dinner time), a pint of champagne. At five minutes to eight, an egg beaten up with a glass of sherry. Between the parts [of the performance], the strongest beef tea that can be made, drunk hot. At a quarter-past ten, soup, and anything to drink that I can fancy. I don't eat more than half a pound of solid food in the whole four-and-twenty hours, if so much.[482]

This is a pretty hefty alcohol intake given how little food accompanied it – indicative, if not of incipient addiction, then of an unhealthy reliance. After his return from America, we find references, in his letters, to being prescribed 'quinine in hot brandy and water', and to taking both laudanum and hydrocyanic acid – the dilute preparation of cyanide which he had used in his youth.[483]

He was pushing himself to the limits.

The challenges Dickens faced during this period should make us think highly of his nerve, his physical courage, whatever we may conclude about other aspects of his behaviour. But they also raise the question of why on earth he kept doing it to himself. Why travel at all, when it made him suffer so much, both physically and mentally?

Perhaps he was motivated not just by the money he received for the tours but also by the praise, the adulation. The crowds didn't want new stories, another novel. They weren't bored with his writing. They didn't want him to innovate. No psychological delicacy for them. Cohesive plotting could go hang. They wanted Twist and Nickleby and Dr Marigold and *A Christmas Carol*. They were quite happy with the unnatural sentiment, and the broad-brush characterisation, the comic caricatures, the monstrous murderers.

On the few occasions on which he ventured alone into fiction during the later 1860s, the results were far from encouraging.

George Silverman's Explanation, a story which first appeared in an American magazine, *Atlantic Monthly*, early in 1868, seems to hit up all the familiar Dickensian tropes. Modern critics have praised its pared-back style, describing it as a miniature Dickens novel. It consists of a handful of disconnected scenes – a slum cellar, a hill-top farm, a community of prosperous Non-conformists, Cambridge, a country parsonage – through which moves a featureless narrator.

Born into poverty, orphaned through illness, cheated (so we gather) by his self-appointed guardian, George Silverman is always trying to do the right thing, and is continually being treated as if he has done the wrong one. Meeting so frequently with those who mistreat or wish to exploit him, he is unable to interact with those who do not; when the rich and beautiful girl whom he tutors falls in love with him, he redirects her affections towards another man, even though he loves her too. Dickens's American publishers paid £1,000 for first dibs on the story and one wonders whether they thought the investment worthwhile. As a psychological portrait it's fascinating, though underdeveloped. As a story, there's nothing to it – nothing is wound up, but then, hardly anything happens.

There are, in fact, better endings, and noticeably more plot, in the stories which make up *A Holiday Romance*, the central conceit of which is that they have been written by four small children. Also published in 1868, this is the product of another deal struck by Dickens with his American publishers, designed for a children's magazine. The first of the stories, in which the children appear as pairs of star-crossed lovers, seems a touch unconvincing, not least because it is told by a character who has reached an age at which the childhood fondness for marriage plans tends to have worn off. The last, set in a world where the grown-ups are the children, and can be sent away to school when they are troublesome, cannot be called successful. The other two, though, are delightful – little jewels. One is a fairy tale which you feel certain you must have read before, so perfectly does it reproduce the genre's rhythms and cadences. The other is a tale of adventure on the high seas, in which a Latin teacher meets with just punishment and the hero storms the bathing machines at Margate to locate his bride. But this, an occasional clever story or section of a story, just a few pages in length, is the best of what Dickens had to offer during this period of his career.

The American trip had exhausted him. But he was, after expenses had been accounted for, nearly £20,000 better off. That's the equivalent of more than £1.8 million today.

In the autumn of 1868, less than half a year after his return from North America, Dickens embarked on his 'farewell tour' of Britain and Ireland, another punishing programme of travel and readings – a planned 100 nights of them – extending across the country and which, it was widely reported, was to net him £10,000 (getting on for a £1 million in today's money). The cheapest tickets cost a shilling (about £5 today) and the audience was told to expect the show to last nearly two hours. He gave two, sometimes three, readings in most places on consecutive nights and had, in addition, regular commitments to appear in London. The schedule sounds draining. In January 1869, for example, he visited Belfast, Dublin, Bristol, Bath, Cheltenham, Torquay and Newport, in Wales. He also seems to have been involved in a second train accident.

George Dolby describes it:

> Whilst running along at a rapid speed, about forty miles from Belfast, we received a severe jolt which threw us all forward in the carriage. Looking out we observed an enormous piece of iron flying along a side line, tearing up the ground and carrying [...] telegraph posts along with it. The brakes were suddenly applied, a lumbering sound was heard on the roof of the carriage, and the plate-glass windows were bespattered with stones, gravel, and mud.
>
> Possibly having the recollection of the dreadful Staplehurst accident in his mind, Mr. Dickens threw himself to the bottom of the carriage, and we all followed his example.[484]

This incident from Dolby's memoir tends to be relegated to foot-notes in Dickens biography, if it appears at all, perhaps because it's less interesting than Staplehurst – less serious and, lacking Ellen, less sexy. There is no mention of it in any of Dickens's surviving letters, nor do the newspapers place him at the scene of any rail accident other than Staplehurst. There was, though, an accident on the railways in Ireland during Dickens's trip there in 1869, on a day he was travelling between Dublin and Belfast – a derailment in which a teenage boiler stoker was scalded by steam, later dying in hospital. It was recorded that 'the engine bounded, as it were, from the rails, plunged a short distance, and capsized beside the adjoining ditch'.[485] The cause was a wheel which came loose and tore up part of the track, not dissimilar to what Dolby describes happening.[486]

What Dickens could have been doing on this section of track, which was near Omagh, not on any usual route between Dublin and Belfast, and why he failed to mention this accident, is unclear, though Dolby did plan journeys to minimise the likelihood of his star turn getting a panic attack and may have done so on this occasion. Perhaps Dickens was unwilling to invite speculation as to why on earth, if he hated travelling by train so much, he was spending almost all his time doing it. More significantly, this episode shows that Dickens was able to keep some stories out of the press.

He began to suffer from nausea, insomnia and physical exhaustion, possibly as a direct result of this second train accident. As winter turned to spring, his doctors began to express serious concern: his foot was troubling him again, and soon other symptoms were added. In April 1869, three-quarters of the way through the 'farewell' tour, he started to experience blood loss from the rectum. Just piles, he thought, but, with his history of fistula, it was enough to drive him to write to his doctor. A few days later he became 'extremely giddy, extremely uncertain of my footing (especially on the left side) and extremely indisposed to raise my hands to my head'.[487] His remaining speaking engagements were cancelled on urgent medical advice, the doctors signing a certificate to the effect that he had been 'seriously unwell', blaming, in equal measure it seems, 'his public Readings and long and frequent railway journeys'.

What Forster calls 'an attack of paralysis' was feared, or even 'apoplexy' – 'threatenings of brain mischief' in any event, and Dickens was scared enough by his collapse that in May 1869 he rewrote his will.[488] But a final twelve 'farewell' readings were rescheduled for January, February and March 1870. Dickens remained an active editor for *All the Year Round*, and devoted patient hours to counselling an acquaintance whose marriage had collapsed.[489] He also began – for the first time in years – to think about a new novel, *The Mystery of Edwin Drood*.

❧

Wilkie Collins thought the story a failure. A 'last laboured effort', he called it, the 'melancholy work of a worn-out brain'.[490] But if *The Mystery of Edwin Drood* is so 'laboured', if its author's creativity was so 'worn-out', why then has it continued to intrigue people? Few unfinished novels can have attracted a larger readership. This 'melancholy work' has inspired writers and directors and continues to baffle critics, who have been entirely unable to agree on what was meant to happen next.

The story centres on a young man – Edwin – who vanishes from the cathedral city of Cloisterham one Christmas Eve, shortly before a planned departure for Egypt. In spite of his youth he has for years considered himself betrothed to a schoolgirl named Rosa, even younger than himself. This is in obedience to the wishes of their respective fathers, both now dead. On the day of his disappearance, the pair decide that they are, after all, not suited. Edwin has previously come to blows with another young man – the wild-tempered Neville, recently arrived in Cloisterham from Ceylon (modern-day Sri Lanka). Meanwhile Edwin's uncle John Jasper, choirmaster at the cathedral, is infatuated with the beautiful Rosa. After Edwin disappears, local suspicion falls on Neville (foreign, violent), while reader suspicion tends to fall on the uncle, since we know him to be an opium addict whose visions, under the influence of the drug, are dark and disturbing. Another beautiful schoolgirl, a drug dealer, an athletic clergyman, a manly sailor and a dusty lawyer are all drawn into the mystery, together with a comedy stonemason, a frustrated playwright and a street urchin.

Scores of solutions to the mystery have been suggested over the last century and a half, by Dickens's friends and family, by the book's illustrator, by literary critics, novelists, lawyers, librettists, mediums and scriptwriters. Edwin is dead! He's alive! Jasper strangled him with the 'black silk scarf' which appears prominently in the text and which Dickens apparently insisted the illustrator include, or tried to, or thinks that he did. The real culprits are Thugee assassins from India! The truth lies in Egypt! There are family feuds and hidden family ties and cross-dressing. There are skeletons both real and metaphorical, the latter rattling themselves right out of their closets in one suggested solution, where it's hypothesised that the uncle harbours a secret incestuous gay passion for his nephew. In another, Neville and Edwin are brothers.

Some writers really let themselves go – one of the first to attempt to finish the story has a murdered monk, discovered in passing, Edwin (half-dead) concealed within the walls of the cathedral, a mysterious Eastern concoction which functions as a primitive truth drug, another murder – this time successful, a little light mesmerism and some telepathy. The cathedral window shatters in a storm. And just in case anyone was getting bored, the writer also includes a number of betrayed and abandoned women, a winsome injured child, four unrequited love affairs, a religious awakening and a dog.[491]

Later attempts have tended more towards the post-modern. Audiences of the 1980s musical *Drood* were asked to pick a criminal from a list of suspects. In a 1989 Italian novel, translated into English as *The D. Case*, a whole host of fictional detectives try their hand at explicating the mystery and uncover a second one, a dark tale of plagiarism and poisoning in which Dickens is murdered by Wilkie Collins.[492] Wilkie also takes a central role in Dan Simmons' *Drood* (2009).

The solutions aren't all equal, but none can be dismissed out of hand. There is no way of knowing, for certain, what represents a significant clue or is just a red herring in the original text. According to Forster, Dickens had lost the knack of knowing exactly how much to write for a monthly number, discovering to his 'horror' that the first two instalments 'were, together, twelve printed pages too short!!!' and being obliged to 'transpose a chapter from number two to number one, and remodel number two altogether!'[493] This seems odd, because though Dickens hadn't written his own serial for nearly five years, he had been constantly dealing with other people's in his capacity as magazine editor and one would have thought that he would have just known what length to write. However, it does indicate that some of the material, at least, might be make-weight, of no real importance to the plot. It's also possible, of course, that Dickens might not himself have decided on the final outcome.

The suggestions that Wilkie Collins had reason to resent Dickens shouldn't be lightly dismissed either.[494] We've seen that Dickens borrowed ideas. *The Mystery of Edwin Drood*, with its emphasis on opium and a missing piece of jewellery, and its characters connected with the East, looks, superficially at least, a lot like Wilkie Collins's 1868 novel *The Moonstone*, which also features a missing jewel, travellers from the Orient and opiates, and had been serialised in Dickens's own magazine. The cathedral setting is likely to have encouraged readers at the time to make comparisons with Anthony Trollope's Chronicles of Barsetshire as well, a series of novels revolving around the fictional Barchester Cathedral which had appeared over the course of the previous decade and a half. Elizabeth Gaskell had died suddenly in 1865, but if she'd still been alive she might have traced similarities between this new novel and an essay of her own which had appeared in *Household Words* in 1851, involving six mysterious disappearances.[495]

And there's yet another text to throw into the mix – a story written by a rising diplomat called Robert Lytton, the son of Dickens's old friend Edward Bulwer-Lytton. This appeared in *All the Year Round* at the end of 1869.[496] It was published as *The Disappearance of John Ackland* – a title suggested by Dickens himself that was slightly similar, we might think, to the title he was to choose for the new novel he had already started work on. There are other, stronger similarities, too. Both stories centre on a man's disappearance. Both have a character christened John and called Jack, in love with a woman he cannot hope to possess. Both feature a young girl at school, a character named Ned (this is one of Edwin Drood's nicknames) and, prominently, a watch. In both stories the missing man's personal effects seem to have been planted in order to deflect suspicion, and a river is searched for a body that isn't found. There are significant differences, too. Lytton's is a short story and set in the United States. The motive for the crime is monetary, the criminal psychologically uninteresting.

In the letter accepting Lytton's story for publication, Dickens offers the younger man some editor's notes, of possible interest in relation to his own method in writing *The Mystery of Edwin Drood*. They are chiefly concerned with sustaining tension: 'Here and there, I think you let the story out too much – prematurely – ,' he writes. It will be better if readers are left 'in doubt [...] until the end'.[497] The letter is affable and we have young Lytton's reply, in which he expressed a flattered willingness to accept whatever changes Dickens suggested.

But a month later Dickens wrote to Lytton again, breaking the news that 'John Ackland has been done before!' A 'correspondent' has 'read the story [...] in Chambers's journal'. Dickens does not blame Lytton at all, he assures him ('This is very unfortunate, but of course can not be helped'), he will however proceed with 'winding the story up [...] as expeditiously as possible'. What seems to be indicated is that the similarity either rests on, or is related to, the role of the jeweller who recognises a watch as the property of the dead man, since it is this which Dickens apologises for cutting ('as published', he admits, the edited version is 'a little hard on [the jeweller] Mr. Doiley').[498]

It's perhaps due to Dickens's editorial interference that *The Disappearance of John Ackland* finishes so abruptly and unsatisfyingly. The evidence of the watch appears with a leaden and unconvincing thud, the baddy hurries off stage and the detectives discover, in quick order, not only John Ackland's body but also an eyewitness to the murder, a man who's lived his life in slavery and who is so terrified and brutalised by the pre-Civil War American South that it doesn't occur to him that he could tell anybody what he has seen his 'master' do.

We can gather from Dickens's next letter that Lytton was upset, perhaps disbelieving. Dickens explains that, though he has 'made no further discovery in detail', his (still nameless) correspondent 'told me what the end of the story was, concerning the watch', convincing him that it must have been 'previously told and printed'.

However, he has decided 'to set no one here on to enquire about it or look it up' and 'If it should never turn up, *tant mieux* [so much the better].'[499] It never has turned up, to date, leading to the suspicion that something else may have been going on here. If it isn't just coincidence, and if Lytton didn't find the nub of the story elsewhere, then the alternatives are that Dickens was either misinformed, mistaken or lying.

Dickens may well, by this point in his career, and with emergent changes to cultural attitudes, have been hyper-sensitised to any breath of plagiarism – enough for him to want to sweep the whole matter under the carpet without looking for proof. But there's a scene in Dickens's novel, just before Edwin vanishes, with a jeweller and a watch. Mightn't he, perhaps, have found in Lytton's story the very solution that he wanted for his own book, the neatest denouement, and finding it, desiring it, stolen it from him, just as he had done with Elizabeth Gaskell?

We'll never know the truth, of course. Dickens didn't live to finish the novel.

Notes

441. *Edinburgh Evening Courant*, 29 July 1861, page 3.
442. *Leeds Times*, 21 September 1861, page 6, reprinted from the London *Guardian*.
443. Letter to Wilkie Collins, 20 July 1862.
444. Letter to Angela Burdett Coutts, 12 February 1864. Which of the Dickens children they were supposedly concerned about is unclear.
445. Letter to W.W.F. de Cerjat, 3 May 1860.
446. London *Sun*, 1 February 1865, page 2.
447. *The Hunchback* (1832) by James Sheridan Knowles. The similarities appear to have been first identified by Earle Davis in his 1963 book, *The Flint and the Flame: The Artistry of Charles Dickens*. Davis suggests Knowles's *The Daughter* (1837) may also have helped to inspire Dickens.

448. 'Our Mutual Friend' [Review], *The Nation*, 21 December 1865, pages 786–7.

449. *Morning Post*, 6 June 1865, page 3.

450. *Pall Mall Gazette*, 9 December 1865, page 5.

451. See London *Sun*, 10 June 1865, page 3, widely reprinted elsewhere.

452. *Globe*, 10 June 1865, page 3; *Carlisle Journal*, 9 June 1865, page 11; same report in *Dublin Evening Mail*, 10 June 1865, page 2.

453. Letter to W.H. Russell, 26 May 1865; letter to Sir Edwin Landseer, 27 May 1865.

454. See letter to Thomas Mitton 13 June 1865; another letter of the same date to his sister Letitia mentions the ladies as well.

455. London *Sun*, 10 June 1865, page 3 and widely reproduced.

456. *Dublin Evening Mail*, 12 June 1865, page 3.

457. St Marylebone, Workhouse and Infirmary Registers, 1864 and 1862–4, accessed via Ancestry.

458. To the Head Station Master, Charing Cross, 12 June 1865.

459. '[I] have even got my voice back; — I most unaccountably brought somebody else's out of that terrible scene.' (Letter to Mrs Lehmann, 29 June 1865.)

460. *The Globe*, 14 December 1866, page 1.

461. *The Globe*, as above.

462. Letter to Elizabeth Gaskell, 25 November 1851.

463. The correspondences have been widely remarked on by critics.

464. *Household Words*, 13 July 1850.

465. *Saunders's News Letter*, 19 December 1865, page 2.

466. Letter to the Editor of the *Athenæum*, 28 March 1866; letter to same, 3 April 1866 (printed, respectively, 31 March and 7 April 1866).

467. Letter to W.W.F. de Cerjat, 26 August 1868.

468. Ralph Harrington, 'Railway Safety and Railway Slaughter: Railway Accidents, Government and Public in Victorian Britain' crunches the figures, which suggest that there had not been a significant change. *Journal of Victorian Culture*, Vol. 8, No. 2 (2003), pages 187–207.

469. Letter to *The Times* newspaper, 26 January 1867, page 7.

470. *Bedfordshire Times and Independent*, 2 February 1867, page 4.

471. *Loughborough Monitor*, 21 February 1867, page 6, and elsewhere.

472. Letter to W.W.F. de Cerjat, 26 August 1868.

473. George Dolby, *Charles Dickens as I Knew Him: The Story of the Reading Tours in Great Britain and America (1866–1870)* (Fisher Unwin, London, 1887), page 74.

474. Letter to W.H. Wills, 6 June 1867.

475. Letter to Angela Burdett Coutts, 12 February 1864.

476. 'It appears to me that an allowance of 250 a year will be handsome for all your wants, if I send you your wine' (letter to Henry Dickens, 15 October 1868).

477. See letters to Mrs J.T. Fields and Georgina Hogarth (both 19 March 1868), and W.C. Macready (21 March 1868).

478. For example, letter to W.C. Macready, 21 March 1868.

479. Letters to W.C. Macready, 1 March 1865; Madam Sainton-Dolby, 7 August 1867; Letitia Austin, 18 August 1867; Georgina Hogarth, 25 February 1869.

480. Letter to Letitia Austin, 18 August 1867.

481. '[…] having some amiable small talk with a neat little Spanish woman who is the premiere danseuse, I asked her, in joke, to let me measure her skirt with my dress glove. Holding the glove by the tip of the forefinger, I found the skirt to be just three gloves long—and yet its length was much in excess of the skirts of 200 other ladies whom the carpenters were at that moment getting into their places for a transformation scene'. Letter to W.C. Macready, 21 March 1868.

482. This letter, to Mamie Dickens, survives transcribed rather than in manuscript, dated 7 April 1868. If anything, it's likely that she would have edited down rather than up.

483. See letter to W.W.F. de Cerjat, 4 January 1869. The transcribed text of a letter from Dickens to his dentist, Samuel Cartwright, refers to his intention to 'abstain from hydrocyanic acid' (2 December 1868, no manuscript).

484. George Dolby, *Charles Dickens as I Knew Him: The Story of the Reading Tours in Great Britain and America (1866–1870)* (Fisher Unwin, London 1887), page 367.

485. *Belfast Morning News*, 13 January 1869, page 3.

486. Reports suggest that 'the flange of the wheel' came loose and tore up 'about two dozen of the metal chairs' – these being fixings for the railway sleepers. *Londonderry Standard*, 16 January 1869, page 3.

487. Letters to F.C. Beard, 13 April 1869 and 19 April 1869.

488. John Forster, *The Life of Charles Dickens*, volume 3, page 422.

489. The journalist and writer Mrs Elliot.

490. Collins' annotations in his own copy of Forster's biography of Dickens.

491. Henry Morford, *John Jasper's Secret; a sequel to Charles Dickens' unfinished novel "the Mystery of Edwin Drood"* (1871).

492. Charles Dickens, Carlo Fruttero, Franco Lucentini, *La verità sul caso D.* (Giulio Einaudi, 1989), *The D. Case: The Truth about the Mystery of Edwin Drood*, trans. Gregory Dowling.

493. Quoted in John Forster, *The Life of Charles Dickens*, volume 3, page 429, apparently 22 December 1869.

494. This has been suggested on several occasions, including by Jerome Meckier in his 1987 book *Hidden Rivalries in Victorian Fiction: Dickens, Realism, and Revaluation*. He also suggests a rivalry with Trollope, and with Gaskell.

495. 'Disappearances', *Household Words*, 7 June 1851. According to family tradition, Gaskell's brother John Stevenson had vanished either *en route* to India or in Calcutta.

496. At this point in his life, Edward Robert Lytton Bulwer-Lytton chiefly went by 'Robert Lytton'. Later he became the Earl of Lytton and an extremely unpopular viceroy of India. His father's success as a novelist had been, to a large extent, eclipsed by Dickens but the two older men remained on friendly terms.

497. Letter to Robert Lytton, 2 September 1869.

498. Letter to Robert Lytton, 1 October 1869.

499. Letter to Robert Lytton, 21 October 1869.

FINAL DAYS (1870)

10

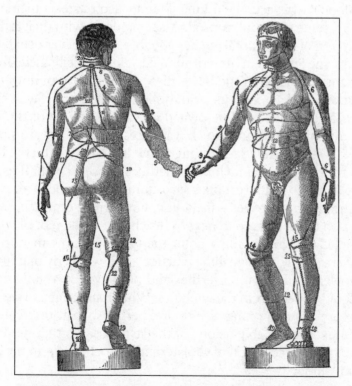

**An illustration from *J.L. Pulvermacher's patent portable
hydro-electric voltaic chains: Sold by J. Steinert, sole agent,
no. 568 Broadway, New York* (1853). (Wellcome Collection
under Creative Commons, Public Domain (CC 0))**

By June 1870, Dickens knew he was dying. Or he was optimistic he was getting better. He was still at the top of his game, or he was fading, written-out. He was living happily, if irregularly, with Ellen, or the relationship had faltered. Three days before his death, he went to Rochester – or was it two? He was alone, or he had someone with him. He stayed at home. He went to a party. One day he was too weak to walk far, on another capable of tackling a steep hill on foot on a hot summer's day.

Dickens's daughters Katie and Mamie were with him over the weekend of 4–5 June, before leaving together for London, but their accounts of events are, at certain points, either incorrect or fanciful. Mamie, for example, misremembers the date that she and her sister left Gads Hill. '[T]his Monday morning, the seventh', she writes. The Monday was actually 6 June. Mamie also relates a memory of Katie's – some beautiful, consoling last moments with their father, a description of him embracing her goodbye, as he never usually did, and how she left him in his writing shed, 'among the branches of the trees, among the birds and butterflies, and the scent of flowers'.[500]

Dickens had a luxurious writing shed – a miniature Swiss chalet which sat on some land he owned on the other side of the main road from his house and which was accessed via a private subway tunnel. We've already seen, though, that his 'Kentish freehold' was by no means the rural idyll he sometimes chose to paint it as. Not only was the nearby turnpike road quite a busy one, a route for pedestrians and vehicles – including, now, a new omnibus service – but also there was a pub next to his chalet, at the foot of what is still called Telegraph Hill, a point then used in army manoeuvres and, increasingly, for signalling practice – as it was early that June.[501]

Flowers and trees, butterflies and birds were certainly not all that could be seen from the windows. What Katie's memory resembles more than anything else, more, perhaps, than the reality, is what must presumably be one of the last passages that her father ever wrote, a description of Cloisterham – Rochester – in the summer sunshine:

A brilliant morning shines on the old city. Its antiquities and ruins are surpassingly beautiful, with a lusty ivy gleaming in the sun, and the rich trees waving in the balmy air. Changes

of glorious light from moving boughs, songs of birds, scents
from gardens, woods, and fields – or, rather, from the one great
garden of the whole cultivated island in its yielding time – pen-
etrate into the Cathedral, subdue its earthy odour, and preach
the Resurrection and the Life. The cold stone tombs of centuries
ago grow warm; and flecks of brightness dart into the sternest
marble corners of the building, fluttering there like wings.

The similarities suggest that Katie found her father's mellifluous
prose offered a happier and more powerful narrative than real life,
that his words overlaid what had actually happened.

There are not as many competing versions of Dickens's last
days as there are solutions to his last novel, but there are several.

One story claims that Dickens was taken ill, not at his house
at Gads Hill, but at Ellen's house in Peckham, and that he was
smuggled the 25 miles back home in a carriage.[502] It has been suggested that Dickens had a substantial sum of money on him – £22
cashed at the pub across the road in exchange for a cheque, £15 or
£16 of which mysteriously vanished, and that the only explanation
is that he must have given it to Ellen. The basis for all of this is
not terribly secure. Partly it rests on a tradition passed on in the
family of J. Chetwode Postans, who became vicar of the church
near Ellen's house in Peckham and who was apparently once told
by the church caretaker that Dickens had died 'in compromising
circumstances', on a different occasion the caretaker insisting that
he had helped to move Dickens's body himself.[503] There is no record
of who this man was, when he made his claims or what the 'compromising circumstances' might have been. Nor, in fact, does the
family tradition ever report that Dickens was moved any significant
distance. Perhaps the caretaker had at one point lived or worked
somewhere around Rochester, or had heard rumours from a servant
of Ellen's. And Ellen's local relations – her uncle, her cousins, little
Howard Cleveland – might be a more plausible destination for the
missing cash, if, indeed, there is any to account for. The evidence
for its existence rests, after all, on the accuracy of an 85-year-old
interviewed nearly two decades after the event.[504]

The biographer Peter Ackroyd, meanwhile, delights in hearing that Dickens was driven to the park at Cobham Hall the day

before he was taken ill, quoting the description of that very park on a summer's day which occurs early in *The Pickwick Papers*, and tracing a perfect circle, a tranquil literary homecoming. But this rather glosses over the fact that Dickens went to Cobham Hall park often when he was at home. It was nearby; it was a pleasant walk, through woods. And it also ignores the fact that the park had gathered other connotations since the publication of *The Pickwick Papers*, having been the location for a horrific murder when a locally born artist, Richard Dadd, suffering from a catastrophic mental breakdown, slit his own father's throat there in 1843.

Dickens certainly knew of the murder; he used to take visitors to show them where it had happened.[505] His friend, the artist Augustus Egg, had worked with Dadd and it's entirely possible that Dickens or some of his siblings might have known the family from their childhood days when they had lived in Chatham.[506] The supposed carriage trip doesn't, suddenly, look quite so tranquil and gentle-into-that-good-night any more, does it?

The twelve 'farewell' readings had occupied much of Dickens's energy at the beginning of 1870. The new novel was progressing, though not as fast as he might have wished – even with his 'borrowings' from Bulwer-Lytton's story. As had happened before, with *Dombey and Son* back in the late 1840s, a long break from writing his own serial publication had apparently left Dickens unable to gauge the required word count accurately. There was the distraction of an audience with the Queen, while busy socialising during the London season left him caught in what he described as 'a tangled labyrinth of engagements'.[507] He was obliged to excuse himself from several when the old trouble with his foot flared up again. But it's difficult, looking at his letters, to see much real regret. He may even have exaggerated the extent of his lameness, because one day we find him proclaiming that he 'could no more walk' the few steps from carriage to building than he 'could fly in', while the next he appears to have managed the train journey down to Gads Hill without any undue difficulty.[508] During May, it seems from his letters that he travelled up and down between Gads Hill and London regularly, foot notwithstanding. There's a possible weekend with Ellen, too.[509]

The foot did hurt him, though. He told Georgina that he had been forced to take laudanum for it, which disturbed his sleep. He scalded himself with poultices hot enough to blister the skin.[510] Lack of exercise left him restless. He had always struggled mentally during periods of physical inactivity. When he was writing, frequent movement, exertion was very close to a necessity. As he complained in the last week of May, 'Deprivation of my usual walks is a very serious matter to me, as I cannot work unless I have my constant exercise.'[511]

To make matters worse, the first weeks of June 1870 saw golden weather. Even Whit Monday – 6 June – was fine, defying the general rule that English public holidays are damp and disappointing. By long tradition this was a time for merrymaking, for gingerbread stalls and roundabouts, sweets and sunburn and over-indulgence. There were fêtes and treats for poor children. Prizes were offered for bicycle races and for climbing greasy poles. Theatres scheduled extra performances. Steamships ferried sightseers to Hampton Court and Richmond. Special excursion trains were laid on to the seaside resorts. At Rosherville Gardens, the popular attraction within very easy reach of Gads Hill, the beer and gin flowed and the fried oysters sizzled. There was a yacht race from Tilbury, across the river from Gravesend, a cricket match on the Lines at Chatham, a fair on the beach of the Medway, at Upnor.

Dickens, though, was tempted by none of these local Whitsuntide amusements, if the family's version of events is to be believed; instead, he spent most of the weekend quietly at home with Georgina, Mamie and Katie. A fashionable new conservatory had just been added to the house and Dickens was proud of it. According to Mamie, the whole of the garden was looking particularly fine, 'the outdoor plants were wonderfully forward in their bloom, my father's favourite red geraniums making a blaze of colour in the front garden' while 'syringa shrubs [i.e. lilac] filled the evening air with sweetest fragrance'.[512] It's possible Dickens may have ventured as far as a party at the dockyard in Chatham, however, and on either the Monday or the Tuesday – there's some disagreement which – he went into Rochester.[513]

From Gads Hill to Rochester is about 45 minutes' walk by the fastest and easiest route along the old turnpike road. The road climbs upwards before falling steeply away, the crest of Strood Hill offering a vista down into the valley below and what were, then, still largely green slopes beyond – to the River Medway, the new bridge which had been built in the 1850s, the blank-eyed castle, grimly Norman, the cathedral behind but, from this vantage point, through a trick of perspective, appearing to sit alongside it.

By the 1860s, the towns and villages around the Medway were growing fast. Building lots were constantly being advertised. But the development was piecemeal, the resulting juxtapositions incongruous. So on his walk Dickens would have passed farms and neat rows of terraced houses, a 'chalk-hole' where three 'diminutive lads' had slept rough the previous year, windmills (the Ordnance Survey map shows five), a meadow, new villas for the newly prosperous and a pub – sometimes identified as a favourite haunt.[514] For a time it was rebranded 'The Dickens Inn', but it has recently revived its previous name, the Crispin and Crispianus, for the twin patron saints of cobblers associated with the area, who survived being drowned only to be beheaded. In 1870, licensing hours were not applied to beer sold for refreshment; it's possible, on a hot day, that Dickens paused there for a drink.

One of the reasons Dickens went to Rochester was to visit the post office – of which more in a moment. Mamie relates, however, that her father's stated intention was to fetch a copy of the *Daily Mail*. She also states that he took the dogs with him; kept as guard dogs, there are a number of references in Dickens's letters to their ill-discipline – biting children, snarling at policemen and soldiers.[515] Other reports don't mention the dogs, but instead have Dickens 'walking with guests who were staying with him', showing them the sights of the city.[516] There is no indication of who these 'guests' might have been, how many there were or whether they were male or female. Perhaps they might, instead, have been chance-met acquaintances or fans. Perhaps Ellen was with him, or even little Howard Cleveland, who by this point seems to have been living just off Rochester High Street.[517]

Local tradition insists that Dickens went to the Vines, a piece of open ground near the cathedral appearing in *The Mystery of Edwin Drood* as the 'Monks' Vineyard' – which is what it was, once upon a time. Nowadays an information board and a plaque in the Vines both enlarge on the Dickens connection, and the claim that it was here that 'Charles Dickens walked on his last visit to Rochester 3 days before his death on the 6th June 1870'. At one end of the Vines sits Restoration House, a stately relic whose front of red bricks conceals mediaeval buildings, and which is near-universally accepted as one of the real-life models for Satis House, Miss Havisham's home in *Great Expectations*. There's been speculation that Dickens intended to use the house again, in *The Mystery of Edwin Drood*, though if he did, he never got round to it.[518]

From among all these competing stories we can extract one solid, unromantic nugget. Dickens might have said he was going to Rochester to buy a newspaper, as Mamie asserts, and he might, while he was there, have carried out some research for his current work-in-progress, but he had another chore to carry out as well.

On 3 June Dickens had written to a company called Pulvermacher &. Co., asking them to send him one of their products, a 'voltaic band' for his 'right foot', and promising to 'remit a cheque [...] by return of post' – that is, when he'd received the product.[519] This device had been recommended to him by an actress, Mrs Bancroft, who, before her marriage, had performed alongside both Maria and Ellen Ternan.[520] The voltaic chain-band or galvanic band was akin to a Slendertone or TENS machine, but constructed rather like an ammunition belt; long enough and flexible enough to be wrapped around an arm or a leg – or a smaller part of the body, such as a foot. It comprised 120 pairs of electrodes linked together – a sufficient number to produce a palpable sensation. Variants were popular for several decades through the middle of the nineteenth century, and advertised as a cure for everything from rheumatism and gout to deafness and erectile dysfunction – and, of course, the euphemistic 'nervous debility', a phrase which seems to have encompassed all venereal disease.[521]

Even at the time, most were dismissed as pure quackery, but there was qualified medical support for the model which Dickens selected.[522] Contemporary medical opinion was that this particular design, made by this particular brand, was effective. A copyright case of 1869 had brought the machines to prominence, inspiring an article in *The Medical Gazette* entitled 'Pulvermacher's galvanic chains and the advertising quacks'. The author admits to having previously dismissed the devices as 'so many semi-scientific baubles of apocryphal merits'. Having looked at them more closely, however, he had discovered that 'the galvanic chain is really an instrument of most ingenious and beautiful construction, and is one of the handiest and most effective which the Medical practitioner can employ'. It worked at 'high intensity', producing 'a succession of interrupted shocks', 'very decidedly but not violently'. It was 'an instrument of power, and precision, and convenience', particularly useful, he suggested, in obstetrics, for resuscitating babies who were born not breathing or 'contracting a lax and bleeding uterus'.[523]

Some of Pulvermacher's claims and testimonials were clearly exaggerated. Paralysed wives walked again, epileptics were cured.[524] Perhaps Dickens felt foolish buying such a thing. Perhaps he was embarrassed by the fact that advertisements for this and similar products openly mentioned supposed benefits to gentlemen who were experiencing trouble in the bedroom department. He often asked Georgina to order small items for him; this order he did himself, also rejecting Mrs Bancroft's offer to arrange the matter for him. When writing to Pulvermacher, he'd mentioned sending a cheque, but in fact wound up paying by what he called a 'P.O. order' (that is, a money order). In 1852, he had edited an article on money orders for *Household Words*. It admitted the usefulness of the concept for those who had no bank account while deriding the stupidity of the people who optimistically sent them off as payment for infallible investments or miracle cures.[525] In this situation, though, he saw the appeal of one. They were, of course, anonymous. Presumably he picked one up from the post office in Rochester whichever day it was he went there, either Monday 6th or Tuesday 7th.

On the 8th, the Wednesday, the day before he died, he wrote to Pulvermacher again, thanking them for the delivery of the machine and explaining that since he had taken out the money order for slightly too large a sum, he would like the excess to be returned to him in postage stamps.[526] It's one of the very last letters he wrote.

Dickens appears to have concealed his purchase from Georgina. If he wanted to conceal his use of it as well, perhaps we should envisage him in his writing chalet, where he would not be disturbed, sitting down at his desk and trying the effects of a 'chain' which delivered – 'decidedly' – 'a succession of [...] shocks'; a design which was strong enough to work on thick uterine walls, and to jerk a new-born heart into action.

A promotional booklet directs how the chain should be positioned in order to treat different issues. In cases of gout, it is to be wrapped around the affected toe and the foot, with the other end on the inside of the ankle. For heart problems, it should be placed with one end on the spine and the other 'in front, on the left side'. If you're afflicted with toothache, you should put it against your gum or 'in the tooth'; if the issue is 'female complaints', you are told to permit the 'current' to 'traverse the parts affected'. A man suffering from 'impotence and general debility of the genital organs' should arrange the chain with one end 'upon the small of the back, and the other under the Testes, upon the Perineum'.[527]

That evening, according to Georgina, Dickens came in from his writing chalet, spoke of feeling unwell, muttered something incoherent about lying down on the ground and collapsed. The next day, he died.

A heart attack, plausibly, an aneurysm or a stroke. What nearly everyone agrees on is that his death was the inevitable, natural result of an underlying illness; that, health-wise, the man had been a ticking time bomb for ages.

There's at least a possibility, though, that a heart attack, or a stroke, could have been precipitated by using Pulvermacher's machine. The fact that the machine actually did something, the coincidence of timing – these seem suggestive. But Pulvermacher & Co. made a point of releasing Dickens's letters to the press within a week of his death, pretending to think that the public might be interested in reading some of the great man's final words.[528] In more than one newspaper, adverts for Pulvermacher's bands were placed on the same page as this nugget of 'news'. They may have thought that all publicity was good publicity.

When buying the machine, Dickens had referred to the ongoing problem with his right foot. But, given the varied purposes to which users were encouraged to put galvanic chains, is it possible that he had a double purpose in mind, that he had bought one hoping to treat both his foot and a longer-lasting, more intimate health issue?

☙❧

In June 1859, eleven years before he died, Dickens wrote to his doctor explaining that his 'bachelor state' had 'engendered a small malady'.[529] Now, this may have been a 'malady' which to our way of thinking no longer really exists: 'spermatorrhoea', the involuntary release of semen or fluid from the penis, which might have covered what we characterise as wet dreams. It's more likely, however, that the problem was a sexually transmitted disease. Suspicion edges towards near certainty when, a few weeks later, in August 1859, we discover Dickens making a rueful joke about 'nitrate of Silver'.[530] There is a footnote in the collected letters at this point in which the editor primly mentions that this substance was 'Used for cauterizing warts and the treatment of ulcers'. And so it was – but it was also, and still is, used as a treatment for gonorrhoea. Newspaper advertisements from the 1850s mention 'Nitrate of Silver and Quinine' as 'a speedy self-cure of Nervous Debility.[531] Sexually transmitted diseases were common, epidemic even, but it was rare for people to openly admit their infection status. References were often euphemistic.

Dickens was still suffering from 'disagreeables' in December 1860, and the following month writes of having taken a 'Vapour Bath', which in the circumstances sounds very much as if it might have been a 'mercurial vapour bath', cutting-edge treatment at the time, not for gonorrhoea but for syphilis.[532]

Is this the secret Dickens had been trying to hide for so many years, that he had contracted syphilis? Or was the truth something even worse – that he had passed it on?

Earlier I said that I would return to look in more depth at Catherine Dickens's sojourn in the spa town of Great Malvern. You'll remember that she was sent there in the spring of 1851. The doctor who treated her, a James Wilson, was a leading proponent of the so-called 'water cure' and so we know that her treatment is likely to have included hot and cold baths, showers, a plain diet and plenty of exercise. We don't know, though, what was wrong with her.

Dickens, you'll remember, drew a picture of his wife as suffering from confusion. Catherine herself described in a letter what might be migraine or cluster headaches ('fullness in the head' and 'violent headaches').[533] These are frequently associated with hormonal changes in women and could plausibly be connected to her most recent pregnancy.

Wilson did claim to treat 'nervous complaints'. However, as the full title of his 1840 book reveals, he considered himself a specialist in the treatment of other conditions too: 'The Water Cure: a New

System for Restoring injured Constitutions to Robust Health, for the radical cure of Gout and Rheumatism, stomach, liver, and nervous complaints, tic, scrofula, syphilis, and their consequences'.[534]

Before Catherine even arrived in Great Malvern, her husband wrote to Dr Wilson in mysterious terms:

> As her case is a nervous one and of a peculiar [i.e. particular] kind, I forbear to describe it, or to state what Dr. Southwood Smith has particularly requested me to mention to you, as rendering great caution necessary, until I have the pleasure of seeing you [...] I do not contemplate her living in your house. Indeed, under any circumstances, I should have my reasons (founded on my knowledge of her) for desiring to settle her in some temporary home of her own [...].[535]

Lillian Nayder suggests Catherine may have been suffering from post-partum depression, but a 'nervous' case 'of a peculiar kind', the details not to be committed to paper; this certainly sounds like Dickens might be hinting at some embarrassing form of 'nervous debility'.[536] There was, we noted, a surprising lack of publicity surrounding Catherine's and Charles's arrival in the town. Most of Dr Wilson's patients stayed in his house (there are a couple of dozen 'visitors' there in the 1851 census), but Catherine didn't and seemingly her husband considered it out of the question for her to do so. She didn't go to London to attend her father-in-law's funeral or offer comfort to the bereaved. Perhaps she was too ill to travel. Or perhaps she had a visible sore and so couldn't be seen out. Baby Dora's sudden death, coinciding as it does with her mother's illness and absence, may also strike us as significant, although the infant death rate was high in the mid-nineteenth century and there were plenty of common diseases which could explain her illness and subsequent demise.

In fact, so many of the earlier symptoms of syphilis resemble those associated with other illnesses and conditions that it is known as the 'great pretender' or 'great imitator'. The first stages are easily missed or pushed to the back of the mind – a flat red spot, a painless ulcer known as a chancre (usually on or around the genitals), perhaps swollen lymph nodes. Often sufferers have a very sore throat. Later comes a rash, classically on the palms of the hands or soles of the feet. After this, the disease can lie hidden for decades. Rashes or isolated sores may recur and then disappear again, and can be sufficient in themselves to reveal someone's infection status; equally, a range of other symptoms may emerge without anyone being the wiser as to the root cause. There may be no further signs at all. Some sufferers will never progress to the dreaded tertiary stage of the disease. There are three types of this. One is 'late benign syphilis' – not all that benign, since it involves lesions developing on the body which can obviously lead to quite serious health problems. Another is cardiovascular syphilis, which typically affects the aorta, the great blood vessel of the heart. The third type is neurosyphilis, which can present as problems in balance and with walking, as stroke, or as full-blown dementia, 'general paresis'.[537]

Syphilis can cause miscarriage but not inevitably so, nor is it always passed on to the foetus during pregnancy, though it can be. It can also be passed on during breastfeeding if there are sores on the breast. In children affected by congenital syphilis, the disease can lie dormant for considerable periods before manifesting itself. It can also become apparent much earlier, at birth or in babyhood, causing general malaise, failure to thrive, convulsions and even sudden death.

So *was* there syphilis in the Dickens family, and if there was, when and how did it get there?

Well, as to when, an educated guess says in the early 1840s.

One health issue associated with syphilis is an increased risk of developing anal fistula, either because of a chancre or ulcer located in the anus or because of a weakened immune system. We know Dickens suffered from anal fistula in 1841 and underwent surgery for it late that year. In spring 1842, during their trip to America, both husband and wife suffered from sore throats which were bad enough to confine them to bed and to be mentioned in multiple letters.[538] Meanwhile Catherine's face swelled up hideously on and off for weeks.[539] It is also on this trip that we find Dickens complaining that his wife, as a result of her supposed clumsiness, had acquired bruises and developed 'great sores and swellings on her feet'.[540] Injuries, or one of the few reliable diagnostic markers of early syphilis infection? Catherine's first miscarriage, in 1837, is readily explained by the stress of her sister Mary's death just before it took place, and by the fact the pregnancy had followed so hard upon the heels of her first; however, there is no other very obvious cause for the one we know happened a decade later.

Walter, born early in 1841, died aged 22, from aortic aneurysm. 'Standard' – sexually transmitted – syphilis is known to be a major cause of this.[541] Congenital syphilis, acquired in the womb, is also associated with it.[542] That there was a relationship between syphilis and aortic aneurysm was suspected from the 1700s.

We may think that this casts a different light on Dickens's decision to conceal the cause of Walter's death both from the press and from many of his own children. There are, undoubtedly, letters missing from around the time that the news of Walter's death reached his father; between 4 and 10 February 1864 only one survives. But when he wrote to give fuller details to Angela Burdett Coutts, who had taken an interest in Walter, he made – as we have seen – a point of suggesting that there was a known inherited problem in the Hogarth family ('his Aunt has the same disorder, and [...] we observe strong traces of it in one of his brothers').[543] The aunt – Georgina – proved, as I've said, remarkably spry and long-lived for someone with a heart problem. This letter is the only place, in the letters that survive, where Dickens mentions the specific cause of Walter's death. Angela Burdett Coutts had been far more sympathetic to Catherine during the separation than had been pleasing to Dickens; that this letter includes a special explanation, overlong, might – again – lead us to wonder about his motivation.

There are other suggestive indications aside from the aortic aneurysm and the hearing loss which Dickens's third son Francis suffered from his late teens and which is a 'common symptom' of congenital syphilis.[544] The offspring of syphilitic parents sometimes exhibit particular physical signs: oddly shaped teeth, abnormally notched; damaged corneas; flattened nasal bones. These signs are sometimes referred to as Hutchinson's triad, named after a specialist in the treatment of syphilis who was active during the 1850s and 1860s (although he was not the first to recognise them). One or two of the smudged photographs which survive of the younger Dickens children show what appear to be decidedly *retroussé* noses – sufficient, at any rate, to bolster rather than allay suspicion. Walter's nose looks distinctively tip-tilted. So, perhaps, to a lesser extent, does Sydney's. And the appearance is particularly marked in the case of Edward Dickens.

The problems with Dickens's foot could be something called Charcot arthropathy, another complication of syphilis. Neurosyphilis can lead to stroke, which Dickens almost certainly suffered from in 1869 and possibly again the day before he died. Sydney Dickens, the seafaring son, survived his father by less than two years, dying at sea on his way home from India. Some of the newspapers give details of his naval career, but there's no reference to what caused his death. The register of deaths at sea notes against his name 'Genl debility', 'general debility' being a catch-all term which sometimes indicated the existence of an underlying systemic health issue.[545] He had just turned 25. When Catherine died in 1879, her death was attributed to 'scirrhus of the cervix', a form of cervical cancer.[546] Internal syphilitic lesions are still sometimes confused with cervical cancer, which is anyway far more common in women who have suffered from sexually transmitted infections.

Dickens's preoccupation with disease and its spread in *Bleak House*, the secrets kept from spouses and children in *A Tale of Two Cities, Little Dorrit* and *Great Expectations*, the guilt-ridden men who appear in his last novels: these all might support the conclusion that he not only knew but also feared exposure.

And in *Hard Times*, written in 1854, Dickens had bemoaned the fate of a working man married to a syphilitic wife. He made a point of stating that the pair had been married for exactly the same length of time that he had been married himself at the time the story was published. Is this really coincidence, or is it, as I've half-intimated before, an accusation against Catherine? Was he getting his defence in because he already wondered whether he might need it?

It's not impossible that Catherine could have contracted syphilis during an affair of her own – it isn't as if she didn't have some excuse for being unfaithful. Dickens might have picked up the infection before they married. Either of them might have been, at some point, the victim of sexual assault. Wet-nurses offer a possible source of infection for the children – and we know from the 1851 census return that one was employed in the Dickens household.

But if the disease did indeed enter the family, we would be naive not to acknowledge that the probability has to be firmly in favour of it doing so as a result of Charles Dickens's own extramarital promiscuity.

I suggested earlier that Dickens got involved in the halfway house for brand management reasons. He might have felt a genuine vocation, though. His dock-town upbringing would have exposed him to the grim realities of street prostitution at a young age and we know that when he was a child in Chatham an 'unfortunate girl of the town' was found dead just around the corner from his home. But in the 1840s he took to wandering into the back-streets and slums and docks of London, looking for likely candidates, and who knows whether all he did there was espouse the benefits of emigration. 'The young lady was *not* interesting,' he writes to one male friend, 'and I was after you in three or four minutes.'[547] He was the one who arranged secret meetings with women who were not his wife. He was the one who enjoyed numerous 'bachelor' trips away with his male friends.

Catherine's decision to leave her husband was a huge step for her to take. So what if he was conducting an affair with an actress? There would have been enormous pressure on her to turn a blind eye. Separating would damage her daughters' marriage prospects and her husband's career. But if Charles had passed on syphilis to his wife and potentially to some of their children, too, if Catherine elected to share that information, then the support she enjoyed from some unexpected quarters (her parents, her sister-in-law Letitia, Angela Burdett Coutts, Dickens's friend Mark Lemon) would suddenly make sense. It might also explain why Dickens and Georgina didn't scotch the rumours about the two of them, as they so easily might have done; not because of Ellen, but because there were worse stories circulating – one of them so 'disgusting and horrible', according to Dickens's own lawyer, 'that I cannot think it desirable that it should be distinctly written down even for the purpose of denial'.[548] This is usually viewed as a reference to rumours of an affair with Georgina, and it could be that it is; it might as easily refer to rumours about syphilis.

In February 2019, Dickens was in the news, the subject of horrified reports about a letter discovered in an archive which claimed that he had tried to have his wife committed to a lunatic asylum when their marriage broke down in 1858. This would have been a dreadful fate, imprisonment without trial or guilt, little chance to plead your case and no one to believe you if you did.[549] Terrible enough in the case of genuine mental illness; monstrous if the real motive was simply someone else's convenience or reputation.

But it wasn't the smoking gun some reports suggested. And nor was it really news, in the sense of being new information. As long ago as 1955, an article was published in an academic journal giving what purported to be a transcript of a letter from one of Catherine Dickens's aunts, making a very similar claim:

> [...] from a recent insertion of a letter which Dickens had written to a friend in America now going the round of the press, in which he talks of his wife occasionally labouring under *mental disorder*, I think it only right to contradict that statement, to such a friend as you; he did indeed endeavour to get the physician who attended her in illness, to sanction such a report, when he sternly refused, saying he considered Mrs. Dickens perfectly sound in mind, consequently he dared not in England assert anything of the kind.

Supposedly written towards the end of summer 1858, the letter makes no insinuations about impropriety between Dickens and Georgina. Instead it suggests that Georgina supported him because she was naive and flattered: she 'is an enthusiast', it runs, 'and worships him as a man of genius' who 'ought not to be judged with the common herd of men'.[550]

As well as asserting that Dickens tried to persuade a doctor to diagnose his wife as mentally unwell, this letter is, if you read it carefully, making another accusation. It states that Catherine and Charles Dickens had been parted by 'a living death' – a common way at the time to describe the general paralysis which was the dreaded end-stage of syphilis.

Proof? No, not that. This is a theory, a hypothesis. But it's one which offers a coherent explanation of the circumstances which surround the collapse of the Dickens's marriage, including the failure to deal effectively with the rumours about Georgina. It suggests a reason why Dickens kept dropping reminders of the rumours about Georgina and Ellen into stories and essays and letters – enough to keep them circulating. When, in the early 1840s, he had been trying to distract from persistent press reports about his mental health, he'd done so by introducing other, competing rumours. When Forster had seemed on the cusp of discovering all about the Lamerts, Dickens had distracted him with a juicy tale of youthful suffering, garnished with snippets of disinformation. This would be a similar approach, though on a grander scale.

It also suggests why a man who was supposedly intent on hiding his illicit relationship at all costs should have chosen to blazon it abroad in his will.

Notes

500. Mamie Dickens, *My Father as I Recall Him* (Cambridge University Press, 2014 [1896]), page 119.
501. 'The officers of the Indian army, and the officers and non-commissioned officers of the various cavalry and infantry regiments, who have been going through a course of instruction in army signalling and telegraphy [...] have recently been despatched in small parties to Sheerness, Gravesend, Higham, Queenborough, &c., and were engaged in signalling back to this garrison by day and night.' (*Morning Post*, 8 June 1870, page 5.)
502. This is sometimes called the 'Peckham conjecture'. Some biographers – notably A.N. Wilson in his recent *The Mystery of Charles Dickens* – have embraced it more enthusiastically than others.
503. See the letters by D.C. Leeson reproduced in the postscript to Claire Tomalin's book *The Invisible Woman*.
504. W.R. Hughes, *A Week's Tramp in Dickens-Land*, Dickensland (Chapman and Hall, 1891), page 207. ·
505. According to the artist W. Powell Frith, 'Dickens was eloquent on the subject of the Dadd parricide, showing us the place where the body was found'. Cited in W.R. Hughes, *A Week's Tramp in Dickens-land*, page 396.
506. The Dadd family lived in Chatham in the 1820s where the father ran a chemist's shop. Richard, being born in 1817, was five years younger than Charles.
507. Letter to John Delane, 23 May 1870.

508. Letter to J.B. Buckstone, 15 May 1870. That is, unless the transcription by W.R.S. Ralston is incorrect.

509. A letter to his printer survives dated 28 May but, unusually, with no address. In a letter to a Mrs Bancroft dated 31 May he explains that he is 'most heartily obliged' for her 'kind note, which I received here only last night, having come here from town circuitously, to get a little change of air on the road'. There might easily be a missing word here, which would change the meaning entirely, and make the *letter* the circuitous traveller which had 'a little change of air'. He makes a similar joke about delayed post elsewhere.

510. Letter to Georgina Hogarth, 12 May 1870.

511. Letter to Mrs Percy Fitzgerald, 26 May 1870.

512. Mamie Dickens, *My Father as I Recall Him* (Cambridge University Press, 2014 [1896]), pages 118–19.

513. *Chatham News*, 11 June 1870, page 4, reports both his attendance at the garden party 'last Saturday' and a visit to Rochester, 'on Tuesday'. The family version of events has him do nothing more on the Tuesday than drive out to Cobham Park.

514. *Maidstone Telegraph*, 24 April 1869, page 6.

515. Mamie Dickens, *My Father as I Recall Him* (Cambridge University Press, 2014 [1896]), page 117.

516. *Chatham News*, 11 June 1870, page 4.

517. As mentioned before, William Ternan was by this point occupying a building in what was then called Theobald Square, just off Rochester High Street, and the 1871 census has Howard Cleveland living in the same household.

518. 'On Tuesday last, a day before the fatal attack, Mr Dickens paid a visit to Rochester, and spent some time in looking at one of the old ivy-clad buildings in that city, an antique house which overlooked the "Vines," a glimpse of which is given in one of the chapters of "Edwin Drood." It was evidently Mr. Dickens' intention to introduce a description of this quaint edifice into his unfinished work.' (*The Scotsman*, 13 June 1870, page 3.)

519. To Messrs Pulvermacher & Co., 3 June 1870.

520. *John Bull*, 18 April 1857, page 1; *Globe*, 22 December 1858, page 2.

521. 'Health and manhood restored!' trumpets an advertisement for one of Pulvermacher's rivals, an 'electric and magnetic [...]

Scientific Appliance', *Wrexham Advertiser*, 18 June 1870, page 2, for example, but published very widely.

522. *Medical Times and Gazette*, Volume 2, July–December 1869, pages 21–2.

523. *Medical Times and Gazette*, as above.

524. These from an advertisement in the *Daily Telegraph and Courier*, 30 May 1870, page 6.

525. W.H. Wills, 'Post-Office Money-orders', *Household Words*, Volume V, Magazine No. 104, 20 March 1852, pages 1–5. In a memorandum drawn up before he left for his second American tour, Dickens left instructions for the wives of two of his support staff to be paid by 'P.O. order' (Memorandum to W.H. Wills, 1867).

526. 'Mr. Charles Dickens begs to enclose Messrs. Pulvermacher and Co. a P. O. order for the band safely received. It has been obtained by mistake for a shilling or two more than the right amount. They can, if they please, return the balance in postage stamps.' Letter to Messrs Pulvermacher & Co, 8 June 1870.

527. *J.L Pulvermacher's Hydro-Electric Voltaic Chains. Sold by J. Steinert, sole agent, no. 568 Broadway, New York* (1853) pages 23–5, pages 21–2. The booklet states that in the last case, the chain should be applied at night and worn while sleeping, but people do not always follow instructions to the letter.

528. See the *Morning Post*, 15 June 1870, page 7.

529. Letter to F.C. Beard, 25 June 1859.

530. Letter to Wilkie Collins, 16 August 1859.

531. For example, *Buxton Herald*, 5 August 1858, page 6.

532. Letters to Georgina Hogarth, 28 December 1860 and 17 January 1861. In a letter to the editor of the medical journal *The Lancet*, a man called Langston Parker explained that he had been 'the first to draw attention to the advantages to be derived from combining the vapour of fumes of various preparations of mercury with aqueous vapour and to recommend a bath, which I denominated the "mercurial vapour-bath" in which the patient was exposed to the influence of three agents – the vapour of some preparation of mercury, heated air, and common steam' (The treatment of syphilis by the 'mercurial vapour bath', *The Lancet*, 1864, volume 2, page 212).

533. Catherine Dickens to Fanny Kelly, 11 March 1851 (quoted in Lillian Nayder, *The Other Dickens: A Life of Catherine Hogarth* (Cornell University Press, 2010), page 177).

534. This is the title given in advertisements, which appeared very widely (for example, *Globe*, 28 June 1842, page 1, and many other publications).

535. Letter to James Wilson, 8 March 1851.

536. Lillian Nayder, *The Other Dickens: A Life of Catherine Hogarth*, page 177.

537. See, for example, the National Institute of Neurological Disorders and Stroke: Neurosyphilis (https://www.ninds.nih.gov/health-information/disorders/neurosyphilis).

538. Among others, letter to Lewis Gaylord Clark, 15 February 1842; letter to George W. Putnam, 1 March 1842.

539. See letter to Frederick Dickens, 22 March 1842.

540. Forster dates the letter 24 April 1842 (*The Life of Charles Dickens*, volume 1, page 378).

541. William C. Roberts *et al.*, 'Syphilis as a cause of thoracic aortic aneurysm', *The American Journal of Cardiology*, Vol. 116, No. 8 (2015), pages 1298–303.

542. I. Matusoff, P.D. White, 'The heart and blood vessels in congenital syphilis', *The American Journal of Diseases of Children*, Vol. 34, No. 3 (1927), pages 390–403; Hallard W. Beard, Robert G. Thompson, 'Aneurysm of the ascending aorta caused by congenital syphilis', *American Heart Journal*, Vol. 56, No. 2 (1958), pages 313–16.

543. Letter to Angela Burdett Coutts, 12 February 1864.

544. C.S. Karmody, H.F. Schuknecht, 'Deafness in congenital syphilis', *Archives of Otolaryngology* Vol. 83, No. 1 (1966), pages 18–27.

545. The Register of Births, Marriages and Deaths at Sea, 1844–1890, Piece 4 (1872–1883), page 175. Accessed via Ancestry.

546. Lillian Nayder, *The Other Dickens: A Life of Catherine Hogarth*, page 340.

547. Letter to Daniel Maclise, 1 April 1850.

548. Letter from Frederic Ouvry to George Smith, 28 May 1858. MS Charles Dickens Museum London.

549. John Bowen offers an accessible version of his argument in *The Times Literary Supplement* of 19 February 2019 ('Unmutual friend').

550. K.J. Fielding, 'Charles Dickens and his wife: fact or forgery?', Études Anglais, Vol. 8, No. 3 (1955), pages 213–18. The letter, if it was genuine, was from Miss Helen Thomson to a Mrs Stark. The date given is August 1858, no manuscript is available.

EPILOGUE: IN MEMORIAM

Dickens's Dream, Robert W. Buss, *c.* 1875. (Charles Dickens Museum)

From the tunnel the train emerges into June morning and hisses to a halt at the small station of Higham. As the steam and smoke clear, unfurling into the air, faintly pearlescent early in the day, here on the north Kent marshes, we can see, at one end of the platform, a knot of people and a coffin.

It is Tuesday 14 June 1870, and Charles Dickens is about to set out on his final journey – to a grave in Poets' Corner in Westminster Abbey.

The coffin is lifted on, the living passengers following, and then, jerking, picking up speed, the train continues on its way to London, to the terminus at Charing Cross. The distance is less than 30 miles as the crow flies but the journey takes about an hour. The train moves westwards, not fast, but determinedly, keeping roughly parallel to the bank of the Thames as it narrows, past Gravesend, Dartford, Woolwich, Greenwich, the buildings clustering ever closer, around, above, below, until it is in the midst of the city, and diving at last across the bridge to the northern bank of the river.

At Charing Cross, the coffin is transferred to a plain hearse and driven 'down the Strand, along Whitehall and King Street to the Abbey door'.[551] There it is met by officials from the Abbey, the mourners emerge from the three mourning coaches and a quiet service is performed, with only a handful of chance passers-by joining in, and 'no choir [...] no anthem, no chanted psalm, no hymn'.[552] The coffin is to be lowered to rest close to that of Handel. It has been decked with flowers – ferns and roses, white and red.[553] The Victorians were much attached to the language of flowers, and nearly all floral arrangements were held to express meaning. This one, from descriptions, suggests sincerity, first love, union and separation. It is likeliest that it was speaking for Catherine, the dead man's widow, though so far as we're aware she didn't attend.[554] Rumours persist that Ellen Ternan did, though I wonder whether even the clergymen who officiated at the Abbey, however urbane, however regardful of Dickens's fame, would really have been willing to countenance the presence of a married man's mistress as a chief mourner, especially given the risk of attracting adverse publicity.[555]

There's some suggestion that Dickens might have indicated a preference to be laid to rest in the burial ground at the foot of Rochester Castle; even a report that it might have been possible.[556] The family themselves seem at one point to have favoured Shorne, close to Gads Hill. The tradition of burying famous writers in Poet's

Corner, in the south transept of Westminster Abbey, was only ever a fairly loose one and had not been adhered to at all closely during the decades preceding Dickens's death. Leon Litvack has convincingly argued that officials from the Abbey conspired to change the family's mind. On the Sunday following Dickens's death, the Bishop of Manchester preached a sermon about him in Westminster Abbey. Added to this were repeated offers and invitations from the Abbey's dean, and the assurance that the funeral could be carried out quietly and privately, even in the very heart of London. Meanwhile, Rochester Cathedral was piling on the pressure, too, grave-diggers poised and ready to spring into action if required. These warring preparations and invitations and applications to the Home Secretary to open closed burial grounds feel uncomfortably insistent, intrusions on the first pangs of a family's private grief.

Dickens had struggled for years to maintain his privacy, with mixed success. By 1870, with improvements in communication technology, privacy was increasingly difficult for anyone to achieve. He was taken ill on the evening of Wednesday 8 June and on Thursday there were reports of it in the press. By the afternoon following his death, telegrams were clattering away, sharing the fact with the world. News of the family's decision to use the Abbey seems to have crept out, too, though who knows by what route.

After the funeral was finished and the mourners had gone, Dickens's grave was left open with a raised platform set up around it, and two vergers were put on crowd-control duties. Londoners arrived to pay their respects to the greatest novelist of their age. Some dropped their boutonnières or small posies on top of the coffin and by the end of the day the grave was filled with flowers.[557]

It's a touching testament to Dickens's power as a writer, to the way he connected with his public. His readings made him available to his fans in a way that was, at the time, entirely new. People felt that they knew him. His stories had offered a space to characters who were poor and dispossessed, had excoriated the selfish, the venal and the hypocritical, had given pleasure, interest and solace to thousands, millions of readers, over decades; they formed a legacy of which, with a few notable exceptions, he ought to have been proud.

This, in the days and weeks that followed his death, was the burden of a hundred newspaper articles and editorials, that a great man was gone, that the whole country, the world, was bereft. The man's embarrassments and failings – personal, literary – were very much glossed over.

Dickens's later years had been occupied largely with the lucrative public readings, attracting sniffy disdain; this was put aside. So too was the suggestion, so long and so frequently repeated, that his glory days as a writer were far behind him. The fact that he had broken with his wife in a blaze of notoriety remained decently undisturbed. Now was really not the time to revisit the allegations of plagiarism which had haunted him throughout his career. The rumours of Dickens's mental health troubles, of his extramarital liaison with a young actress, of a possible illicit sexual relationship with his sister-in-law were not raked over. No one wanted to speak ill of the dead.

No one, it seems, except for the dead man himself.

In the spring of 1869, just after Dickens had been forced to abandon his 'farewell tour' around Britain, he'd written to his solicitor explaining that he wanted to update his will. Clearly the small stroke or cardiac episode he'd experienced had caused him serious alarm.

Wills are powerful drivers of plot in Dickens's stories, but they're also revealing of the people who make them. In *Bleak House*, a legal battle over a will tears apart an entire extended family and wastes a fortune. There are so many versions of the will which kick-starts *Our Mutual Friend* that the novel can offer us absolutely no reassurance that they've all been found. One of the wills featured in *Little Dorrit* is so poorly drafted that the identity of the beneficiary can't be determined, legally, until two other people have died. The father of Oliver Twist not only names his pregnant mistress in his will, he phrases the document in terms which make it practically certain that his older, legitimate son is going to wind up hating the younger.

Dickens had worked for a time in a solicitor's office. He knew what wills could do, had written entire novels about the problems an ill-judged or poorly worded one might lead to. He had at this point eight surviving children, the youngest still a minor.

His personal life was far from straightforward. He hadn't shared a house with his wife for more than a decade but she was still his wife. There was Ellen Ternan to be considered, and Georgina. Yet he didn't arrange to see his lawyer and talk through his plans in person. Instead he outlined his intentions in a letter, asking that they be drafted into the proper legal form but insisting on his desire to add in the details and 'write the whole will' himself.[558] Perhaps he wanted to minimise opportunities for his solicitor to attempt to dissuade him from the course he had planned. Many solicitors would have expressed reservations.

Take, for example, the bequest Dickens earmarked for Georgina, his sister-in-law. She was left £8,000 (equal to about 100 times as much today) and, besides, a good deal of 'personal jewellery', 'all the little familiar objects' from his 'writing-table' and 'room', and 'all' his private papers. She was also made an executrix. Her co-executor was John Forster, entrusted with Dickens's manuscripts just as he had been entrusted with the official version of Dickens's life story. The pair were made guardians to Dickens's minor children – only one, by this point, Edward, who was already living in Australia.[559] They were also given the right to realise Dickens's assets however they chose, including by selling his copyrights, with no suggestion that they consult the wishes of the family before making their decisions. A decade earlier, Dickens had thought of Charley, his oldest son, as the obvious choice to be one of the executors but though Charley was now a man in his thirties with a wife and children of his own, he had been deemed incapable, or unworthy, of managing his father's legacies.[560] Nor was he the only close relation who had cause to feel rejected or aggrieved. Dickens's sole surviving sibling, Letitia, received nothing at all from her brother, not even a token to remember him by. Possibly this was a punishment for remaining on good terms with Catherine, as she had done. Catherine was left money, but only in trust and for her lifetime.

The month before Dickens died, he added a minor codicil to his will, directing that his financial stake in a magazine was to go to Charley. This may have been a sop, an attempt at a consolation prize. But if he had wanted to change anything else he had written, that was his chance. He didn't take it. He meant every word.

It's no oversight, then, that the very first bequest listed is £1,000, 'free of legacy duty', to 'Ellen Lawless Ternan, late of Houghton Place, Ampthill Square'. Just that; no protests about Ellen's virtue and no fond or appreciative words either. We know that Dickens had already settled property on her. If he had wanted to give her more, he could easily have done so privately. There was no need to mention her at all. Doing so was, effectively, a bald admission that he *had* had a relationship with her, and it was an admission which was being made, not only to his family but also to the entire world, not just once but forever. There is no way on earth that Dickens can have failed to realise that the details of his will would be published and pored over in the newspapers after his death, and studied by anyone who wrote about him in the future. He had been famous all his adult life. He had been thinking about this moment for years.

Many newspapers reproduced the whole or nearly the whole text of the will, verbatim. The summaries all made a point of mentioning Ellen. A few publications proffered snide little paragraphs about her: 'As Mr. Charles Dickens' will has been published at length,' they say, 'it may not be indecorous' to identify 'Miss Ternan whose name appears first', and to confirm that she was indeed the young woman readers might have remembered from the reports which had circulated some years before.[561]

Meanwhile *The Saturday Review* published a tirade against Dickens, reproduced in other newspapers. He had, it said, invited 'the whole world to survey his private and domestic concerns', and a sorry sight they were, too:

> [...] Profuse and unctuous and stilted in his expressions of gratitude to his wife's sister, liberal in the provision he had made for that lady, not forgetful of another lady, he has reduced his wife's income by one-half after his death [...] His heart might be all charity and all love to the whole human race, but it was chilly enough to one dispossessed lady, that lady his own wife – who, whether she has wrongs or sorrows, at least kept them to herself. To Miss Ternan and Miss Hogarth [Georgina] Mr Dickens very likely had duties and he has cheerfully recognised them by word and deed. Are we told to believe that all

his duties to his wife were summed up by giving her an annuity
without a single word of recognition [...]?[562]

The partisanship displayed here is strikingly unusual, as is the anger.
The year was, after all, 1870. There might have been a queen on the
throne, but everywhere else men ruled. The divorce laws remained
totally unequal. Married women had only just been granted the
right to keep hold of their earnings and it would be another dozen
years before parliament deigned to give them full independent legal
rights over their own property.[563] To come down so firmly on the
side of Dickens's wife, to criticise openly a popular, beloved author
who had been dead less than two months, is astonishing. The piece
even ends with a complaint about Dickens's expressed desire for no
memorial save the plainest and most restrained of tombs, calling it
'bad taste', the 'offensive' 'ostentation of unostentatiousness', 'the
pride that apes humility' – this last phrase borrowed from a poem
called, variously, *The Devil's Thoughts* or *The Devil's Walk*, where it
is identified as Satan's 'darling sin'.[564] The implication, surely, is
that Dickens was going to have a hard time getting into heaven.

As previously discussed, the names of Ellen Ternan and her
sisters Fanny and Maria were mentioned in the press in connection
with the breakdown of the Dickens's marriage, though the majority
of newspaper editors preferred to keep to hints and circumlocu-
tions. But in the early 1870s, after Dickens's death, after his will
had been published, no one seemed much inclined to conceal
Ellen's identity any more. There wasn't really any point. In 1874,
an anonymous short article appeared in the *Arcadian*, an American
publication, written by a 'London correspondent' and entitled
'Dickens's Platonic Affair'.[565] Though the writer makes a point of
stating that the relationship 'was said to have been purely platonic,
and I have never met anybody who was disposed to dispute this
belief', the detailing of how and where Dickens and Ellen had met
and become 'mutually infatuated', how she had left the stage 'at
Dickens' wish', had been 'the final cause of the rupture between
Dickens and his wife', together with the concluding assurance that
Mrs Dickens 'has always enjoyed' the 'respect and affection' of her
children, rather encourages readers to believe that the affair wasn't
in the least platonic.

The will seems to have been interpreted not only as admitting to the affair with Ellen but as hardly discouraging suspicions that there had been one with Georgina, as well. Perhaps Dickens had not intended his words to be read like that.

When you come down to it, though, he had been writing and performing for the public for three and a half decades. He had edited story after story for his magazines, penned articles, speeches and plays as well as prose fiction. He understood how to manipulate the feelings and responses of an audience.

Though early biographers connived with the family to try to write Ellen out of the story, with the result that she did fade from sight for a while, the rumours – as Michael Slater has demonstrated – never vanished completely.[566] Since the death of the last of Dickens's legitimate children in the 1930s, we've constantly been rediscovering the affair and the well-worn narrative of Dickens's mid-life crisis. Almost every news story about Dickens, every biography, comes back to it. Once you've talked about that, and the debtors' prison and the boot-polish factory, the charity work, the travelling, Mary and Georgina Hogarth, not to mention the books and the writing, there's usually not that much room left for anything else.

Which is, I would argue, more or less what Dickens intended. You have to hand it to him.

❧

In the opening scene of *Great Expectations*, the young orphan hero Pip imagines what his departed family might have looked like, based on the appearance of their tombstones, inferring that his father was 'a square, stout, dark man, with curly black hair', his mother 'freckled and sickly'.

Dickens's own grave offers scope for no such fancies – it is startlingly, aggressively plain. The gravestone is black marble, largish, but its surface is marked by only ten words: 'Charles Dickens, born 7th February 1812 died 9th June 1870'. Even his middle names are excluded. There is no place of birth, no Bible verse, no expression of grief, no reference to explain why he was laid to rest in Poet's Corner in Westminster Abbey. This was an attempt to follow his wishes. He left instructions about his gravestone, stating that his name should be inscribed 'in plain English letters on my tomb, without the addition of "Mr." or "Esquire"'. Just like the young man in *Little Dorrit* who obsesses over the wording on his grave, he'd thought about it a lot.

From a point when his career had barely got off the ground, from an age when most people still view their own death as impossibly distant, Dickens had been anxious about what people would say about him in the future. At the age of 25, in the middle of writing the prison scenes in *The Pickwick Papers*, he had rejected the offer of some local colour from a man connected with the Fleet prison. The reason he gave was that, however much he embroidered on the information, however carefully he wove it into his fiction, 'the World would be informed one of these days – after my death perhaps – that I was not the sole author of the *Pickwick Papers*'.[567] The suicide of Robert Seymour, initially Dickens's collaborator on the Pickwick project, the enmity of the Seymour family, strong enough to be maintained for decades, contextualise this particular expression of anxiety. But the anxiety didn't go away. It's visible in every lie that Dickens told about himself, the faux-autobiographical stories he peddled, the reputational management he engaged in long before it had a name.

In the mid-1850s, after the death of Charlotte Brontë, Dickens apparently wrote to reject an offered article on her which had been pitched to his magazine, doubting whether he – and, by implication, anyone else – had 'any right' to the details of her private life. The extract from the letter also expresses 'a particular objection to that kind of interest in a great mind, which prompts a visitor to take "a good look" at the mortal habiliments in which it is arranged, and afterwards to catalogue them, like an auctioneer'. Dickens suggests that Brontë 'would have shrunk from this account of her trials, and that such as she wanted given, she has given herself'.[568] He had already determined that anyone interested in his own 'great mind' would read the account that he wanted them to read.

In 1858, mired in the scandal of his marriage breakdown, Dickens had expressed his 'hope that my Books will speak for themselves and me, when I and my faults and virtues, my fortunes and misfortunes, are all forgotten'.[569] In 1860, he had chosen to burn 'every letter [he] possessed' and continued to make a point of destroying every one he received that touched on anything except 'absolute business'.[570] But he had already spent years before this drip-feeding Forster information, telling him fibs, writing his own autobiography at one remove. Few academics, nowadays, treat the resulting book as completely reliable, but though Forster was not, perhaps, a very diligent biographer, most of the problems in the book stem from Dickens.

This was a man fearful of his letters being put to 'improper uses' – that is, made available to what he called 'a public audience that has no business with them'.[571] He had spent decades worrying about how to control his image.

What business do we have, as a 'public audience', as readers, with information that Charles Dickens didn't want us to know, with his personal secrets? Well, if he'd lied less, been less manipulative and controlling, less of a showman, less intent on dazzling and distracting everyone from the truth, if he hadn't got Forster to tell his story for him, we would, I think, be less confident that we had a right to expose him. But he did lie.

While affecting to be on intimate, confiding terms with his readers, he lied to us in every way imaginable – outright, by omission, by misdirecting us, by encouraging us to misdirect ourselves.

It's understandable that Dickens wanted to exert authorship over the public narrative. Fame is overwhelming; few people enjoy it. And everyone has episodes in their lives they would prefer to keep to themselves. A wish to draw a veil here, to hide a sensitive spot there; we can all identify with that.

Forget, for a moment, though, understanding, forget what we do or don't owe to Charles Dickens; what about what we owe to his parents, to Catherine, to Harriet, to the Lamerts, to the truth?

Late in 1869, Dickens wrote of being 'disgusted' with a 'Mrs. Stowe' over an article she had published.[572] 'Disgust' is a word he seldom used; for him, it was a very strong one. Harriet Beecher Stowe, best known as the author of the abolitionist but problematic *Uncle Tom's Cabin* (1851–2), had excited this response by penning an article about the marital breakdown between Lord and Lady Byron.[573] It's a robust defence of the latter who, in this version of the story, turns out to have been entirely justified in separating from a debauched 'devil' of a husband, a man who was not only abusive and doubtfully sane, but had embarked on an incestuous 'intrigue'. In the article, Stowe makes Lady Byron's silence heroic, while exposing the dishonest way Lord Byron portrayed his wife and their relationship, the wrong conclusions he encouraged readers of his letters, and poetry, to arrive at. No matter how pretty the flowers of rhetoric, Stowe suggests, no matter how popular the writer, his narrative should not be permitted to stand unquestioned.

Though expressed in staunchly mid-Victorian terms, this is not a million miles away from the modern idea that the character of a painter or a writer or an actor is of paramount importance, that art cannot be separated from the artist, nor the message from the messenger. And what happens to Dickens's work then? He's already come in for justifiable criticism for his treatment of his wife and for racism – as well as the examples I've mentioned in this book, there is one startlingly repellent letter advocating genocide, written in the context of the 1857 Indian Uprising, and some upsetting descriptions of African American prison inmates, not much in line with either Dickens's public rejection of slavery or his much-vaunted charitableness.[574] He has also been criticised for some of the language and imagery used in magazine essays, offensive to several different ethnic groups, and for his support of Edward Eyre, governor of Jamaica during the brutal suppression of the Morant Bay rebellion in 1865. Add accusations that Dickens gave his wife and children syphilis, concealed a probably disabled sibling and seems to have tried to use anti-Semitism to prevent the discovery of his Jewish relations and that might be it for a lot of people: game over.

And what about those readers who are willing to soldier on?

Following Forster, following the narrative Dickens left for us, we've believed in a life that's different from the one he actually led; in some places, very different. Take the story of the boot-polish factory; that, it turns out, may not have happened – not, at any rate, quite as described. It's been one of the central pillars of Dickens's biography, though. What happens if we start to chip away at its foundations? What happens when we consider the possibility that, even though we've discovered a decent candidate for Ellen's child by Dickens, perhaps his marriage didn't end because of her, that she may have been, in part, a convenient excuse, a distraction from a truth which, though all too common, was too horrifying to be discussed in polite Victorian society? We've spent decades viewing *David Copperfield* as Dickens's autobiographical novel. How do we respond to the discovery that several of his other novels may come as close, or perhaps closer, to representing his experiences? How harshly should we judge him for his repeated plagiarism and for shoring up his own brand and reputation by dragging others through the mud – among them Ellen, Catherine, his sister-in-law Georgina and, as a result of censoring out his sister Harriet, his parents?

Look at it another way, though: Dickens's lies show his genius as a storyteller. Some of the holes in his standard, accepted biography are gaping, but who cares when the plot is so emotive, the archetypes so powerful? The suffering child, the lover driven to extremes by love: we recognise them both. Dickens has carried us away and we've let him, succumbing to the magic of what he had to show us though we knew perfectly well, all the time, that it couldn't possibly be real.

And as we uncover more of Dickens's lies, we uncover even more complexity and skill in his writing. There is truly remarkable craftsmanship in his weaving together of truth and fiction, personal memory and literary tropes, outrageous sentimentality and cold-blooded commercialism. And there's so much to discover still, so many new angles to explore.

Dickens's first fans knew very little about him. Since the publication of Forster's biography, we've thought we understood his childhood; since the 1930s, we've believed we had uncovered his secrets. But we didn't. We hadn't.

Now, though, when we read north-Kent-set *The Mystery of Edwin Drood* or *Great Expectations*, we'll be able to incorporate the information about Ellen's extensive connections to the area into our reading. When Dickens writes about fraudsters, we'll be on the alert for references to his father. His sibling deaths won't look sickly saccharine any more, nor will characters with disabilities necessarily seem a hackneyed attempt at extorting sympathy from the audience.

Dickens was an anti-Semite, a racist who expressed a belief in innate British superiority – and his acknowledged mistress was half-Irish, with what appear to have been Jewish relatives, one of them the mother of Howard Cleveland, as good a candidate as has yet emerged for the child who is supposed to have been born of the affair in the early 1860s. Perhaps the pen name of Boz might have been a nod to the origins of Dickens's Jewish uncle Matthew, once Moses. Besides, television casting directors ought to play closer attention when adapting Dickens than they sometimes have done, because the diversity among his characters is – even to modern ways of thinking – not that bad. There are multiple characters with disabilities, both physical and intellectual, and beyond the anti-Semitic figures in *Oliver Twist* and *The Old Curiosity Shop* are a number of other minority ethnic characters, such as the presumably partly Sinhalese twins who feature in *The Mystery of Edwin Drood*. Dickens produced both a Jewish heroine, the Marchioness, in *The Old Curiosity Shop*, and a part-Roma one – Estella, the heroine of *Great Expectations*. Jaggers, the lawyer in the same novel, is clearly not meant to be read as Anglo-Saxon.[575]

It appears overwhelmingly likely that Dickens contracted syphilis and passed it on, making his treatment of many of his children, and of his wife, in later life, appear still more monstrous than it has done before. Yet how many of us, hand on heart, could swear we would have behaved better in the circumstances, unaware, perhaps for years, with patchy knowledge of how the disease operated, with no antibiotics and, as time went on, weighed down under an ever-increasing press of guilt?

A son who magnified his parents' explicable failings into unforgivable ones; an unblushing plagiarist tormented with guilt over the death of his first collaborator; a brother who mourned the loss of his sister secretly, for years; a man who laughed to scorn any suggestion that his mental health was chancy, though it appears that sometimes it was.

An admirer of many women, who treated none of them well. An author who tricked one of his most faithful friends into writing a biography in which truth and untruth are so closely interwoven that almost nothing in it can be wholly relied on.

A consummate storyteller; the creator of Oliver Twist, of Miss Havisham, Pickwick, Scrooge and Tiny Tim and hundreds of others. A liar who has succeeded in making us believe his lies for a century and a half.

This is Charles Dickens.

Notes

551. *Daily Telegraph and Courier*, 15 June 1870, page 5.

552. *Bell's Weekly Messenger*, 20 June 1870, page 3.

553. See, for example, *The Graphic*, 18 June 1870, page 7, which talks of red and white roses 'spread about' over the coffin. There are also references to a 'chaplet' or wreath of camellias, but June is on the late side for them; perhaps it was in fact a wreath of white roses. Some reports suggest that members of Dickens's family, perhaps his children, put the flower arrangements on the coffin with their own hands.

554. Red roses stood, as they do now, for passionate love; white roses for innocent first love. To spread or scatter both perhaps signifies the separation. Fern stands for sincerity. A garland of white roses suggests innocence and the 'reward of virtue'. Meanwhile camellia japonica would signify 'My heart bleeds for you'. Lucy Hooper, *The Lady's Book of Flowers and Poetry* (New York, 1846); H.G. Gardiner, *The Language and Poetry of Flowers* (London, 1871).

555. See, for example, Robert Garnett, 'The mysterious mourner: Dickens's funeral and Ellen Ternan', *Dickens Quarterly*, Vol. 25, No. 2 (June 2008). Some people get very excited about the fact that, though several of the reports mention 'fourteen' mourners, only thirteen are listed by name. Actually a fourth mystery mourning carriage crops up in some reports as well. It's possible that both the fourth carriage and the fourteenth mourner are straightforward mistakes on the part of reporters.

556. *Chatham News*, 18 June 1870, page 4.

557. According to the *Irish Times*, Friday 17 June 1870, page 3. Numerous other reports agree.

558. Letter to Frederick Ouvry, 25 April 1869.
559. It was pretty standard for a will to specify children, plural, including in situations where there was only one. Even if Howard Cleveland was Dickens's biological son, it would have been impossible for him to will guardianship of a boy who was, legally, nothing to do with him.
560. See letter to Frederic Ouvry, 27 September 1861.
561. See *Newcastle Guardian and Tyne Mercury*, 30 July 1870, page 5, reproduced from a publication called the *London Figaro*. The report also appeared in the *Sun*. *The Era* decided, apropos of nothing, to take this moment to remind its readers that 'Miss Ellen Ternan' had appeared as 'Hippomenes' in the burlesque *Atalanta* at the Haymarket in 1857 (31 July 1870, page 11).
562. *Saturday Review*, 30 July 1870. Quoted and cited in *The Era* 7 August 1870, page 6, and elsewhere.
563. Before the passing of the 1870 Married Women's Property Act, husbands had been entitled to any money their wives earned.
564. Possibly by Samuel Taylor Coleridge and Robert Southey, originally.
565. At quoted and cited in *Hamilton Daily Times* (Ontario), 6 August 1874, page 1; *Newcastle Chronicle*, 29 August 1874, page 6; *Renfrewshire Independent*, 17 October 1874, page 1.
566. Michael Slater, *The Great Charles Dickens Scandal* (Yale University Press, 2012).
567. Letter to George Beadnell, probably July 1837.
568. Partial transcript of a letter apparently to Frank Smedley, date conjectured to be 5 May 1855. Samuel J. Davey catalogue No. 31.
569. Letter to W.W.F. de Cerjat, 7 July 1858.
570. Letter to W.C. Macready, 1 March 1865.
571. As above
572. Letter to W.C. Macready, 18 October 1869.
573. Readily accessible through the website of *The Atlantic*, the magazine in which it was first published in September 1869.
574. I have no desire to repeat these passages. Much is sadly fairly typical for the period, but Dickens's letter to Emile de la Rue, dated 23 October 1857, is shocking.
575. We are told that Estella's mother 'had some gipsy blood in her', while repeated reference is made to Jaggers' 'dark' or 'exceedingly

dark complexion', a description found regularly in newspapers from the period, sometimes attached to people from Cornwall and Ireland, but more frequently used to denote individuals whose ancestry is Jewish, Roma, Mediterranean, Asian or African, or who appear biracial.

BIBLIOGRAPHY

Ackroyd, Peter, *Dickens* (1990)

Allen, Michael, *Charles Dickens's Childhood* (1988)

Allen, Michael, 'The Dickens/Crewe Connection', *Dickens Quarterly*, Vol. 5, No. 4 (December 1988)

Allen, Michael, 'Suicide, Fraud and Debt: John Dickens's Last Days at Chatham', *Dickens Quarterly*, Vol. 33, 4 (December 2016)

Aylmer, Felix, *Dickens Incognito* (1959)

Bowen, John, 'Unmutual friend', *Times Literary Supplement* (19 February 2019)

Brontë, Charlotte, *Jane Eyre* (1847)

Bunnett, Henry Jones, *A Description Historical and Topographical of Genoa* (1844)

Carlton, William J., 'Dickens's Literary Mentor', *Dickens Studies*, Vol. 1, No. 2 (May 1965)

'Clutterbuck, Lady Maria' (pseud.), *What Shall We Have for Dinner? Satisfactorily Answered By Numerous Bills of Fare for From Two to Eighteen Persons* (1851)

Collier, John Payne, *An Old Man's Diary, Forty Years Ago, Part IV, for the last six months of 1833* (1872)

Collins, Wilkie, *The Frozen Deep* (performed 1857)

Collins, Wilkie, *The Moonstone* (1868)

Cruikshank, George, *The Artist and the Author* (1872)

Denne, Samuel and William Shrubsole, *The History and Antiquities of Rochester and its Environs* (second edition, 1817)

Dickens, Charles, *American Notes for General Circulation* (1842)

Dickens, Charles, *Barnaby Rudge* (1841)

Dickens, Charles, *The Battle of Life* (1846)

Dickens, Charles, 'The Begging Letter Writer', *Household Words* (18 May 1850)

Dickens, Charles, *Bleak House* (1852–3)

Dickens, Charles, 'Chatham Dockyard', The Uncommercial Traveller, *All the Year Round* (29 August 1863)

Dickens, Charles, *A Child's Dream of a Star* (1850)

Dickens, Charles, *A Child's History of England* (1851–53)

Dickens, Charles, *The Chimes* (1844)

Dickens, Charles, *A Christmas Carol* (1843)

Dickens, Charles, *The Cricket on the Hearth* (1845)

Dickens, Charles, *David Copperfield* (1849–50)

Dickens, Charles, *Dombey and Son* (1846–48)

Dickens, Charles, 'Dullborough Town', The Uncommercial Traveller, *All the Year Round* (30 June 1860)

Dickens, Charles, *George Silverman's Explanation* (1868)

Dickens, Charles, *Great Expectations* (1860–61)

Dickens, Charles, *Hard Times* (1854)

Dickens, Charles, *The Haunted Man* (1848)

Dickens, Charles, *A Holiday Romance* (1868)

Dickens, Charles, *Is She His Wife?* (first performed 1837)

Dickens, Charles, *Little Dorrit* (1855–7)

Dickens, Charles, 'The Lost Arctic Voyagers', *Household Words* (2 December 1854)

Dickens, Charles, *Martin Chuzzlewit* (1842–44)

Dickens, Charles (ed.), *Memoirs of Joseph Grimaldi* (1838)

Dickens, Charles, *The Mystery of Edwin Drood* (1870)

Dickens, Charles, *Nicholas Nickleby* (1838–39)

Dickens, Charles, *The Old Curiosity Shop* (1840–41)

Dickens, Charles, *Oliver Twist* (1837–38)

Dickens, Charles, *Our Mutual Friend* (1865)

Dickens, Charles, *The Pickwick Papers* (1836–37)

Dickens, Charles, *Pictures from Italy* (1846)

Dickens, Charles, *Sketches by Boz* (1836)

Dickens, Charles, *Sketches of Young Couples* (1840)

Dickens, Charles, *Sketches of Young Gentlemen* (1838)

Dickens, Charles, *A Tale of Two Cities* (1859)

Dickens, Charles, *To Be Read at Dusk* (published in *The Keepsake*, 1852)

Dickens, Charles, *The Village Coquettes* (libretto, 1836)

Dickens, Charles, 'City of London Churches,', *All the Year Round*, (5 May 1860)

Dickens, Charles, 'Nurses' Stories', The Uncommercial Traveller, *All the Year Round* (8 September 1860)

Dickens, Charles, *The Letters of Charles Dickens: 1820–1870*, electronic edition, 12 Vols (eds Madeline House, Graham Storey, Kathleen Tillotson) (1965–2002) [includes Dickens's *Diary*, 1838–41]

Dickens, Charles and Wilkie Collins, *The Lazy Tour of Two Idle Apprentices* (1857)

Dickens, Charles and Wilkie Collins, *A Message from the Sea* (1860)

Dickens, Charles and Wilkie Collins, *No Thoroughfare* (play and novel, 1867)

Dickens, Charles and Wilkie Collins, *The Perils of Certain English Prisoners* (1857)

Dickens, Charles and Wilkie Collins, *The Wreck of the Golden Mary* (1856)

Dickens, Charles and Richard H. Horne, 'One Man in a Dockyard', *Household Words* (6 September 1851)

Dickens, Charles and multiple authors: *Dr. Marigold's Prescriptions* (1865); *The Haunted House* (1859); *The Holly-Tree Inn* (1855); *A House to Let* (1858); *Mrs Lirriper's Legacy* (1864); *Mrs Lirriper's Lodgings* (1863); *Mugby Junction* (1866); *The Seven Poor Travellers* (1854); *Tom Tiddler's Ground* (1861)

Dickens, Mary ('Mamie'), *My Father as I Recall Him* (1896)

Dolby, George, *Charles Dickens as I Knew Him: The Story of the Reading Tours in Great Britain and America (1866–1870)* (1887)

Dolmetsch, Carl R., 'Dickens and the Dead Heart', *Dickensian*, Vol. 55 (January 1959)

Fielding, K.J., 'Charles Dickens and his Wife: Fact or Forgery?', Études Anglais, Vol. 8, 3 (1955).

Forster, John, *The Life of Charles Dickens*, 3 Vols (1871–1874)

Gaskell, Elizabeth, 'Disappearances', *Household Words* (7 June 1851)

Gaskell, Elizabeth, *Mary Barton* (1848)

Gaskell, Elizabeth, *North and South* (1854–55)

Grubb, Gerald, 'Dickens's Marchioness Identified', *Modern Language Notes*, LXVIII (1953)

Hollington, Michael (ed.), *The Reception of Charles Dickens in Europe* (2013)

Horne, Richard H. (ed.), *A New Spirit of the Age* (1844)

Horne, Richard H., 'Dust; or Ugliness Redeemed', *Household Words* (13 July 1850)

Hughes, William R., *A Week's Tramp in Dickensland* (1891)

Kitton, Frederic, *A Supplement to Charles Dickens by Pen and Pencil* (1890)

Knowles, James Sheridan, *The Hunchback* (first performed 1832)

Langton, Robert, *The Childhood and Youth of Charles Dickens* (1883)

Lester, C.E., *The Glory and the Shame of England* (1841)

Long, William F., 'What Happened to Lucy Stroughill', *Dickens Quarterly*, Vol. 29, No. 4 (December 2012)

Long, William F., 'Defining a Life: Charles's Youngest Sister, Harriet Ellen Dickens (15 September 1818–19 August 1827)', *The Dickensian*, Vol. 1110, iss. 492 (Spring 2014)

Lytton, Robert, 'The Disappearance of John Ackland,' *All the Year Round* (1869)

Mayer III, David, *Harlequin in His Element: The English Pantomime, 1806–1836* (2013)

Macready, W.C., *The Diaries of William Charles Macready, 1833–1851* (ed. William Toynbee) (1912)

Meckier, Jerome, *Hidden Rivalries in Victorian Fiction: Dickens, Realism, and Revaluation* (1987)

Miller, Lucasta, *L.E.L.: The Lost Life and Scandalous Death of Letitia Elizabeth Landon, the Celebrated 'Female Byron'* (2019)

Morford, Henry, *John Jasper's Secret; a sequel to Charles Dickens' unfinished novel "the Mystery of Edwin Drood"* (1871)

Nayder, Lillian, *The Other Dickens: A Life of Catherine Hogarth* (2011, 2012)

Philips, Watts, *The Dead Heart* (first performed 1859)

Philips, Watts, *Nobody's Child* (first performed 1867)

Rossi-Wilcox, Susan M., *Dinner for Dickens: The Culinary History of Mrs. Charles Dickens' Menu Books* (2005)

Ruck, Brian, 'Illegitimacy in Dickens, and the riddle of Ellen Ternan', *The Dickensian* (Winter 2022)

Slater, Michael, *The Great Charles Dickens Scandal* (2012)

Storey, Gladys, *Dickens and Daughter* (1939)

Stowe, Harriet Beecher, 'The True Story of Lady Byron's Life', *The Atlantic* (September 1869)

Tomalin, Claire, *The Invisible Woman: The Story of Nelly Ternan and Charles Dickens* (1990)

Wills, W.H., 'Post-Office Money-orders', *Household Words*, Vol. V, Magazine No. 104 (20 March 1852)

Wilson, A.N., *The Mystery of Charles Dickens* (2020)

Wilson, James, *The Water Cure: A New System for Restoring Injured Constitutions to Robust Health* (1840)

Wood, Andy, 'In debt and incarcerated: the tyranny of debtors' prisons', [https://www.thegazette.co.uk/all-notices/content/100938]

INDEX